Lecture Notes in Artificial Intelligence 6599

Subseries of Lecture Notes in Computer Science

LNAI Series Editors

Randy Goebel
University of Alberta, Edmonton, Canada
Yuzuru Tanaka
Hokkaido University, Sapporo, Japan
Wolfgang Wahlster
DFKI and Saarland University, Saarbrücken, Germany

LNAI Founding Series Editor

Joerg Siekmann
DFKI and Saarland University, Saarbrücken, Germany

Rem Collier   Jürgen Dix
Peter Novák (Eds.)

Programming
Multi-Agent Systems

8th International Workshop, ProMAS 2010
Toronto, ON, Canada, May 11, 2010
Revised Selected Papers

 Springer

Series Editors

Randy Goebel, University of Alberta, Edmonton, Canada
Jörg Siekmann, University of Saarland, Saarbrücken, Germany
Wolfgang Wahlster, DFKI and University of Saarland, Saarbrücken, Germany

Volume Editors

Rem Collier
University College Dublin, College of Science
School of Computer Science and Informatics
Belfield, Dublin 4, Ireland
E-mail: rem.collier@ucd.ie

Jürgen Dix
Technische Universität, Institut für Informatik
Julius-Albert-Straße 4, 38678 Clausthal-Zellerfeld, Germany
E-mail: dix@tu-clausthal.de

Peter Novák
Czech Technical University, Faculty of Electrical Engineering
Department of Computer Science and Engineering
Karlovo namesti 13, 121 35 Prague 2, Czech Republic
E-mail: peter.novak@fel.cvut.cz

ISSN 0302-9743   e-ISSN 1611-3349
ISBN 978-3-642-28938-5   ISBN 978-3-642-28939-2 (eBook)
DOI 10.1007/978-3-642-28939-2
Springer Heidelberg Dordrecht London New York

Library of Congress Control Number: 2012933801

CR Subject Classification (1998): I.2, D.2, C.2.4, I.2.11, I.2.5, I.6, D.1

LNCS Sublibrary: SL 7 – Artificial Intelligence

Typesetting: Camera-ready by author, data conversion by Scientific Publishing Services, Chennai, India

Printed on acid-free paper

Springer is part of Springer Science+Business Media (www.springer.com)

Preface

These are the proceedings of the International Workshop on Programming Multi-Agent Systems (ProMAS 2010). It was the eighth of a series of workshops that has the main objective of giving an overview of current research on programming multi-agent systems and providing an interactive discussion forum for agent researchers.

The ProMAS workshop series aims at promoting and contributing to the establishment of multi-agent systems as a mainstream approach to the development of industrial-strength software. More specifically, the workshop facilitates the discussion and exchange of ideas concerning the concepts, techniques, and tools that are important for establishing multi-agent programming platforms that are useful in practice and have a theoretically sound basis.

In its previous editions, ProMAS constituted an invaluable occasion bringing together leading researchers from both academia and industry to discuss issues on the design of programming languages and tools for multi-agent systems. We are very pleased to be able to again present a range of high-quality papers from ProMAS 2010. After seven successful editions of the ProMAS workshop series, which took place at AAMAS 2003 (Melbourne, Australia), AAMAS 2004 (New York, USA), AAMAS 2005 (Utrecht, The Netherlands), AAMAS 2006 (Hakodate, Japan), AAMAS 2007 (Honolulu, Hawai'i), AAMAS 2008 (Estoril, Portugal) and AAMAS 2009 (Budapest, Hungary), the eighth edition took place on May 11 in Toronto, Canada, in conjunction with AAMAS 2010, the main international conference on autonomous agents and multi-agent systems. For ProMAS 2010 we finally accepted six high-quality submissions for presentation at the workshop.

In addition, we invited one distinguished scientist, Sarit Kraus, to give an invited talk on "Human–Computer Negotiation: Learning from Different Cultures."

Following the workshop, we set up a new submission, evaluation and revision process for publishing these proceedings. The authors of the papers accepted for the workshop were invited to submit revised papers. In addition we invited a few more papers from people active in the area. Each paper was reviewed by two members of the Program Committee and by the editors. Authors were then requested to further revise their submissions. After a careful selection, we accepted seven papers plus one invited paper for these proceedings.

The workshop addressed a broad range of mostly practical topics. While two papers deal with the decision component of agent systems, three papers deal with practical examples of programming languages and two papers deal with the interaction with the environment.

We thank the authors whose contributions made this book possible. We also thank the members of the Program Committee for their dedication in successive rounds of reviewing papers.

As for previous editions, we hope that the work described in these proceedings will contribute to the overall goal of stimulating the uptake of agent programming languages and the adoption of agent-based tools for real-world applications.

January 2010

Rem Collier
Jürgen Dix
Peter Novák

Papers in This Volume

These proceedings contain one invited paper, by Michal Pěchouček, Michal Jakob and Peter Novák, entitled "Towards Simulation-Aided Design of Multi-Agent Systems." This paper gives a vision of how powerful a tool hybrid simulations can become in the future. This is grounded in several case studies done at Michal Pěchouček's lab in Prague.

The first regular paper in these proceedings is the one by Joost Broekens, Koen Hindriks, and Pascal Wiggers on "Reinforcement Learning as Heuristic for Action-Rule Preferences." The authors note that many action selection mechanisms in agent-oriented programming are based on rules and leave a great potential for optimization. However, this is difficult to achieve in BDI-like concepts. The authors propose a learning method for sets of rules based on reinforcement.

The second paper, "Towards Reasoning with Partial Goal Satisfaction in Intelligent Agents," by M. Birna van Riemsdijk and Neil Yorke-Smith presents an abstract framework for representing the partial satisfaction of goals. The representation is not based on logic but on metric functions that represent the progress that has been made toward achieving a goal.

In "Evaluating Agent-Oriented Programs: Towards Multi-Paradigm Metrics," Howell R. Jordan and Rem Collier consider metrics for the software engineering process in multi-agent systems. The paper is an attempt toward multi-paradigm structural metrics, which can be applied seamlessly to both agents and the object-oriented environments in which they live. Applications to Jason written in AgentSpeak and Java are given.

In "Atomic Intentions in Jason+," Daniel Kiss, Neil Madden, and Brian Logan deal with interactions between atomic intentions and plan failures in Jason. Atomic intentions in Jason are normally not atomic when considered in conventional programming or in databases. The authors therefore introduce a new semantics and its implementation, Jason+, and claim that this leads to more robust agent programs.

Hugo Carr, Alexander Artikis, and Jeremy Pitt deal, in "Software Support for Organised Adaptation," with *emergence* as a mechanism for coordinating hundreds of agents. The authors define a new programming environment, PreSage-MS, a rapid prototyping and animation tool designed to facilitate experiments in organized adaptation of metric spaces of agent teams.

In the paper "Action and Perception in Agent Programming Languages: From Exogenous to Endogenous Environments" by Alessandro Ricci, Andrea Santi, and Michele Piunti, the authors discuss action and perception models in agent programming languages and note that they cannot deal well with endogenous environments. They describe models specifically designed for such environments and evaluate them using CArtAgO.

Finally, in "An Interface for Agent-Environment Interaction," Tristan Behrens, Koen V. Hindriks, Rafael H. Bordini, Lars Braubach, Mehdi Dastani, Jürgen Dix, Jomi F. Hübner and Alexander Pokahr treat the problem of how exactly agents and environments interact. While there are many interesting environments available, there is no standard that would enable agents to easily interface with them. The paper is a first step toward an environment interface standard. The standard has been implemented and evaluated in a number of agent platforms.

Organization

The ProMAS 2010 workshop was held on May 11, 2010, in Toronto, Canada. The workshop was part of the AAMAS 2010 Workshop Program.

Program Chairs

Rem Collier	University College Dublin, Ireland
Jürgen Dix	Clausthal University of Technology, Germany
Peter Novák	Czech Technical University in Prague, Czech Republic

Steering Committee

Rafael Heitor Bordini	Federal University of Rio Grande do Sul, Brazil
Mehdi Dastani	Utrecht University, The Netherlands
Jürgen Dix	Clausthal University of Technology, Germany
Amal El Fallah Seghrouchni	University of Paris VI, France

Program Committee

Matteo Baldoni	University of Turin, Italy
Juan Botia Blaya	Universidad de Murcia, Spain
Olivier Boissier	Ecole des Mines de St Etienne, France
Guido Boella	University of Turin, Italy
Lars Braubach	University of Hamburg, Germany
Louise Dennis	University of Liverpool, UK
Ian Dickinson	HP Labs, Bristol, UK
Mauro Dragone	University College Dublin, Ireland
Michael Fisher	University of Liverpool, UK
Jorge Gómez-Sanz	Universidad Complutense de Madrid, Spain
Vladimir Gorodetsky	Russian Academy of Sciences, Russian Federation
James Harland	RMIT, Australia
Koen Hindriks	Delft University of Technology, The Netherlands
Benjamin Hirsch	TU-Berlin, Germany
Jomi Fred Hübner	Federal University of Santa Catarina, Brazil
João Leite	Universidade Nova de Lisboa, Portugal
Viviana Mascardi	University of Genova, Italy
John-Jules Meyer	Utrecht University, The Netherlands
David Morley	SRI International, USA

Berndt Müller	University of Glamorgan, UK
Jörg Müller	Clausthal University of Technology, Germany
Andrea Omicini	University of Bologna, Italy
Frederic Peschanski	LIP6 - UPMC Paris Universitas, France
Michele Piunti	ISTC - CNR and DEIS Universitá di Bologna, Italy
Agostino Poggi	University of Parma, Italy
Alexander Pokahr	University of Hamburg, Germany
Alessandro Ricci	DEIS, Universitá di Bologna, Italy
Birna van Riemsdijk	Delft University of Technology, The Netherlands
Ralph Rönnquist	Intendico Pty Ltd, Australia
Sebastian Sardina	RMIT University, Australia
Ichiro Satoh	National Institute of Informatics, Japan
Munindar P. Singh	NCSU, USA
Kostas Stathis	Royal Holloway, UK
Leon van der Torre	University of Luxembourg, ILIAS, Luxembourg
Paolo Torroni	University of Bologna, Italy
Cao-Son Tran	New Mexico State University, USA
Gerhard Weiss	Maastricht University, The Netherlands
Wayne Wobcke	University of New South Wales, Australia
Neil Yorke-Smith	SRI International, USA
Yingqian Zhang	Delft University of Technology, The Netherlands

Auxiliary Reviewers

Alberti, Marco

Behrens, Tristan M.

Bulling, Nils

Verwer, Sicco

Table of Contents

Part I

Invited Paper

Towards Simulation-Aided Design of Multi-Agent Systems*

Michal Pěchouček, Michal Jakob, and Peter Novák

Agent Technology Center
Dept. of Cybernetics, Faculty of Electrical Engineering,
Czech Technical University in Prague
Czech Republic

Abstract. With the growing complexity of multi-agent applications and environments in which they are deployed, there is a need for development techniques that would allow for early testing and validation of application design and implementation. This is particularly true in cases where the developed multi-agent application is to be closely integrated with an existing, real-world system of multi-agent nature.

Drawing upon our previous experiences with development of complex multi-agent applications, we propose *simulation-aided design of multi-agent systems* (SADMAS), a methodology tightly integrating simulations of the target system into the MAS application development process. In its heart lies the use of *mixed-mode simulation*, a simulation where parts of the deployed application operate in the target environment and parts remain simulated. We argue, that employing SADMAS process contributes to reduction of risks involved in development of complex MAS applications, as well as it helps to accelerate the process. Besides describing the capstones of the SADMAS approach and consequences of its application, we also illustrate it's use on a case-study of a next-generation decentralised air traffic management system.

1 Introduction

In today's world, we are increasingly surrounded by and reliant on complex systems and infrastructures. Often, these systems behave far from the optimum or even highly undesirably. Roads in our cities are congested, plane trips frequently delayed, computer networks routinely overrun by worms and electricity grids fail in split-second cascade reactions. The systems have also grown increasingly decentralised, interconnected and autonomous, with more and more decisions originating at the level of individual subsystems rather than being strictly imposed top-down.

The paradigm of *multi-agent systems* is being increasingly successfully applied in modelling and engineering of complex distributed systems. Examples of

---

* The presented work was supported by the Czech Republic Ministry of Education, Youth and Sports, grant no. MSM6840770038.

R. Collier, J. Dix, and P. Novák (Eds.): ProMAS 2010, LNAI 6599, pp. 3–21, 2012.

current and future applications of the paradigm include e.g., *civilian air traf-fic* with the requirement to double the capacity of the airspace within next ten years; *smart energy grids* automatically balancing energy production and con-sumption between interconnected yet independent producers and consumers; *disaster and emergency management operations*, which in the future will rely on the coordination of heterogeneous ad-hoc teams of semi-autonomous robotic entities and networks of unattended sensors; or *intelligent buildings* comprised of large numbers of interconnected autonomous sensors and actuators adapting to the activities of their human occupants.

Development and deployment of such *complex multi-agent systems* is a chal-lenging task. Large numbers of spatially distributed active entities characterised by complex patterns of mutual interaction and feedback links give rise to dy-namic, non-linear emergent behaviours which are very difficult to understand, capture and, most importantly, control. We argue that because of the complexity of the above-described types of applications, it is no longer possible to develop such systems in a linear, top-down fashion, starting from a set of requirements and proceeding to a fully developed solution. Instead, more evolutionary, itera-tive methodologies are needed to successfully approach the problem of develop-ment of complex multi-agent systems.

In this paper, we give a preliminary outline of the *simulation-aided design of multi-agent systems (SADMAS)* approach, a development methodology rely-ing in its core on the exploitation of a series of gradually refined and accurate simulations for testing and evaluation of intermediary development versions of the engineered application. In particular, we propose and argue in favour of us-ing *mixed-mode simulations* in which the implemented application is evaluated against a partly simulated environment. That is, some aspects of the test envi-ronment are real parts of the target system while some remain simulated. Over time, the extent of the simulation will be decreasing until the application fully interacts with the target system itself. We argue that this approach helps to ac-celerate the development of complex multi-agent applications, while at the same time keeps risks and costs associated with destruction or loss of the tested assets low. Our goal is not to give the ultimate answer to the problem of developing complex systems, but rather to synthesise our past experiences with building such systems and to initiate a discussion on the role simulations can play in making engineering of such systems more efficient.

In the following section, we introduce the conceptual framework, the pro-cesses of the SADMAS approach, and discuss the scope of its applicability. Sub-sequently, Section 3 distills our past experiences with the early version of the SADMAS approach. We put forward a set of methodological principles to be respected during application development, in order to facilitate successful ap-plication of the SADMAS methodology. Finally, in Section 4, we discuss tool support for the SADMAS approach, in particular the core features an ideal simulation platform facilitating the introduced methodological principles should provide. Finally, sections 5 and 6 conclude the paper by a discussion of related work and some final remarks.

Throughout the paper, the discourse is accompanied by a running example exemplifying the main principles of the SADMAS approach in a case-study application in the air-traffic management domain developed in our research centre. Before diving into the core of the paper, let us first introduce the case-study problem.

1.1   Running Case Study: Free-Flight-Oriented Air Traffic Control

The ever-growing volume of air traffic is approaching the stage when the current techniques for its management begin to constrain its further expansion. The main limiting factor is congestion of the predefined, reserved flight corridors used by air traffic controllers for long-distance routing of flights in the airspace. An additional grand challenge stems from the need to integrate autonomous unmanned aerial assets with manned air traffic. Small unmanned aerial vehicles (UAVs) are often used for tasks such as policing and emergency area surveillance, and need to be able to operate near airports with heavy civilian air traffic. Current air traffic management systems cannot efficiently support integration of such UAVs and at the same time handle future higher traffic densities. Sophisticated, intelligent technology is needed to enable further growth of the global, manned and unmanned air traffic.

A promising solution concept is represented by the *free-flight*-oriented approach which suggests moving away from the current centralised traffic control based on the predefined flight corridors towards decentralisation. In the extreme, the free-flight air traffic control should be based on on-line negotiation schemes and consequently moved on board of the (un-)manned aircrafts. This radical shift is expected to provide a more efficient use of the available airspace and improve support for dynamic flight trajectory re-planning, as well as collision avoidance. Autonomous decision making in such scenarios is especially important in the case of dynamic, partially unmanned operations in police and military settings.

As the running example for the following discourse, we will use *AgentFly* application, an agent-based free-flight-oriented air traffic management and control system developed in Agent Technology Centre of the Czech Technical University in Prague [17,13]. The aim of the project is to i) propose and implement decentralised flight control algorithms, subsequently ii) evaluate them in an experimental planning system for civilian air traffic control simulating the real traffic in the US National Airspace (NAS), and finally also iii) port and evaluate the proposed control algorithms on board of real aircrafts of different types (fixed-wing aeroplanes, as well helicopters).

2   Simulation-Aided Design of Multi-Agent Systems

At the core of the SADMAS approach lies the use of multi-agent simulations for iterative application evaluation. Results of the evaluations subsequently serve as a driver for further advancement of the process. In the following, we introduce the core concepts of the approach, sketch the application development process it induces and finally elaborate on conditions for its applicability.

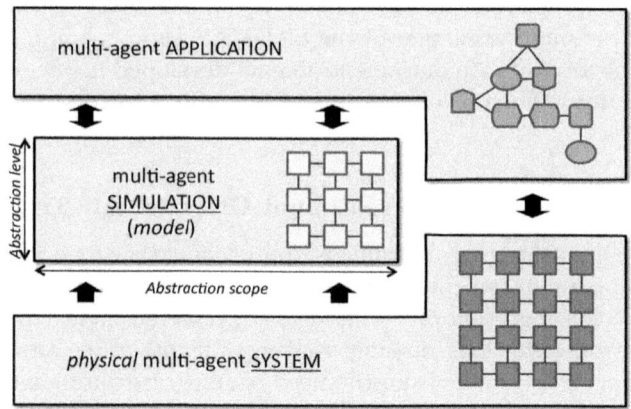

Fig. 1. Conceptual scheme of the SADMAS approach

2.1   Core Concepts

The SADMAS approach revolves around the following three multi-agent concepts:

target system: a real-world system which should be controlled by means of the developed *multi-agent application;*

multi-agent simulation: an agent-based simulation of the target system. In general, the simulation can have different (a) *level of abstraction* (how much is the target system simplified) and (b) *scope of abstraction* (which parts of the target system are simplified);

multi-agent application: a decentralised, multi-agent software system designed to control some (or all) aspects of the target system.

2.2   Development Process

One of the main problems of using simulations as an intermediate tool for testing and evaluating of implemented application, which is nothing particularly novel *per se*, is maintaining the relevance of the simulation with the target system. In result, it might easily happen that while the implemented application runs smoothly in the simulated environment, it breaks down upon its deployment in the target system. We argue, that one of the main reasons for such failures is the breaking of *relevance* when moving from the simulation to the target real-world system. As an example of such a failure, consider a situation when in the simulation of an air traffic management system developers assume perfect communication links used in the multi-agent negotiation. Even though the assumption is not unreasonable as such, the real reliability of communication links could be e.g., 95%, the actual deployment of the application validated against such a simulation could result in severe problems late in the deployment stages of the project. Since it is often extremely difficult, if not plainly impossible, to detect all such misalignments right at the beginning of the project, the development process should ensure that they are discovered as soon as possible in early stages of the development process. The SADMAS approach is based on incremental development of the application hand-in-hand with a series of ever more accurate simulations it is evaluated against. On the top level, the overall process of developing a multi-agent application using the SADMAS approach consists of the following steps:

1. Collect the (multi-agent) *application* requirements, assuming it will control, or interact with, the physical (multi-agent) *system*.
2. Repeat the following steps iteratively:
   (a) Choose the appropriate *simulation level of abstraction* and *application feature coverage* for the particular process iteration. The choice of the appropriate level of abstraction of the application iteration directly results in determining which parts of the simulation will be replaced with interfaces to the real-world *target system*.
   (b) Building upon the simulation from the previous iteration of the process, construct a refined multi-agent *mixed-mode simulation* (cf. Subsection 4.4) of the target system. The simulation should focus on the critical features of the iteration, such as the nature of inter-agent interactions and interaction with the environment so that it respects the chosen level of abstraction of the process iteration.
   (c) Based on the requirements collected in (1) design and develop the *application* (multi-agent control mechanism) w.r.t. the chosen application feature coverage.
   (d) Test, debug and evaluate the *application* (or application variants) developed in (2c) on the multi-agent simulation constructed in the step (2b).
   (e) Iteratively repeat the steps (2c) and (2d) until sufficient level of application reliability w.r.t. the chosen set of features on the chosen level of abstraction is reached.
3. Once the simulation is either completely replaced with the physical target system, or sufficiently tested, perform final evaluation and verification of the application directly interacting with the target system and *deploy* the application.

From some point on in the development process, the simulation refinement should result in replacement of some aspects of the simulation with direct interfaces to the target system. With the advancing stage of the application development, it is increasingly tested against relevant aspects the real-world target system. The consecutive replacement of aspects of the simulation with interfaces to the physical target system leads to subsequent refinements and adaptations of the mixed-mode simulations eventually resulting in complete replacement of the initial simulation of the target system with the system itself. By keeping the tight alignment between the intermediate states of the system simulation and the application, the process ensures, resp. maintains relevance of the developed application w.r.t. the target system and the chosen level of abstraction at the process iteration.

In many cases, the implementation of the step (2c) will not lead to a straight-forward process. Rather, in order to find the proper set of partial solutions to cover the target feature set at the appropriate level of abstraction, the developer will be often forced to implement several versions of the application. Only after performing the evaluation step (2d), on the basis of the collected experimental results the implementer is able to decide which solution version will be carried to the next iteration of the process. Thus, the proposed approach is not strictly linear, such as e.g., the waterfall model inspired processes.

Figure 2 visualises the iterative process described above and highlights the role of mixed-mode simulation in the overall architecture. In order to ensure that the application can be ported seamlessly through the series of ever more accurate simulations without significant additional expenses, the design of the multi-agent application has to meet several requirements which we expand upon later in Section 3.

2.3   Scope of Applicability

In order for the SADMAS approach to be applicable to a particular problem domain, it is critical to analyse the relationship of the target system vs. the requirements on the developed application. In particular, the target system in which the application will be deployed has to be of multi-agent nature and should manifest some kind of emergent, collective behaviour on its own. Furthermore, we assume that the developed application will be deployed in hardware and situated in the target system. Due to its reliance on safe simulation-based evaluation, the SADMAS approach is particularly suitable for applications in which at least one of the following conditions hold

- the cost of an individual HW unit is high, and risk of a failure that may result in loosing an asset is not negligible;
- application testing may result in undesirable, possibly harmful changes of the environment, such as when the safety of material resources and/or humans would be endangered;
- the cost of running the HW experiments is high and proportional to the number of deployed assets; or finally
- the application operates in an environment which strongly influences the behaviour of the application, i.e., it is difficult and/or costly to set up test conditions so that all critical aspects of the application can be evaluated.

Example problem domains for target systems, potentially suitable for application of the SADMAS methodology, include air traffic, public transport system, energy grids including consumers and producers, or peer-to-peer file sharing network. The possible developed applications in such domains include automated aircraft, resp. vehicle flight planning and collision avoidance mechanisms, control and

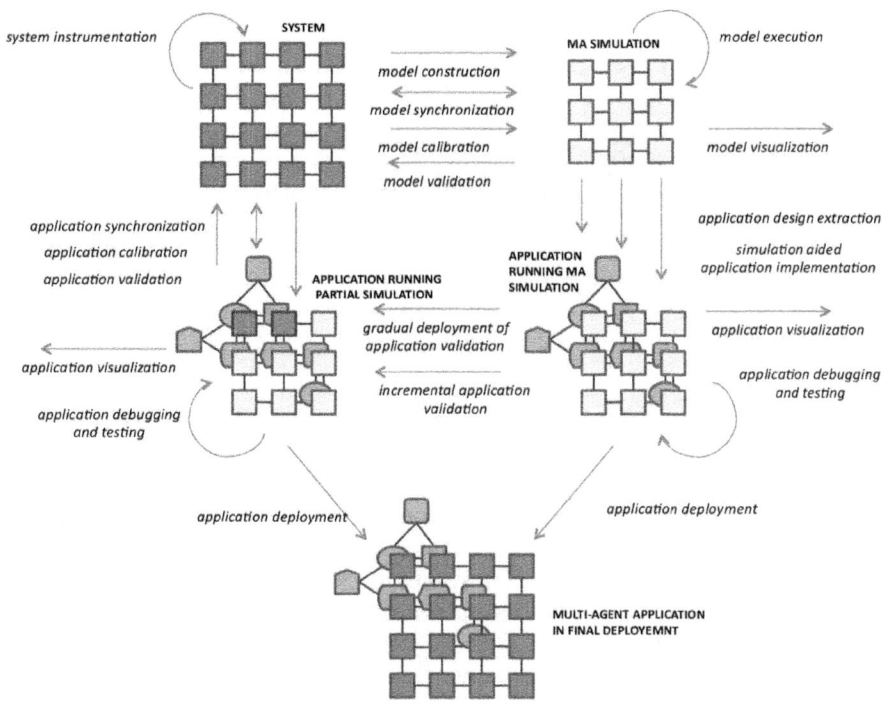

Fig. 2. Relations and processes between the components of the SADMAS approach

management mechanisms for negotiating electricity consumption and production between entities on the smart grid.

The scope of simulations used as the intermediary testing platform would typically differ between different stages of the development process. The development may initially be done completely in an isolated simulation, while later its parts would be replaced by the real-world system and eventually, in the ultimate deployment setup, the application would solely interact directly with the target system.

AgentFly case-study analysis: Let us analyse the *AgentFly* case-study using the core concepts of the SADMAS approach. The *target system* is clearly the NAS air traffic system and the related infrastructure. Let's simplify the problem and consider only unmanned aeroplanes. These assets usually operate in geographically bounded environments containing various special-use air-zones, termed *no-fly zones*. The operation of an aircraft is determined by i) the take-off location, ii) the landing location and iii) set of time-space geographical waypoints, e.g., specifying a surveillance pattern. The multi-agent *application* comprises the set of autopilot control algorithms on board of each asset. The application should control the movements of a number of aircrafts along collision-free trajectories that pass through the specified geographical waypoints, while avoiding the no-fly zones. The functionality of the application can be decomposed into two layers:

- *individual planning layer* aiming at planning a smooth 4-dimensional (space and time) trajectory passing through the waypoints for the aircraft; and
- *multi-agent planning layer* aiming at collision avoidance of a set of aircrafts, i.e., detecting potential future collision and using peer-to-peer negotiation in order to determine the set of deconfliction manoeuvres.

The application further needs to fulfil a number of non-functional requirements, in particular i) near-real-time responsiveness, ii) scalability to a very high number of assets and iii) reliability. These requirements make it impossible to design the application in isolation from the target system.

3   Design Considerations of the SADMAS Approach

The SADMAS application development process leads to several issues, which should be considered and tackled early on in the development process. Below, we introduce some of the most important ones. Concretely, we discuss the bottom-up system evolution, an important stance to be adopted in the development process. We continue with stressing the need to support elaboration tolerance both of the application design, as well as the mixed-mode simulation used for evaluation of the application iterations. Finally, we conclude with a set of issues ensuring cross-platform portability of the application w.r.t. the target deployment infrastructure.

3.1   Bottom-Up System Evolution

Ideally, the SADMAS process will proceed from testing of the first application prototype against a full environment simulation, through replacements of the rudimentary and simpler interfaces to the physical target system, eventually to replacement of the simulation with the target system itself. In consequence, the design of both the application and the simulation cannot be based on a blueprint resulting from a green-field-style top-down analytical procedure. The discussion of the scope of applicability of the SADMAS process (Subsection 2.3) implies that typically, the nature of the implemented application will be such that it is being constructed *into* an existing target system, rather than being developed from scratch including its environment. In result, the overall behaviour of the application, together with the target system cannot be characterised in separation and must be considered as a whole. As an example, consider the running example, the *AgentFly* air traffic management system, which will be typically seamlessly deployed into the already set up and strictly regulated airspace infrastructure. From the point of view of a single agent within the system, an unmanned aircraft, the behaviour of the other aircrafts is a part of the environment behaviour. However, these aircrafts are in fact components of the implemented application on par with the agent in consideration. The iterative SADMAS process is based on tight coupling between the application and simulation development and stresses growing accuracy of the simulation w.r.t. the target system. That is, it supports the bottom-up approach to maintaining the relevance of the simulation to the deployment environment by gradual replacement of ever more significant parts of the simulation with the real-world APIs. Thus it provides a solid support for the evolutionary application development principle.

In AgentFly: The planning and collision avoidance application in *AgentFly* has been designed in an evolutionary manner respecting the bottom-up approach to interaction with the environment. The principle objective was to delegate the aircraft planning autonomy on board of the UAVs and thus minimise the role of the centralised point of control. Several variants of the negotiation mechanism used for collision avoidance have been developed (including the pair-wise and the multi-party negotiation schemes) and evaluated on a high-fidelity simulation of UAV flight and sensor behaviour. Experiments on a range of synthetic, as well as real-world inspired scenarios provided empirical evidence that the simpler and more robust pair-wise collision avoidance algorithms are sufficient even in the most extreme cases.

3.2   Elaboration Tolerance

As a consequence of the SADMAS process, at any specific development iteration, the application and simulation releases must be frozen and ideally further iterations should not require change reverse, or backward modifications of the features implemented in previously frozen releases. The strong emphasis of the process on evolutionary development implies that already the initial application design and layout provides sufficient flexibility w.r.t. future changes and adaptations. That is, more than with other application development methodologies, SADMAS approach calls for strong emphasis on *elaboration tolerance* of both, the design, as well as the actual implementations of the application and the simulation. Paraphrasing the origin of the term in [12], a design is elaboration tolerant to the extent that it is convenient to modify it to take into account new phenomena or changed circumstances. In particular, transposed to multi-agent application development domain, this leads to a requirement that the design should be based on component-based practises with well-thought-of set of APIs, that, ideally, do not change during the development process.

While nowadays the call for flexibility of software design is relatively obvious and straightforward (mostly due to maintenance reasons), often it is difficult to ensure the flexibility w.r.t. right kind of future modifications. Without going deeper into this issue, we see a potential for methodological support assisting multi-agent systems programmers and designers to understand the elaboration tolerance implications on their designs in order to assist them to make the right and informed decisions in the early stages of the application development process.

In AgentFly: The planning algorithms developed in *AgentFly* project [18] have been designed so that they perform general, yet extremely efficient on-the-fly planning in complex 4D space (spatio-temporal planning). While this design decision did not break elaboration tolerance and kept options open w.r.t. the potential uses of the algorithms in various types of aircrafts, at certain stage we realised that the data structures used in planning algorithms were too closely linked with the implemented planning algorithms tailored for Cartesian 3D co-ordinates. At the point, when the systems needed to scale up to the level of US National Airspace, there was a requirement to upgrade the planning algorithms from Cartesian coordinates to GPS coordinate system, which however turned out to be a major issue. Due to the efficiency requirements, elaboration toler-ance have not been met and was not foreseen in this aspect of code development. This design issue finally resulted in major implementation difficulties as large portions of the already constructed application had to be modified accordingly.

3.3   Cross-Platform Portability and Deployment Issues

As a consequence of the gradual shift of the series of mixed-mode simulations towards interfacing with the real-world target system, the SADMAS process also dictates gradual transfer of the application from synthetic settings to deployment on the target platform. In particular, e.g., in the air-traffic management domain this means gradual porting of the core algorithms for collision avoidance from synthetic personal computer environment to the actual hardware platform where it will be finally deployed, i.e., the embedded computers running on board of the target aircrafts. In order to ensure that such a gradual deployment of the application to the real-world system is possible, several additional design and implementation considerations should be respected.

Technically, the elaboration tolerant application development must be supported from early stages on. The decisions include appropriate choices of programming platforms, tools and supporting infrastructure so as to aim at maximum cross-platform portability of the application, as well as the relevant aspects of the mixed-mode simulation.

As far as the application design is concerned, we argue that in the multi-agent systems context, the initial application design should strive for maximum decen-tralisation of decision making of the application components, the agents. That is, the multi-agent application logic has to be implemented so that it respects the actual constraints and properties of the target system, such as bandwidth, latency, etc.

In order to comply with general real-time properties of many real-world ap-plication domains, full asynchronicity of the application components, the agents, should be striven for whenever possible. Even though in general it is non-trivial and even relatively difficult to implement and especially debug asynchronous sys-tems, we argue, these difficulties must be overcome in order to be able to routinely propose and implement elaboration tolerant multi-agent application designs. We see a great potential in methodological guidelines and design patterns aiming at assisting developers to work out fully asynchronous multi-agent systems.

Finally, the design of the mixed-mode simulation must enable and facilitate the iterative gradual replacement of individual modules with interfaces for interaction with the real-world system. It should ensure from the project beginning on that the individual interfaces to the environment are clearly separated and defined in a general way so that they closely correspond to the respective aspects of the target real-world system. This clear separation and modularisation will later in the process enable the gradual and piece-wise replacement of the API's to simulated modules with interfaces to the actual sensors and actuators of the application to the target system.

Again, while each of the above considerations belongs to standard best practises of engineering of complex software systems, often they are not respected, or difficult to consider in development utilising simulations. It is important to consider in the earliest stages of application development the relevance of not only the application design w.r.t. the target system, but also of the design of the multi-agent simulation w.r.t. the target system. It is thus vital to keep a strong separation between the design of the application w.r.t. the design and implementation of the simulation itself. Only this way the developer can avoid the situation when the implemented application works flawlessly when evaluated against a complex simulation, however breaks down when finally deployed to the target system. Often the primary problem lies not in the design of the application itself, but in the level of abstraction assumed by the design of the simulation which simplified some crucial aspect of the target system too far from the real-world conditions.

In AgentFly: The main constraint in the design of the autonomous collision avoidance system is the bandwidth and reliability of aircraft-to-ground communication links, which prevents deployment of a centralised solution. The collision avoidance mechanism was therefore designed in a fully decentralised manner. Although each negotiation is managed by a master plane, this plane is chosen dynamically from within the collision pair and/or group. From the beginning, the mechanisms was designed as fully asynchronous and its computational and memory requirements were kept in line with the parameters of aeroplane's onboard computers. Altogether, these made the process of migrating the mechanism from simulated aircrafts to real hardware UAV platforms relatively straightforward.

4   Requirements on a SADMAS Platform

One of the key components of an ideal pragmatic SADMAS toolkit is a platform for construction, calibration and execution of the series of mixed-mode simulations used for evaluating the iterations of the developed application. In the following, we discuss some of the properties such a platform should feature in order to facilitate the SADMAS process.

4.1   Adjustable Simulation Fidelity

The simulation has to accurately and reliably replicate those aspects of the target system that are critical for the real-world operation of the developed application. Key aspects that need to be modelled include computation and communication capabilities of the target system, such as throughput limitations, communication delays, and communication link failures. In the case of multi-robot applications, interaction with the environment, i.e., sensors, actuators and physics of the component on which the application is to be deployed, need to be also modelled with sufficient fidelity, as it is done in robotic simulators (e.g., [11]).

High-fidelity simulations require high amount of resources, both at run-time but also at the design time when a sufficiently detailed model of the target system has to be designed, implemented and properly calibrated. The level of abstraction chosen for the simulation should be balanced with i) the ability to scale to the required size of the target systems and ii) obtain enough data about the behaviour of the target system to facilitate precise calibration of the simulation model. Depending on the focus of the application, the level of detail required may vary for different aspects of the target system and/or different parts of the simulation. Multi-scale simulation techniques [10] can be employed for this purpose.

In AgentFly: The lesson learnt from *AgentFly* development was that the granularity of the simulation does not need to be defined *a priori* and that it is rather important to decide upon the right level of fidelity for specific scenarios. Low simulation granularity does not make it believable and would not facilitate the application migration from the simulation environment to the final system. On the other hand way too high fidelity may become a resource overkill (both financially, as well as w.r.t. human resources involved). For the original *AgentFly* simulation, the application was modelled as a collective of micro UAVs flying in perfect conditions. At that stage, the development team was putting its focus into the fidelity of the physical dynamic model of the flying asset. In later stages, during *AgentFly* extension to support air traffic management in the US National Airspace, the fidelity of the simulation had to be refined towards providing i) a high precision aeroplane model based on the *Total Energy Model* of the BADA (Base of Aircraft DAta) aeroplane performance standards (cf. [7]), ii) full models of the geographical environment including landing, take-off locations, no-fly zones and special purpose air traffic sectors; and finally iii) full models of the weather. The design of the home-developed simulation platform *A-globe Simulation* [15] turned out to be flexible enough to accommodate the corresponding adjustments of the simulation without major frictions.

4.2   Rich Environmental Modelling

The problem domains the SADMAS approach is suitable for usually concern agents situated in and interacting with a real-world physical environment.

 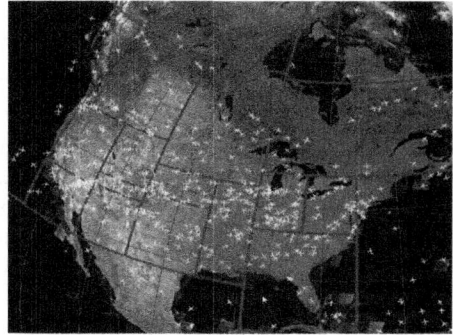

Fig. 3. Left: rich environment model in *Tactical-AgentFly* simulation. Right: dynamic partitioning of the environment in *AgentFly* simulation.

An ideal SADMAS simulation platform has to provide abstractions and run-time support for simulating rich virtual environments. Depending on the type of application, different modes of interaction with environment have to be accommodated, including perception (via sensors) and acting (via actuators) in the environment, possibly also agent mobility within the environment. Possibly, some applications may require modelling of the environment dynamics itself (e.g., weather), and this might also need to be simulated with sufficient precision.

Rich environmental models are supported by robotic simulation platforms and engines for simulating digital virtual worlds. However, most existing popular multi-agent-based simulation platforms (e.g., [5,20]), so far only focus at highly abstracted environments (graphs, grids), though recently support for GIS concepts has been added. Structurally complex environments involving object such as buildings are still generally unsupported in general-purpose multi-agent-based simulation platforms.

In AgentFly: Important part of air traffic simulation is a detailed modelling of the landscape, the ground terrain and also weather, in particular wind. In the simulation used for testing collaborative UAV-based surveillance control mechanisms [13], we had to model urban terrain, sensors and both the physical, as well as logical movement of ground units. Figure 3 provides a snapshot of the simulation visualisation involving the urban environment with a number of ground agents and two UAVs collaboratively performing surveillance and tracking tasks over the area.

4.3   Simulation Scalability

In many application domains, with the advancing SADMAS process iteration, the size of the simulated target (sub-)system will significantly grow. To accommodate to the variable simulation size, an ideal SADMAS simulation platform design should emphasise scalability. Both, in terms of growing number of entities and components of the multi-agent application, as well as the increasing size and accuracy of the simulated environment. To support the scalability on the simulation model level, the platform should therefore also support scalability w.r.t. the growing number computational resources.

The multi-agent-based approach to simulation provides natural decomposition of the computation process. However, there are two main factors that may prevent scalability of the simulation. Firstly, it is the super-linear growth in communication requirements between agents with their growing number, and secondly, naive employment of the centralised environment simulation design. The first factor is application-specific and closely linked to the way individual agents in the target system interact with each other during their operation; there are no universal techniques by which the problem can be generally addressed. The bottleneck represented by the centralised environment simulation design could be eliminated by distribution of fragments of the simulation, i.e., partitioning the environment into a number of zones which are each hosted on a separate computational core. Distributed agent-based simulations are a relatively new concept and platform support for them is relatively limited. We can distinguish between two types of distribution: i) agents only and ii) agents and environment distribution. The latter is more complex because it requires partitioning the environment state and correctly synchronising it across multiple machines.

In AgentFly: As a part of the collaboration with the FAA (US Federal Aviation Administration), it was requested to model the entire US National Air Space traffic comprising of approximately 75,000 flights a day. Due to high-fidelity of the simulation required (cf. the above subsections), simulating such a number of flights turned out to be impossible on a single machine. A fully distributed simulation was therefore developed, where both the application logic and simulation of the environment was distributed. In the latter case, this was achieved by dynamically partitioning the environment into a number zones. The Figure 3 depicts the dynamic fragmentation of the environment where each zone was dedicated to a single host computer. With the growing number of simulated aircrafts in the airspace, the environment was re-fragmenting and re-distributing in order to ensure load-balancing of the entire distributed simulation among the hosts of the computational cluster running it.

4.4   Mixed-Mode Support

Mixed-mode simulation, the core element of the SADMAS approach, denotes a simulation with a capability to replace part of the simulation by the respective physical component whose state, its sensory inputs and actuator outputs, are reflected back into the simulation using a phantom simulated entity. Mixed-mode simulation enables a series of intermediate steps in the validation of the developed application, between a fully simulation-based evaluation and evaluation on a fully deployed application. In a mixed-mode simulation, parts of the application logic can be tested on a real hardware platform in situations which involve multiple entities (e.g., an autonomous car driving through a congested city), without the

Fig. 4. *AgentFly* UAV hardware platforms. Left, Procerus fixed-wing aircraft with the development toolkit; Right, *LinkQuad* vertical take-off and landing quad-rotor aircraft.

need to have all the entities physically available. The latter could be either too costly, or potentially dangerous either for the assets involved, or the deployed environment itself.

Mixed-mode simulation might be the only way to evaluate the developed application (prior to a full-scale deployment) in scenarios where the target system is beyond our control and cannot be easily used for evaluation, such as e.g., in urban traffic or human crowds. A fundamental requirement that mixed-mode execution thus imposes on the simulation platform is the ability of the simulation to run in, at least, real-time (one wall-clock second corresponds to one simulation second). The agent-based tools and platforms would need to support various levels of state synchronisation so that an easy plug-and-play, resp. replace-and-forget functionality is provided.

In AgentFly: AgentFly has been successfully tested on physical hardware platform, *Unicorn* UAV test platform by Procerus Technologies [19] and we are currently working on porting the relevant application fragments to the Linksys *LinkQuad* vertical take-off and landing aircraft (cf. Figure 4). We already performed a series of successful experiments with *AgentFly* planning algorithms running on the platforms and we are currently adapting the *AgentFly* simulation platform to be able to accommodate a mixed-mode simulation with several physical flying assets (2 Unicorn UAVs and 1 LinkQuad aircrafts).

The second *AgentFly* mixed-mode line of evaluation is w.r.t. the large-scale air-traffic management systems of the US National Airspace. There we are working towards mixed-mode mixed-mode simulations of the domain populated with a number of computational models of the controllers, with several controllers instantiated with real human air traffic controllers provided by FAA.

4.5   Evaluation Modes

The SADMAS process is in its heart evaluation-driven. It dictates advancement to the next development process iteration only when the actual release performs sufficiently well against the current choice of implemented features and level of abstraction embodied in the iteration of the mixed-mode simulation. Different modes in which the simulation is used result in several different simulation execution modes which should be supported by an ideal SADMAS simulation platform:

single instance mode: the goal is to execute a single simulation run in a minimum time. This requirement arises whenever the simulation is used during interactive development and testing of the application. In this case, minimisation of simulation time improves the productivity of the programmer.

batch mode: the goal is to execute a batch of simulation runs as fast as possible. This need arises when performing extensive simulation-based evaluations which involve simulating the system in different configurations.

real-time mode: the goal is to execute the simulation in real-time. This final requirement arises when performing mixed-mode simulation against the real-world target system.

If a single host is incapable of running the simulation sufficiently fast, the only way to perform the single instance and real-time modes is by distributing the simulation over multiple machines. We discuss the system distribution above, in Subsection 4.3.

As long as a single simulation instance can fit into a memory of a single machine, the batch-mode evaluation is often best performed by *not* distributing the simulation run, but fitting as many, possibly smaller-scale, simulation runs on a single host. Our experience shows, that such a setup generally leads to lower overheads, while we were still able to retrieve reasonable experimental data from the batch-mode simulations; though this might not hold universally.

In AgentFly: The actual development and debugging of *AgentFly* relied on the single-instance execution mode. The need for batch-mode evaluation arose and became prominent in testing efficiency of the developed collision avoidance methods. The capability of the multi-agent application has been tested on a series of super-conflict scenarios in which a number of aircrafts are set to collide in a single space point. In these scenarios, various aspects of the application performance were tested, such as i) total length of the flight trajectory, ii) flight safety expressed in the number of near misses, iii) bandwidth requirement or iv) total computational time. For such experimental setups involving real hardware assets, the possibility of employing mixed-mode simulations is crucial in order to minimise the potential risks of the project.

5 Discussion and Related Work

Some of the issues raised in the Section 3 on application design considerations have been addressed in the field of agent-based software engineering. Example methodologies include *Adelfe* [3], a methodology for the design of adaptive software situated in unpredictable environments. *Gaia* [21], general methodology that supports both the micro-level, agent structure, as well as the macro-level, agent society and organisational aspects of agent development. *Prometheus* [14] methodology provides hierarchical structuring mechanisms which allow design to be performed at multiple levels of abstraction. Such mechanisms are crucial to the pragmatics of large-scale complex systems development. *Tropos* [4] methodology puts major focus on agent-oriented requirements engineering perspective.

Though some of the agent-oriented software engineering methodologies provide support for evolutionary application development, they assume the testing is done directly against the target environment. They do not explicitly support simulation-based development cycle in which the testing of the developed multi-agent application is first done on simulations of the target system. We argue, that the here introduced methodology of *Simulation-Aided Design of Multi-Agent Systems* is orthogonal to the existing methodological approaches and can be relatively easily combined with them. While traditional multi-agent systems development methodologies are to be applied to the overall application design, the SADMAS approach rather guides developers through the intermediary development life-cycle of the project and ensures that 1) the application is continuously evaluated against relevant and sufficiently accurate simulated environments, and as a consequence of this, 2) attention is paid to the relevance of the application w.r.t. relevant aspects of the environment continuously throughout the application life-cycle. Here we speak about both knowingly crucial issues and aspects of the target system, as well as those which are potentially crucial, however not easily recognised as such in the early phases of application development.

Although, to our knowledge, no general-purpose simulation-oriented agent-based software-engineering methodologies exist, the SADMAS idea has been partially applied in specific sub-domains. A good example is the *Anthill* framework [1] for design, implementation and evaluation of peer-to-peer applications based on ideas such as multi-agent and evolutionary programming. Besides the air traffic domain referenced throughout the paper, some of the core ideas of the SADMAS approach have also been employed in the general traffic and transportation domains, e.g., for designing agent-based demand-responsive transport coordination mechanism [8], for increasing maritime security [9] and for designing multi-agent control of smart grids [16]. In none of the above cases, however, the mixed-mode simulation technique has been used.

Regarding the relationship to general-purpose software engineering methodologies, to an extent, the SADMAS process is similar to Test-Driven Development [2], although SADMAS comes with a significantly more complex test evaluation mechanism employing a simulations. To an extent, the stress of the SADMAS approach on frequent evaluation against more and more accurate simulation models of the target system integrates elements of *continuous integration* [6] approach.

Let us finish with a remark on the cost-effectiveness of the SADMAS approach. At the first sight, the implementation of mixed-mode simulations increases the overall cost of development due to introduction of an additional development step which brings in rather non-trivial costs. The additional costs of mixed-mode simulation can be hardly expressed *a priori* and are very application domain specific. However, we argue that in the cases when the risks involved throughout the application development life-cycle are relatively high, the SADMAS approach can significantly reduce the overall project risks, and safe costs in the face of severe costs in the case of project failure due to either loss of physical assets, or harm done to the target system possibly involving humans (cf. also Section 2.3).

6   Conclusions and Outlook

With the increasing size and complexity of environments and target systems with which multi-agent applications have to interact, there is a growing need to support incremental, evolutionary development processes. In particular, in the context of engineering of large-scale complex and non-linear systems, where all the consequences of individual design decisions are hard to predict *a priori*, there is a need to rapidly evaluate the individual design and implementation decisions without requiring full-scale deployment to the target real-world environment. Such support can be provided by having a multi-agent-based simulation of the target environment available and using it as a testbed during the development of the application. With the advancing application development stages, mixed-mode simulations should be used as an intermediate step between application validation against pure simulation and full deployment to the target system. The *Simulation-Aided Design of Multi-Agent Systems* approach proposed in this paper builds on these ideas and in certain application domains has a potential to significantly reduce risks involved and even speed up the development process.

References

1. Babaoglu, O., Meling, H., Montresor, A.: Anthill: A framework for the development of agent-based peer-to-peer systems. In: International Conference on Distributed Computing Systems (ICDCS), pp. 15–22 (2002)
2. Beck, K.: Test Driven Development: By Example. Addison-Wesley Professional (November 2002)
3. Bernon, C., Gleizes, M.P., Peyruqueou, S., Picard, G.: ADELFE: A Methodology for Adaptive Multi-agent Systems Engineering. In: Petta, P., Tolksdorf, R., Zambonelli, F. (eds.) ESAW 2002. LNCS (LNAI), vol. 2577, pp. 156–169. Springer, Heidelberg (2003)
4. Bresciani, P., Perini, A., Giorgini, P., Giunchiglia, F., Mylopoulos, J.: Tropos: An agent-oriented software development methodology. Autonomous Agents and Multi-Agent Systems 8, 203–236 (2004)
5. Collier, N.: RePast: An extensible framework for agent simulation. Technical Report 36, The University of Chicago, Social Science Research (2003)
6. Duvall, P.M., Matyas, S., Glover, A.: Continuous Integration: Improving Software Quality and Reducing Risk. Addison-Wesley Professional (July 2007)
7. The European Organisation for the Safety of Air Navigation. EUROCONTROL BADA (2011),
   http://www.eurocontrol.int/eec/public/standard_page/proj_BADA.html

8. Horn, M.E.T.: Multi-modal and demand-responsive passenger transport systems: a modelling framework with embedded control systems. Transportation Research Part A: Policy and Practice 36(2), 167–188 (2002)
9. Jakob, M., Vaněk, O., Urban, Š., Benda, P., Pěchouček, M.: Employing Agents to Improve the Security of International Maritime Transport. In: Proceedings of the 6th workshop on Agents in Traffic and Transportation, ATT 2010 (May 2010)
10. Jakovljevic, G., Basch, D.: Implementing multiscale traffic simulators using agents. In: 26th International Conference on Information Technology Interfaces, vol. 1, pp. 519–524 (June 2004)
11. Koenig, N., Howard, A.: Design and use paradigms for Gazebo, an open-source multi-robot simulator. In: Proceedings of the 2004 IEEE/RSJ International Conference on Intelligent Robots and Systems (IROS 2004), vol. 3, pp. 2149–2154 (September 2004)
12. McCarthy, J.: Elaboration tolerance (1999),
    http://www-formal.stanford.edu/jmc/elaboration.html
13. Pavlíček, D., Jakob, M., Semsch, E., Pěchouček, M.: Occlusion-aware multi-uav surveillance of multiple urban areas. In: 6th Workshop on Agents in Traffic and Transportation, ATT 2010 (2010)
14. Padgham, L., Winikoff, M.: Prometheus: A practical agent-oriented methodology. Agent-Oriented Methodologies, 107–135 (2005)
15. Pěchouček, M., Šišlák, D., Pavlíček, D., Volf, P., Kopřiva, Š.: AGENTFLY: Distributed Simulation of Air Traffic Control Using Unmanned Aerial Vehicles. In: Proceedings of 2nd Conference for Unmanned Aerial Systems, UAS (March 2010)
16. Pipattanasomporn, M., Feroze, H., Rahman, S.: Multi-agent systems in a distributed smart grid: Design and implementation. In: IEEE/PES Power Systems Conference and Exposition, PSCE 2009, pp. 1–8 (2009)
17. Šišlák, D., Volf, P., Pěchouček, M.: Agent-Based Cooperative Decentralized Airplane-Collision Avoidance. IEEE Transactions on Intelligent Transportation Systems (99), 1–11 (2009)
18. Šišlák, D., Volf, P., Pěchouček, M.: Agent-Based Cooperative Decentralized Airplane-Collision Avoidance. IEEE Transactions on Intelligent Transportation Systems (99), 1–11 (2010)
19. Procerus Technologies. Procerus Technologies: Fly Light with world's smallest UAV Autopilot (2011), http://procerusuav.com/
20. Wilensky, U.: Netlogo. Technical report, Center for Connected Learning and Computer-Based Modeling, Northwestern University (1999),
    http://ccl.northwestern.edu/netlogo/
21. Zambonelli, F., Jennings, N.R., Wooldridge, M.: Developing multiagent systems: The gaia methodology. ACM Trans. Softw. Eng. Methodol. 12(3), 317–370 (2003)

Part II

Reasoning

Reinforcement Learning as Heuristic for Action-Rule Preferences

Joost Broekens, Koen Hindriks, and Pascal Wiggers

Man-Machine Interaction department (MMI)
Delft University of Technology

Abstract. A common action selection mechanism used in agent-oriented programming is to base action selection on a set of rules. Since rules need not be mutually exclusive, agents are often underspecified. This means that the decision-making of such agents leaves room for multiple choices of actions. Underspecification implies there is potential for improvement or optimalization of the agent's behavior. Such optimalization, however, is not always naturally coded using BDI-like agent concepts. In this paper, we propose an approach to exploit this potential for improvement using reinforcement learning. This approach is based on learning rule priorities to solve the rule-selection problem, and we show that using this approach the behavior of an agent is significantly improved. Key here is the use of a state representation that combines the set of rules of the agent with a domain-independent heuristic based on the number of active goals. Our experiments show that this provides a useful generic base for learning while avoiding the state-explosion problem or overfitting.

Categories and subject descriptors: I.2.5 [**Artificial Intelligence**]: Programming Languages and Software; I.2.11 [**Artificial Intelligence**]: Distributed Artificial Intelligence—*Intelligent Agents.*

General terms: Agent programming languages; Robotics; AI; Methodologies and Languages.

Keywords: Agent-oriented programming, rule preferences, reinforcement learning.

1   Introduction

Agent platforms, whether agent programming languages or architectures, that are rule-based and use rules to generate the actions that an agent performs introduce the problem of how to select rules that generate the most effective choice of action. Such agent programming languages and architectures are based on concepts such as rules, beliefs, and goals to generate agent behavior. Here, rules specify the agent's behavior. A planning or reasoning engine tries to resolve all rules by matching the conditions and actions with the current mental state of the agent. Multiple instantiations of each rule can therefore be possible. An agent can select any one of these instantiations, resulting in a particular action. So,

R. Collier, J. Dix, and P. Novák (Eds.): ProMAS 2010, LNAI 6599, pp. 25–40, 2012.

the rule-selection problem is analogous to but different from the action-selection problem [13]. Rule selection is about which uninstantiated rule to choose; action selection, in the context of rule-based agent frameworks, is about which instantiated rule to chose. In this paper, when we refer to rule we mean uninstantiated rule, i.e, rules that still contain free variables.

Rule-based agent languages or architectures typically underspecify the behavior of an agent, leaving room for multiple choices of actions. The reason is that multiple rules are applicable in a particular situation and, as a result, multiple actions may be selected by the agent to perform next. In practice, it is often hard to specify rule conditions that are mutually exclusive. Moreover, doing so is undesirable as the BDI concepts used to develop agents often are not the most suitable for optimizing agent behavior. An alternative approach is to optimize agent behavior based on learning techniques.

In this paper we address the following question: how to automatically prioritize rules in such a way that the prioritization reflects the utility of a rule given a certain goal. Our aim is a generic approach to learning such preferences, that can be integrated in rule-based agent languages or architectures. The overall goal is twofold; to optimize the agent's behavior given a predefined set of rules by an agent programmer, and to help agent programmers to gain insight into the rule preferences and use these to further specify the agent program. As such, we focus on a useful heuristic for rule preferences. We have chosen reinforcement learning (RL) as heuristic as it can cope with delayed rewards and state dependency. These are important aspects in agent behavior as getting to a goal state typically involves a chain of multiple actions, and rules can have different utility depending on the state of the agent/environment.

We present experimental evidence that reinforcement learning can be used to learn rule priorities that can subsequently be used for rule selection. This heuristic for rule priorities works very well, and results in sometimes optimal agent behavior. We demonstrate this with a set of experiments using the GOAL agent programming language [5]. Key in our approach is that the RL mechanism uses a state representation based on a combination of the set of rules of the agent and the number of active goals. Our state representation is as abstract as possible while still being a useful base for learning. We take this approach for two main reasons: (1) we aim for a generic learning mechanism; RL should be a useful addition to all programs, and the programmer should not be bothered by the state representation or state-space explosions; (2) an abstract state helps generalization of the learning result as a concrete state representation runs the risk of over fitting on a particular problem instance.

It is important to immediately explain one aspect of our approach that is different from the usual setup for reinforcement learning. In reinforcement learning it is common to learn the *action* that has to be selected from a set of possible actions. In our approach, however, we will apply reinforcement learning to select an *uninstantiated rule* from a set of rules in an agent program. An uninstantiated rule (called *action rule* in GOAL, see also Listing 1) is a generic rule defined by the agent programmer.

```
if goal(tower([X|T])), not(bel(T=[])) then move(X,table)
```

is an example of such a rule. We refer to an instantiated rule as a completely resolved (grounded) version of an action rule generated by the reasoning engine responsible for matching rules to the agent's current state. This also means that the action in an instantiated rule may be selected for execution, as the conditions of the rule have been verified by the engine.

```
if goal(tower([a,b])), not(bel([b]=[])) then move(a,table)
```

is an example of an instantiated rule and the action move(a,table) is the corresponding action that may be selected. One instantiated rule thus is the equivalent of one action (as it is completely filled in). Many different instantiated rules may be derived from one and the same program rule, depending on the state. An uninstantiated rule is more generic as it defines many possible actions. We focus on learning preferences for uninstantiated rules.

The paper is organized as follows. Section 2 discusses some related work and discusses how our approach differs from earlier work. In Section 3 we briefly introduce the agent language GOAL and use it to illustrate the rule selection problem. Section 4 presents our approach to this problem based on reinforcement learning and presents an extension of GOAL with a reinforcement learning mechanism. In Section 5 experimental results are presented that show the effectiveness of this mechanism. Finally, Section 6 concludes the paper and discusses future work.

2   Related Work

There is almost no work on incorporating learning mechanisms into agent programming. More generally, BDI agents typically lack learning capabilities to modify their behavior [1], although several related approaches do exist.

With regards to related work, several studies attempt to learn rule sets that produce a policy for solving a problem in a particular domain. Key in these approaches is that the rules themselves are learned, or more specific, rule instantiations are generated and evaluated with respect to a utility function. The best performing rule instantiations are kept and result in a policy for the agent. The evaluation mechanism can be different, for example genetic programming [9] or supervised machine learning [7]. In any case, the main difference is that our approach tries to learn rule preferences, i.e., a priority for pre-existing rules given that multiple rules can be active, while the previously mentioned approaches try to learn rule instantiations that solve a problem.

Other studies attempt to learn rule preferences like we do. However, these approaches are based on learning preferences for instantiated rules [10][4], not preferences for the uninstantiated, generic, rules. Further, the state used for learning is often represented in a much more detailed way [10][4]. Finally, as the state representation strongly depends on the environment, the use of learning mechanisms often involves effort and understanding of the programmer [10].

Reinforcement learning has recently been added to cognitive architectures such as Soar [8] and Act-R [2]. In various respects these cognitive architectures are related to agent programming and architectures. They use similar concepts to generate behavior, using mental constructs such as knowledge, beliefs and goals, are also based on an sense-plan-act cycle, and generate behavior using these mental constructs as input for a reasoning- or planning-based interpreter. Most importantly, cognitive architectures typically are rule-based, and therefore also need to solve the rule (and action) selection problem. For example, Soar-RL has been explicitly used to study action selection in the context of RL [6]. Soar-RL [10] is the approach that comes closest to ours in the sense that it uses a similar reinforcement learning mechanism (Sarsa) to learn rule preferences. As explained above, the key difference is that we attempt to learn uninstantiated rule preferences, while Soar-RL learns preferences for instantiated rules [10]. Another key difference is that we use an abstract rule-activity based state representation complemented with a 'goals left to fulfill' counter, as explained in section 4.2.

Finally, [1] present a learning technique based on decision trees to learn the context conditions of plan rules. The focus of their work is to make agents adaptive in order to avoid failures. Learning a context condition refers to learning when to select a particular plan/action, while learning a rule preference refers to attaching a value to a particular plan/action. Our work is thus complementary in the sense that we do not learn context conditions, but instead propose a learning mechanism that is able to guide the rule selection mechanism itself.

3   The Agent Language GOAL

In this Section we briefly present the agent programming language GOAL and use it to illustrate the rule selection problem in agent languages and architectures. For a more extensive discussion of GOAL we refer the reader to [5]. The approach to the rule selection problem introduced in this paper is not specific to GOAL and may be applied to other similar BDI-based platforms. As our approach involves a domain-independent heuristic based on counting the number of goals that need to be achieved, the language GOAL is however particularly suitable to illustrate the approach as declarative goals are a key concept in the language.

GOAL, for Goal-Oriented Agent Language, is a programming language for programming *rational agents*. GOAL agents derive their choice of action from their beliefs and goals. A GOAL agent program consists of five sections: (1) a knowledge section, called the *knowledge base*, (2) a set of beliefs, collectively called the *belief base*, (3) a set of *declarative* goals, called the *goal base*, (4) a *program section* which consists of a set of *action rules*, and (5) an *action specification section* that consists of a specification of the pre- and postconditions of actions of the agent. Listing 1 presents an example GOAL agent that manipulates blocks on a table.

The knowledge, beliefs and goals of a *GOAL* agent are represented using a knowledge representation language. Together, these make up the mental state of

Table 1. Agent for Solving a Blocks World Problem

```
 1  main stackBuilder {
 2    knowledge{
 3      block(a), block(b), block(c).
 4      clear(table).
 5      clear(X) :- block(X), not(on(Y,X)).
 6      tower([X]) :- on(X,table).
 7      tower([X,Y|T]) :- on(X,Y), tower([Y|T]).
 8    }
 9    beliefs{
10      on(a,table), on(b,table), on(c,a).
11    }
12    goals{
13      on(a,b), on(b,c), on(c,table).
14    }
15    program{
16      if goal(tower([X|T])),
17        bel((T=[Y|T1], tower(T)); (T=[], Y=table))
18        then move(X,Y).
19      if goal(tower([X|T])), not(bel(T=[]))
20        then move(X,table).
21    }
22    actionspec{
23      move(X,Y) {
24        pre{ clear(X), clear(Y), on(X,Z) }
25        post{ not(on(X,Z)), on(X,Y) }
26      }
27    }
28  }
```

an agent. Here, we use *Prolog* to represent mental states. An agent's knowledge represents general conceptual and domain knowledge, and does not change. An example is the definition of the concept tower in Listing 1. In contrast, the beliefs of an agent represent the *current state of affairs* in the environment of an agent. By performing actions and possibly by events in the environment, the environment changes, and it is up to the agent to make sure its beliefs stay up to date. Finally, the goals of an agent represent *what* the agent wants the environment to be like. For example, the agent of Listing 1 wants to realise a state where block a is on top of block b. Goals are to be interpreted as *achievement goals*, that is as a goal the agent wants to achieve at some future moment in time and does not believe to be the case yet. This requirement is implemented by imposing a rationality constraint such that any goal in the goal base must not believed to be the case. Upon achieving the *complete* goal, an agent will drop the goal. The agent in Listing 1 will drop the goal on(a,b), on(b,c), on(c,table) if this configuration of blocks has been achieved, and only if the *complete* configuration has been achieved. Note that if only one of these elements has been achieved, that element will not be a goal to be achieved anymore (called an a-goal), so the program will not consider the element as an active goal, but the overall goal on(a,b), on(b,c), on(c,table) is still in the active goal base.

As GOAL agents derive their choice of action from their knowledge, beliefs and goals, they need a way to inspect their mental state. GOAL agents do so by means of *mental state conditions*. Mental state conditions are Boolean combinations of so-called basic *mental atoms* of the form **bel**(ϕ) or **goal**(ϕ). For example, **bel**(tower([c,a])) is a mental state condition which is true in the initial mental state specified in the agent program of Listing 1.

A GOAL agent uses so-called *action rules* to generate possible actions it may select for execution. This provides for a rule-based action selection mechanism, where rules are of the form **if** ψ **then** $a(t)$ with ψ a mental state condition and $a(t)$ an action. A mental state condition part of an action rule thus determines the states in which the action $a(t)$ may be executed. Action rules are located in the program section of a GOAL agent. The first action rule in this section of our example agent generates so-called *constructive moves*, whereas the second rule generates actions to move a *misplaced* block to the table. Informally, the first rule reads as follows: if the agent wants to construct a tower with X on top of a tower that has Y on top and the agent believes that the tower with Y on top already exists, or believes Y should be equal to the table, then it may consider moving X on top of Y; in this case the move would put the block Y *in position*, and it will never have to be moved again. The second rule reads as follows: if the agent finds that a block is misplaced, i.e. believes it to be in a position that does not match the (achievement) goal condition, then it may consider moving the block to the table. These rules code a strategy for solving blocks world problems that can be proven to always achieve a goal configuration. As such, they already specify a *correct* strategy for solving blocks world problems. However, they do not necessarily determine a unique choice of action. For example, the agent in Listing 1 may either move block d on top of block b using the first action rule, or move the same block to the table using the second action rule. In such a case, a GOAL agent will nondeterministically select either of these actions. It is important for our purposes to note here that the choice of rule is at stake here, and not a particular *instantiation* of a rule. Moreover, as in the blocks world it is a good strategy to prefer making constructive moves rather than other types of moves, the behavior of the agent can be improved by preferring the application of the first rule over the second whenever both are applicable. It is exactly this type of preference that we aim to learn automatically.

Finally, to complete our discussion of GOAL agents, actions are specified in the action specification section of such an agent using a STRIPS-like specification. When the preconditions of the action are true, the action is executed and the agent updates its beliefs (and subsequently its goals) based on the postcondition. Details can be found in [5].

As illustrated by our simple example agent for the blocks world, rule-based agent programs or architectures may leave room for applying multiple rules, and, as a consequence, for selecting multiple actions for execution. Rule-based agents thus typically are *underspecified*. Such underspecification is perfectly fine, as long as the agent achieves its goals, but may also indicate there is room for improvement of the agent's behavior (though not necessarily so). The problem of optimizing the behavior of a rule-based agent thus can be summarized as follows, and consists of two components: First, solving a particular task efficiently depends on using the appropriate rule to produce actions (the rule selection problem) and, second, to select one of these actions for execution (the action selection problem). The latter problem is actually identical to selecting an *instantiated* rule where all variables have been grounded, as instantiated rules that are applicable yield unique actions that may be executed. Uninstantiated rules only yield *action templates* that need to be instantiated before they can be executed.

In this paper we explore a generic and fully automated approach to this optimization problem based on learning, and we propose to use reinforcement learning. Although reinforcement learning is typically applied to solve the action selection problem, here instead we propose to use this learning technique to (partially) solve the rule selection problem. The reason is that we want to incorporate a *generic* learning technique into a rule-based agent that does not require domain-specific knowledge to be inserted by a programmer. As we will show below, applying learning to the rule selection problem in combination with a domain-independent heuristic based on the number of goals still to be achieved provides just such a mechanism.

4   Learning to Solve the Rule Selection Problem

In this Section, we first briefly review some of the basic concepts of reinforcement learning, and then introduce our approach to the rule selection problem based on learning and discuss how we apply reinforcement learning to this problem. We use the agent language GOAL to illustrate and motivate our choices.

4.1   Reinforcement Learning

Reinforcement Learning is a mechanism that enables machines to learn solutions to problems based on experience. The main idea is that by specifying *what* to learn, RL will figure out *how* to do it. An approach based on reinforcement learning assumes there is an environment with a set of possible states, S, a reward function $R(S)$ that defines the reward the agent receives for each state in the environment, and a set of actions A that enable to effect changes to the environment (or an agent in that environment) and move the environment from one state to another according to the state transition function $T(S, A) \rightarrow S$. An RL mechanism then learns a value function, $V(S, A)$, that maps actions in states to values of those actions in that state. It does so by propagating back the reinforcement (reward) received in later states to earlier states and actions, called *value propagation*. RL should do this in such a way that the result of always picking the action with the highest value will lead to the best solution to the problem (the best sequence of actions to solve the problem is the sequence with the highest cumulative reward). Therefore, RL is especially suited for problems in which the solution follows only after a sequence of actions and in which the information available for learning takes the form of a reward (e.g. pass/fail or some utility value).

In order for RL to learn a good value function, it must explore the state space sufficiently, by more or less randomly selecting actions. Exploration is needed to gather a representative sample of interactions so that the transition function T (in case the model of the world is not known) and the reward function R can be learned. Based on T and R, the value function V is calculated. After sufficient exploration, the learning agent switches to an exploitation scheme. Now the value function is used to select the action with highest predicted cumulative reward (the action with the highest $V(s, a)$). For more information on RL see [12].

4.2   GOAL-RL

The idea is to use RL to learn values for the rules in an agent program or architecture, so that a priority of rules can be given at any point during the execution of the agent. Here, we use GOAL to illustrate and implement these ideas, and we call this RL-enabled version GOAL-RL. The basic idea of our contribution is that the GOAL interpreter determines which rules are applicable in a state, while RL learns what the values for applying these same rules are in that state. GOAL will then again be responsible for using these values in the context of rule selection. Various selection mechanisms may be used, e.g., selecting the best rule greedy, or selecting a rule based on a Boltzmann distribution, etc. This setup combines the strengths of a qualitative, logic-based agent platform such as GOAL with the strengths of a learning mechanism such as reinforcement learning.

State representation. RL needs a state representation for learning. Unfortunately, using the agent's mental state or the world state, as is typically done in RL, quickly leads to intractably large state spaces and makes the solutions (if they can be learned at all) domain and even problem-instance specific. Still, our goal is to create a domain-independent mechanism that takes the burden of finding a good rule selection mechanism away from the programmer.

We propose the following approach. Instead of starting to train with a state representation that is as close as possible to the actual agent state, and make that representation more abstract in case of state explosion problems, as is common in RL, we start with a representation that is very abstract, while still being meaningful and specific enough to be useful for learning rule preferences. The benefits of this choice are twofold. First, a trained RL model based on such an abstract state and action representations is potentially more suitable for reuse in different domains and problem instances (learning transfer). Second, by using an abstract state our approach is less vulnerable to large state-spaces and the state-space explosion problem, and, consequently, will learn faster.

The state representation we propose is composed of the following two elements. First, our state representation contains the set of rule-activation pairs itself (i.e. the list of rules and whether a rule is applicable or not). However, for many environments this representation does not contain enough information for the RL algorithm to learn a good value function. Essentially, what is missing is information that guides the RL algorithm towards the end goal. A state representation that only keeps track of the set of rules that are and are not applicable does not contain any information about the approriateness of rules in a particular situation. We add such information by including a second element in the state representation: a version of a well-known progress heuristic used also in planning. The heuristic, which is easily implemented in an agent language or architecture that keeps track of the goals of an agent explicitly, is to count the number of subgoals that still need to be achieved. This is a particularly easy way to compute the so-called *sum cost heuristic* introduced in [3]. Due to its simplicity this heuristic causes almost no overhead in the learning algorithm. This heuristic information is in fact a number that is added to the state used by the reinforcement learning mechanism in order to guide the learning. Adding a heuristic like this will keep the mechanism domain independent, but gives useful information to the RL mechanism to differentiate between states.

Even with this heuristic many states differentiated by the agent itself are conflated in the limited number of states used by the reinforcement learner. Such a state space reduction will sometimes prevent the algorithm from finding optimal solutions (as many RL mechanisms, including the one we use, assume a Markovian state transition). Explicitly adding active goals to the state space is difficult, as these goals are instantiated goals and therefore problem-instance specific, resulting in the need for retraining the RL model for every new problem instance of a particular type of problem (e.g., for each possible instance of the blocks world). Perhaps the abstract (uninstantiated) goals could be used. We feel state representation is definitely an issue for further research. It should be noted, though, that we are not aiming for a perfect learning approach that is always able to find optimal solutions. Instead, we aim for an approach that provides two benefits: it is generic and therefore poses no burden on the programmer, and the approach is able to provide a significant improvement of the agent's behavior, even though this may still not be optimal (optimal being the smallest number of steps possible to solve a problem). The approach to learn rule preferences thus should result in significantly better behavior than that generated by agents that do not learn rule preferences. In the remainder of this paper, we will study and demonstrate how well the domain-independent approach is able to improve the behavior of agents acting in different domains.

In more detail, the approach introduced here consists of the following elements. A state s is a combination of the number of subgoals the agent still has to achieve and the set of rule states. A rule state is either 0, 1 or 2, where 0 means the rule is not active, 1 means there is an instantiation of the rule in which the rule's preconditions are true and 2 means there is an instantiation in which also the preconditions for the action the rule proposes are true meaning the rule fires. For example, if a program has a list of 3 rules, of which the last two in the program fire while the agent still has 4 subgoals to achieve, the state equals to $s = 022 : 4$. An action is represented by a hash based on the rule (in our case simply the index of the rule in the program list; so the action uses the same hash as the rule in the rule-activation pairs used for the state). For example, if the agent would execute an action coming from the first rule in the list, the action equals to $a = 0$, indicating that the agent has picked the first rule for action generation. In our setup, the reward function R is simple. It defines a reward $r = 1$ when all goals are met (the goal list is empty) and $r = 0$ otherwise. The current and next state-action pairs (s, a) and (s', a') are used together with the received reward r' as input for the value function V. A transition function T is learned based on the observed state-action pairs (s, a) and (s', a'). The transition function is used to update the value function according to standard RL assumptions, with one exception: the value for a state-action pair (s, a) is updated according to the probabilistically correct estimate of the occurance of (s', a'), not the maximum. In order to construct the probabilities, the agent counts state occurrences, $N(s)$, and uses this count in a standard weighting mechanism. Values of states are updated as follows:

$$RL(s, a) \leftarrow RL(s, a) + \alpha \cdot (r - RL(s, a)) \tag{1}$$

$$V(s, a) \leftarrow RL(s, a) + \gamma \cdot \sum_i V(s_{a_i}, a_i) \frac{N(s_{a_i}, a_i)}{\sum_j N(s_{a_j}, a_j)} \tag{2}$$

So, a state-action pair (s, a) has a learned reward $RL(s, a)$ and a value $V(s, a)$ that incorporates predicted future reward. $RL(s, a)$ converges to the reward function $R(s, a)$ with a speed proportional to the learning rate α (set to 1 in our experiments). $V(s, a)$ is updated based on $RL(s, a)$ and the weighted average over the values of the next state-action pairs reachable by action $a_{1...i}$ (with a discount factor of γ, set to 0.9 in our experiments). So, we use a standard model-based RL approach [12], with an update function comparable to Sarsa [11].

5   Experiments

In order to assess if rule preferences can be learned using RL with a state representation as described, we have conducted a series of experiments. The goal of these experiments was to find out the sensitivity of our mechanism with respect to (a) the problem domain (we tested two different domains), (b) different problem instantiations within a domain (e.g. random problems), (c) rules used in the agent program (different rule sets fire differently and thus result in both a different state representation and different agent behavior), (d) different goals (a different goal implies a different reward function because $R(s) = 1$ only when all goals are met).

In total we tested 8 different setups. Five setups are in an environment called the *blocks world*, in which the agent has to construct a goal state consisting of a predefined set of stacks of numbered blocks from a start state following standard physics rules (block cannot be removed from underneath other blocks). The agent can grab a block from and drop a block at a particular stack. In principle, it can build infinitely many stacks (the table has no bounds). The agent program lists two rules.

Three setups were in the *logistics domain* in which the agent has to deliver two orders each consisting of two different packages to two clients at different locations. In total there are three locations, with all packages at the starting location and each client at a different location. A location can be reached directly in one action. The agent can load and unload a package as well as goto a different location. The agent program lists five rules.

5.1   Setup

Each experiment consisted of a classic learning experiment in which a training phase of 250 trials (random rule selection) was followed by a exploitation phase of 30 trials (greedy rule selection based on learned values). Such a separation between exploration and exploitation is typical for RL experiments, although online (exploitation during exploration) can also be used. However, online learning has additional issues (such as how to balance exploration/exploitation) that we do not want to address in this paper. For each experiment we present a bar graph showing the average number of actions needed to solve the problem during the training phase (reflecting the goal agent as it would perform on average without learning ability) and during the exploitation phase (reflecting the solution including the trained rule preferences). As a measure of optimality we also show the minimum number of actions needed in one trial to get to a goal state as observed during the first 250 trials (which is the optimal score as it equals the minimum number of steps to reach a solution, except in Figure 3 as explained later). This number is shown in the bar graphs as reference number for the optimality of the learned solution.

5.2   Blocks World Experiments

Five experiments were done using the blocks world. As described in section 3, there are two rules for the $GOAL$ agent, one rule designed to correctly stack blocks on goal stacks (constructive rule) and the other designed to put ill-placed blocks on the table (deconstructive move). Given these two rules, it is easy to see (and prove) that given a choice between the constructive and deconstructive move, the constructive move is always as good as the deconstructive one. It involves putting blocks at their correct position. These blocks do not need to be touched anymore. A deconstructive move involves freeing underlying blocks. This might be necessary to solve the problem, but the removed blocks might also need to be moved again from the table to their correct place at a goal stack.

The first experiment is a test, constructed to find out if the $GOAL$-RL agent can learn the correct rule preferences for a fundamental three-blocks problem. In this problem, three blocks need to be put on one stack starting with C, BA (B on top of A) ending with the goal stack ABC (A on B on C). The agent should learn a preference for the constructive move (a move putting a block on another block, in our case $B > C$), as this allows a solution of the problem in two moves ($B > C$ and $A > BC$), while the deconstructive move (a move putting a block on the table, in our case $B > Table$) needs three ($B > Table$ then $B > C$ and $A > BC$). Indeed, the agent learns this preference, as shown in Figure 1.

The reward in the last experiment comes rather quickly, and the state transitions are provably Markovian, so the positive learning result presented here is not surprising. In the second experiment, we tested if a reward given at a later stage together with a more complex state-space would also give similar results. We constructed a problem of which it is clear that constructive moves are better than deconstructive moves: the inverse-tower problem. Here, the agent is to inverse a tower $IHGFEDCBA$ to $ABCDEFGHI$. Obviously, constructive moves are to be preferred as they build a correct tower, while deconstructive moves only delay building the tower. The rules used by the agent are the same as in the previous experiment. As can be seen in Figure 1, the $GOAL$-RL agent is able to learn the correct rule preferences and thereby produce the optimal solution.

As one of the reasons for choosing an abstract state representation is to find out if this helps learning a solution to multiple problem instances with a problem domain, not just the one trained for, we set up a third experiment based on tower building problem in which the starting configuration is random. This means that at each trial the agent is confronted with a different starting configuration but always has $ABCDEFGHI$ as goal stack. Being able to learn the correct preferences for the rules in this case involves coping with a large amount of environment states that are mapped to a much smaller amount of rule-based states. We have kept the goal static to be able to interpret the result. If the goal is to build a high tower, constructive moves should be clearly preferred over deconstructive ones. Therefore we know that in this experiment the constructive move is clearly favorite and the learning mechanism should be able to learn this. As shown in Figure 2 the agent can indeed learn to generalize over the training samples and learn rule preferences. Note that if we would have taken a state representation more directly based on the actual world (e.g., the current blocks configuration), this generalization is difficult as each new configuration is a new state, and in RL unseen states cannot be used to predict values (unless a RL mechanism is used that uses some form of state feature extraction). Therefore, this result that shows that our approach is able to optimize rule selection in a generic way.

Up until now, the two rules of the agent are relatively smart. Each rule helps solving the problem, i.e., each rule moves forward towards the goal, as even the deconstructive rule never removes a block from a goal stack. In the next experiment we changed the deconstructive move to one that always enables the agent to remove a block form any stack. This results in a *dumb* tower building agent as it can deconstruct correct towers. For this agent to learn correct preferences, it needs to cope with much longer action sequences before the goal is reached as well as many cycles in the state transitions (e.g., when the agent undoes a constructive move). As shown in Figure 2, left and middle, the agent can learn the correct rule preferences and converge to the optimal solution. This is an important result as it shows that the mechanism can cope with different rule sets solving the same problem, as well as optimize agent behavior given a rule set that is clearly sub-optimal (the *dumb* deconstructive move).

In our last experiment with the blocks world, we evaluated whether the learning mechanism is sensitive to the goal itself. It is based on the inverse tower problem, with one variation: instead of having one high tower as goal, we now have three short towers ABC, DEF, GHI as goal stacks as well as a random starting configuration. This variation thus de-emphasizes the merit of constructive moves for the following reason. In order to solve the problem from any random starting configuration, the agent also has to cope with those situations in which one or two long towers are present at the start. These towers need to be deconstructed. As such, even though constructive moves are never worse than deconstructive moves, deconstructive moves become relatively more valuable. As shown in Figure 2, right, the agent still improves the agent behavior significantly, but is not able to always learn the optimal solution. As such our learning approach provides a useful heuristic for rule preferences. The decrease in learning effectiveness is due to the abstractness of the state representation. In the previous experiments, the agent's RL mechanisms could know where it was building the tower, as the number of active subgoals (incorrectly placed blocks) decreases with each well-placed block. In this experiment, however, the number of active subgoals does not map to the environment state in the same fashion (all three towers contribute to this number, but it is impossible to deduce the environment state based on the number of subgoals: e.g., the number 6 does not reflect that tower one and two are build and we are busy with tower three). This means that there is more *state-overloading* in the last experiment, more risk at non Markovian state transitions, hence the RL mechanism will perform worse.

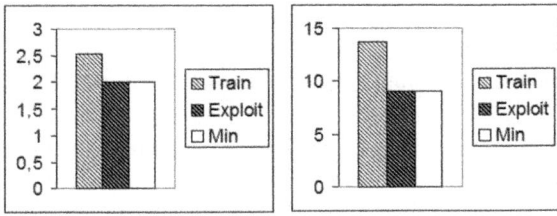

Fig. 1. Left: three-block test. Right: inverse tower.

5.3 Logistics Domain Experiments

In this set of three experiments we test the behavior of our mechanism in a different domain. The domain is called the *logistics domain*. As explained above, this domain involves a truck that needs to distribute from a central location two different orders containing two different items to two clients, making it a total of four items to be delivered. A truck can move between three locations (client 1, client 2 and the distribution center). The agent has two goals: deliver order 1, and deliver order 2. It can pick up and drop an item. When two items are delivered, a subgoal is reached. The agent has five rules, two of which handle pickup, one handles dropping, 1 handles moving to a client, and one handles moving to the distribution center.

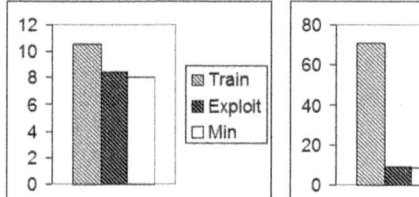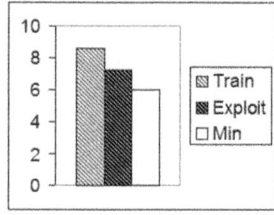

Fig. 2. Left: random start tower. Middle: random start tower dumb. Right random start 3 towers.

In the first experiment, we tested if the agent can learn useful preferences in this domain. As Figure 3, left and middle, shows, it can. This suggests that our results are not specific to a single domain.

In the second experiment, we modified the rule that controls moving to clients such that it also allows the truck to move to clients when empty (the *dumb* delivery truck). This mirrors the dumb tower builder in the blocksworld as it significantly increases the average path to the goal state and it introduces much more variation in the observed states (more random moves). As shown in Figure 3, left and middle, the agent can also learn rule preferences that enable it to converge to the optimal solution. We would like to note that the average learning result is better than the minimum result observed during exploration. This shows that the learned rule preferences perform a strategy that is better than any solution tried in the 250 exploration trials. In other words, learning based on rule-based representations can generalize to a better solution than observed during training.

In the last experiment we manipulated a last important factor: the reward function $R(s)$. In the previous two experiments, the agent was positively reinforced when the last item had been delivered. In this experiment, the agent is reinforced when it returns to the distribution center after having delivered the last item. As shown in Figure 3, right, this results in a suboptimal strategy, although still far better a strategy than the standard *GOAL* agent. This shows that the mechanism is influenced by the moment the reward is given, even if from a logical point of view this should not matter. The reason for this is simple (and resembles the one proposed for the slightly worse performance in the last blocksworld experiment). Due to our abstract state representation, the RL mechanism of the agent cannot differentiate between a state in which it just returned to the distribution center after delivering the *last* item of the last order versus the *first* item of the last order. This means that both environment states are mapped to the same RL state. This RL state receives a reward, and therefore returning to the distribution center gets rewarded. As such, the agent emphasizes returning to the distribution center and learns the suboptimal solution in which it picks up an item and brings it to the client as soon as possible in order to get to the center ASAP because that is where the reward is. The best strategy is of course to pick both items for a client and then move to the

client. However, as the RL mechanism cannot differentiate between two important states, it cannot learn this solution. This clearly shows a drawback of a too
abstract state representation. However, the drawback is relative, as the agent
still performs much better than the standard *GOAL* agent, showing that even
in this case our mechanism is useful as a rule preference heuristic.

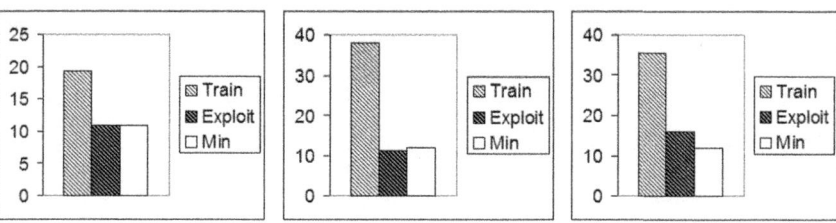

Fig. 3. Left: delivery world. Middle: delivery world dumb. Right: delivery world manipulated $R(s)$.

6   Conclusion

In this paper we have focused on the question of how to automatically prioritize
rules in an agent program. We have proposed an approach to exploit the potential
for improvement in rule-selection using reinforcement learning. This approach
is based on learning state-dependent rule priorities to solve the rule-selection
problem, and we have shown that using this approach the behavior of an agent
is significantly improved. We demonstrate this with a set of experiments using
the *GOAL* agent programming language, extended with a reinforcement learning
mechanism. Key in our approach, called *GOAL*-RL, is that the RL mechanism
uses a state representation based on a combination of the set of rules of the
agent and the number of active goals. This state representation, though very
abstract, still provides a useful base for learning. Moreover, this approach has
two important benefits: (1) it provides for a generic learning mechanism; RL
should be a useful addition to all programs, and the programmer should not be
bothered by the state representation or state-space explosions; (2) an abstract
state helps generalizing the learning result as a concrete state representation runs
the risk of over fitting on a particular problem instance. One of the advantages
is that it does not involve the agent programmer or the need to think about
state representations, models, rewards and learning mechanisms. In the cases
explored in our experiments the approach often finds rule preferences that result
in optimal problem solving behavior. In some case the resulting behavior is not
optimal, but is still significantly better than the non-learning agent.

Given that we have implemented a very generic, heuristic approach there is
still room for further improvement. Two topics are particularly interesting for
future research. First, we want to investigate whether adding other domain-
independent features and making the state space in this sense more specific may
improve the learning even more. Second, we want to investigate whether the use

of different learning mechanisms that are better able to cope with non Markovian worlds and state overloading such as methods based on a partially observable Markov assumption (POMDP) will improve the performance.

Acknowledgments. This research is supported by the Dutch Technology Foundation STW, applied science division of NWO and the Technology Program of the Ministry of Economic Affairs. It is part of the Pocket Negotiator project with grant number VICI-project 08075.

References

1. Airiau, S., Padham, L., Sardina, S., Sen, S.: Enhancing adaptation in bdi agents using learning techniques. International Journal of Agent Technologies and Systems 1(2), 1–18 (2009)
2. Anderson, J.R., Lebiere, C.: The atomic components of thought. Lawrence Erlbaum, Mahwah (1998)
3. Bonet, B., Loerincs, G., Geffner, H.: A robust and fast action selection mechanism for planning. In: Proceedings of AAAI 1997, pp. 714–719 (1997)
4. Deroski, S., De Raedt, L., Driessens, K.: Relational reinforcement learning. Machine Learning 43(1), 7–52 (2001)
5. Hindriks, K.V.: Programming Rational Agents in GOAL. In: Multi-Agent Programming: Languages, Tools and Applications, ch. 4, pp. 119–157. Springer, Heidelberg (2009)
6. Hogewoning, E., Broekens, J., Eggermont, J., Bovenkamp, E.G.P.: Strategies for Affect-Controlled Action-Selection in Soar-RL. In: Mira, J., Álvarez, J.R. (eds.) IWINAC 2007. LNCS, vol. 4528, pp. 501–510. Springer, Heidelberg (2007)
7. Khardon, R.: Learning action strategies for planning domains. Artificial Intelligence 113, 125–148 (1999)
8. Laird, J.E., Newell, A., Rosenbloom, P.S.: Soar: an architecture for general intelligence. Artif. Intell. 33(1), 1–64 (1987)
9. Levine, J., Humphreys, D.: Learning Action Strategies for Planning Domains Using Genetic Programming. In: Raidl, G.R., Cagnoni, S., Cardalda, J.J.R., Corne, D.W., Gottlieb, J., Guillot, A., Hart, E., Johnson, C.G., Marchiori, E., Meyer, J.-A., Middendorf, M. (eds.) EvoIASP 2003, EvoWorkshops 2003, EvoSTIM 2003, EvoROB/EvoRobot 2003, EvoCOP 2003, EvoBIO 2003, and EvoMUSART 2003. LNCS, vol. 2611, pp. 684–695. Springer, Heidelberg (2003)
10. Nason, S., Laird, J.E.: Soar-rl: integrating reinforcement learning with soar. Cognitive Systems Research 6(1), 51–59 (2005)
11. Rummery, G.A., Niranjan, M.: On-line q-learning using connectionist systems. Technical report, Cambridge University Engineering Department (1994)
12. Sutton, R., Barto, A.: Reinforcement Learning: An Introduction. MIT Press, Cambridge (1998)
13. Tyrrell, T.: Computational Mechanisms for Action Selection. Phd, University of Edinburgh (1993)

Towards Reasoning with Partial Goal Satisfaction in Intelligent Agents

M. Birna van Riemsdijk[1] and Neil Yorke-Smith[2,3]

[1] EEMCS, Delft University of Technology, Delft, The Netherlands
m.b.vanriemsdijk@tudelft.nl
[2] SRI International, Menlo Park, CA, USA
[3] American University of Beirut, Lebanon
nysmith@aub.edu.lb

Abstract. A model of agency that supposes goals are either achieved fully or not achieved at all can be a poor approximation of scenarios arising from the real world. In real domains of application, goals are achieved over time. At any point, a goal has reached a certain level of satisfaction, from nothing to full (completely achieved). This paper presents an abstract framework that can be taken as a basis for representing partial goal satisfaction in an intelligent agent. The richer representation enables agents to reason about *partial* satisfaction of the goals they are pursuing or that they are considering. In contrast to prior work on partial satisfaction in the agents literature which investigates partiality from a logical perspective, we propose a higher-level framework based on metric functions that represent, among other things, the progress that has been made towards achieving a goal. We present an example to illustrate the kinds of reasoning enabled on the basis of our framework for partial goal satisfaction.

Categories and subject descriptors: I.2.11 [**Artificial Intelligence**]: Distributed Artificial Intelligence—*Intelligent Agents*.

General terms: Design; Theory.

Keywords: goal reasoning, partial satisfaction, agent programming.

1   Introduction and Motivation

We begin from the observation that existing cognitive agent programming frameworks (e.g., [35,4,10])—i.e., programming frameworks in which agents are endowed with high-level mental attitudes such as beliefs and goals—take a 'boolean' perspective on goals: unless achieved completely, the agents have failed to achieve them. Following Zhou et al. [37], we argue that many scenarios would benefit from a more flexible framework in which agents can reason about *partial goal satisfaction*. As others have recognized, it is important that agents can be programmed with this reasoning ability, because often it is not possible for an agent to achieve a goal completely, in the context of all its commitments situated in

R. Collier, J. Dix, and P. Novák (Eds.): ProMAS 2010, LNAI 6599, pp. 41–59, 2012.

the resource-bounded real world. A notion of partiality allows to express that only part of the goal is achieved, and it facilitates, among other possibilities, changing goals such that only a part has to be achieved.

While prior work proposes a logic-based characterization of partiality, in this paper we aim for a general framework for partial goal satisfaction that also allows quantitative notions of partiality. In particular, we propose a framework based on metric functions that represent, among other things, the progress that has been made towards achieving a goal. Agents rescuing civilians from a dangerous area, for example, may have cleared none, some, or all of the area. Progress may be expressed in terms of different kinds of metrics, such as utility, or in terms of a logical characterization. This richer representation enables an agent or group of agents to reason about partial satisfaction of the goals they are pursuing or that they are considering. The more sophisticated behaviour that can result not only reflects the behaviour expected in real scenarios, but can enable a greater total level of goal achievement. For example, an agent might realize that it cannot completely clear a sub-area and inform teammates of the situation; in turn, they adjust their behaviour appropriately, e.g., by coming to assist.

This paper aims to further establish partial goal satisfaction as an important topic of research, and to provide a step towards a metric-based approach that also allows for quantitative notions of partial achievement. We discuss related work and give an example scenario (Sections 2 and 3). Then, we develop an abstract framework for partial goal satisfaction and identify *progress appraisal* (the capability of an agent to assess how far along it is in achieving a goal [6]) and *goal adaptation* (the modification of a goal [20,27,37]) as the basic types of reasoning that the framework should support (Sections 4 and 5). We sketch how reasoning using partial goal satisfaction may be embedded into a concrete computational framework using the example scenario (Section 6).

Although we provide an abstract framework rather than a concrete proposal on how to embed partial goal satisfaction in cognitive agent programming frameworks, we believe the proposed framework forms an important step towards this aim by identifying the main ingredients that we believe should be part of a framework for partial goal satisfaction. Through this, we lay foundations for future work, which will address the important technical challenges that have to be faced to concretize the framework and render it suitable for programming a cognitive agent.

2   Background and Related Work

Before introducing a framework for partial goal satisfaction, we survey the surrounding literature. In this section, we discuss several areas of research that are related to partial goal satisfaction.

Goal representation. In cognitive agent programming, the concept of a goal has received increasing attention in the past years. Different goal types have been distinguished (see, e.g., [34,2] for a discussion), including achievement goals and maintenance goals. The former, which have received the most attention in the literature, form the focus of this paper. In the literature, the focus of research has been on declarative goals, i.e. goals that represent properties of states (goals-to-be) [35,4,10]. We take the same perspective in this paper.

Achievement goals in logic-based cognitive agent programming languages are often represented as a logical formula, expressing a property of the state of the multi-agent system that the agent should try to achieve [35,36,4,34,10]. The agent considers the goal to be achieved, if it believes a state has been reached in which the formula is satisfied, according to the semantics of the logic employed. This logic-based approach can induce a binary way of thinking about goals, in which the goal is either achieved or not achieved. While we do not reject that point of view, we suggest in this paper that a framework in which levels of goal satisfaction can be represented enables several useful kinds of reasoning.

Partial achievement. The concept of partial achievement of a goal appears in limited extents in the literature. Whereas goals in agent frameworks and programming languages are not customarily defined to allow for partial satisfaction, philosophically, Holton argues for the existence of "partial intentions" [13], a concept spanning both desires and goals.

In the foundational work of Rao and Georgeff [23] an intention (goal) is dropped if it is achieved, not desired, or now believed by the agent to be impossible. Singh [29] drops a goal if another more important task arises. In these and works that followed them, goal achievement remains a boolean concept.

Haddawy and Hanks made an early study [9], in which a function from propositions to a real number represents the degree of satisfaction of a goal. Indeed, various authors have associated goals with a utility, priority, or preference, in the agents literature (e.g., [15,11,18], among others) and in the AI planning literature (e.g., [5]), although usually for the purpose of deciding which goals to prioritize or which subset to pursue, or which plan or action to select.

Zhou and Chen adopt instead a logical approach, defining a semantics for partial implication of desirable propositions from a symbolic point of view [36]. Zhou et al. [37] investigate partial goal satisfaction on the basis of this logical semantics, viewing a goal as achieved when a (possibly disjunctive) proposition is achieved according to the logic. They examine in particular application of different notions of partial implication to goal modification in the context of belief change. Although recognizing its value, we do not approach partial satisfaction viewing goals as logical formulas to be achieved. We discuss the relationship between the approaches later.

While van der Hoek et al. [33] explore a related concept, in their logical analysis of BDI intention revision, we aim for more a fine-grained and broader concept. Morley et al. [21] investigate dynamic computation of resource estimates as a partially-complete goal is executed. Again, the representation of a generic concept of partial achievement is not the focus of their work.

Partial plans and goal/plan adaptation. There is a fair amount of work on reasoning with partial *plans*, for instance in plan formation or negotiation

(e.g., [20,7,17]), as well as in the AI planning literature (e.g., [30]). In the area
of multi-agent planning and negotiation, researchers have examined inter-agent
communication (e.g., about problems in goal achievement). Kamar et al., for
instance, investigate helpful assistance of teammates in pursuit of a plan that
could be partially complete [17], and Kamali et al. [16], for instance, investigate
information timing. Goal adaptation has received less attention than the concept
of goal or plan selection (e.g., [20]), or plan adaptation, the benefits of which are
well established [22].

3   Example Scenario

In this section, we illustrate by means of an extended example the benefits that
a framework for partial goal satisfaction may bring. The scenario is from the
domain of crisis management. An accident has occurred in a chemical plant and
hazardous chemicals have leaked into the area. The emergency response team
must prevent anyone from entering the vicinity of the plant, and evacuate those
who are currently in the area. A team of agents will execute a joint plan according
to their training. Securing the area is done by setting up road blocks on the three
main roads leading to the plant; the third road block can be installed in one of
two different places. The two houses within a 3 km radius of the plant must be
evacuated. The forest within the range of the chemical leak must be searched
and any people brought to safety.

Fig. 1 depicts a *goal-plan tree* (GPT) [32,3,21] for the emergency response
team in the scenario. A goal-plan tree consists of alternating layers of goal nodes
and plan nodes. Goals are depicted in rounded boxes, and plans in square boxes.
Goals descending from a plan node are conjunctive: all must be achieved for the
plan to be successful. An OR node indicates disjunctive subgoals: achievement
of any one renders the plan successful. Thus, the plan *EstablishRoadblocks* is
successful when goals rb_1 and rb_2 and at least one of rb_{3a} and rb_{3b} are achieved.
Primitive actions (leaf goal nodes) are depicted in italicized rounded boxes. The
numerical attributes on leaf nodes will be discussed later.

This scenario would benefit from agents being able to reason with partial goal
satisfaction. A basic type of reasoning is *progress appraisal* [6]. Progress appraisal
is the capability of an agent to assess how far along it is in achieving a goal, i.e.,
which part of a goal it has already achieved. In the scenario, for example, it
may be important for the commander to keep headquarters up-to-date on her
progress in setting up the road blocks.

Another, more advanced, type of reasoning with partial goal satisfaction is
goal negotiation, which has been identified as a key challenge for agents research
[19]. Assume, for example, that the team does not have enough members to
secure the area and evacuate the forest. The commander may engage in goal
negotiation with headquarters, to try to adapt the *publicSafety* goal so only the
part that is achievable for the team will have to be pursued. Note that the ability
to do *goal adaptation* is thus necessary in order to engage in goal negotiation. The
commander suggests to set up only road blocks 2 and 3. However, neglecting road

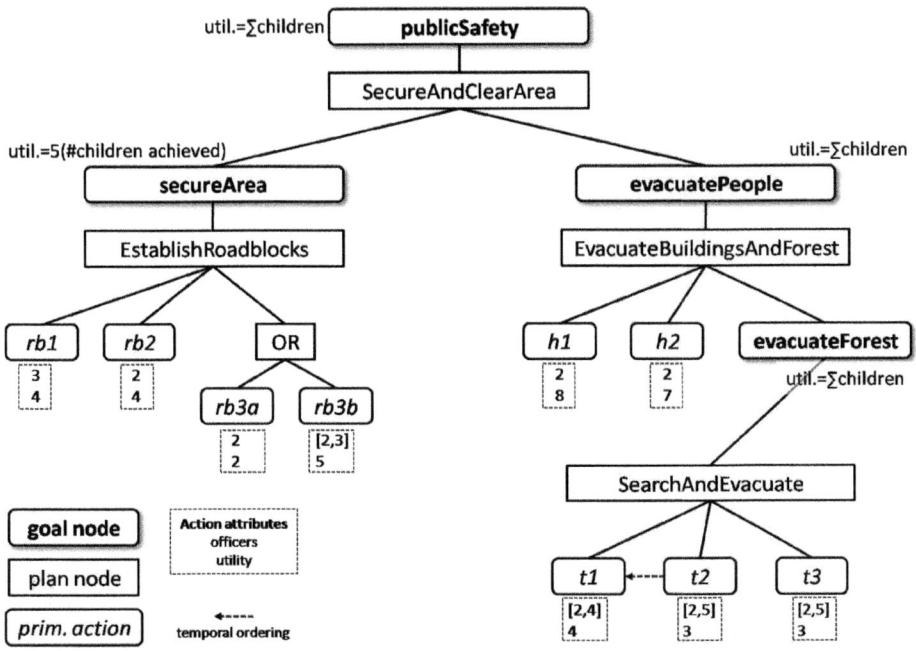

Fig. 1. Goal-plan tree for the scenario

block 1 is not an option according to headquarters, since people may (re-)enter the area, which would lead to a hazardous situation and further evacuation duties. The latter decision is based on an analysis of the importance of achieving the various subgoals. The commander agrees with headquarters that another team will be sent to set up road block 1. Both goal negotiation and adaptation thus require agents to reason about the parts of which a goal is composed.

These kinds of reasoning may occur not only before a goal is adopted, but also during pursuit of a goal. For example, the commander may notice that searching the forest is taking more time than expected, and the team will not be able to search the entire forest before darkness sets in. Rather than abandoning *evacuateForest* entirely because the goal cannot be achieved completely, the team can perform an inferior search of it and achieve it only partially. A decision of whether this is acceptable, or whether it would be better to abandon the forest altogether, depends on an analysis the gains made by achieving the goal only partially—which in this case might be substantial since any person brought to safety is an accomplishment.

This paper provides a high-level framework for partial goal satisfaction that allows a quantitative instantiation, aimed at enabling the kinds of reasoning such as discussed above. After introducing the framework, we mention several other kinds of reasoning that benefit from such a framework for partial satisfaction.

4 Abstract Framework for Partial Goal Satisfaction

In this section, we define a new and abstract notion of goal, that allows the expression of partial satisfaction (Section 4.1). We define notions that are fundamental to frameworks for goals, namely achievement and achievability, for our new notion of goal (Section 4.2), and relate the new definition to the usual binary definition of goal (Section 4.3).

4.1 Goal Template and Goal Instance

At the heart of conceptualizing partial goal satisfaction is identifying how to define partiality. For this, it is essential to define when a goal is *achieved* (satisfied completely): we cannot define partiality without knowing what complete satisfaction means. In pursuit of our interest in a quantitative framework, moreover, one needs a metric in terms of which (complete) satisfaction is expressed. This metric will be endowed with a partial ordering, to allow an agent to determine whether a goal is getting closer to completion. We call such a metric the *progress metric* of a goal, and denote it as a set A with partial order $\leq$.[1]

A goal specifies a minimum value $a_{min} \in A$ (called the *completion value*) that should be reached in order to consider the goal to have been completely satisfied. For example, the progress metric for the goal *evacuateForest* might be defined in terms of time, where complete satisfaction is achieved when the forest has been searched for two hours (until it gets dark); or the metric may be defined of a (boolean) proposition such as *isSearched(forest)*; or it may be defined in terms of the number of subgoals achieved (e.g., searching tracks 1–3), where complete satisfaction means that all tracks have been searched, etc.

Two notes are in order. First, a *minimum* value is specified since we define achievement as the agent reaching at least this level of satisfaction (see below for details). In some cases the agent may exceed the completion value, never exactly attaining it—for example, if six people are estimated to be in the forest, but really there are seven, and if the last two are found together as a pair, then the attained progress metric value may jump from five to seven.

Second, we may wish to mandate that the partial order $\leq$ is total w.r.t. the completion value a_{min}, i.e., that any value $a \in A$ can be compared with a_{min} according to $\leq$. This ensures that, if the agent can appraise the current attained value of the progress metric, then it can compare that value with a_{min} and conclude whether or not the goal has been achieved. In our examples, $\leq$ will typically be a total order, which automatically ensures a_{min} is comparable with all other values of A.

One may consider a wide range of domain-independent metrics, such as TIME (where A may be a set of dates and times with associated order), UTILITY (where A may be the real numbers with the usual ordering), NUMBER OF SUBGOALS, besides domain-dependent metrics such as NUMBER OF ROAD BLOCKS or NUMBER OF PEOPLE BROUGHT TO SAFETY (where A is the natural numbers). Besides

---

[1] Combinations of metrics might be considered, but for simplicity, here we assume quantities such as progress are defined in terms of a single metric.

the metric chosen as the progress metric, the agent (or designer) might have interest in others: e.g., progress may be defined in terms of tracks searched, but time taken could be an additional relevant factor in the team's decisions. An avenue for future exploration is the relation between domain-independent and domain-dependent metrics.

Progress appraisal. As seen earlier, a fundamental reasoning concerning partial goal satisfaction is *progress appraisal*. An agent should thus be able to determine in a given situation where it is with respect to a progress metric $(A, \leq)$. For example, if TIME is the metric, the agent needs to be able to determine how long it has spent so far. In the case of TIME, the computation from the current state to the time spent is relatively direct, assuming agents have access to a clock and have recorded the start time. The computation may be more involved for other metrics. In the case of UTILITY, for example, more computation might be needed to determine the current appraised value of utility in terms of other, measurable quantities (i.e., other metrics besides the progress metric). However, in all cases, an agent should be able to determine, given its beliefs about the current state, at least an estimation of the value of the progress metric for a goal.

Formally, for a goal with progress metric $(A, \leq)$, we require an agent to have for each goal a *progress appraisal function* $\phi : S \rightarrow A$, where S is the set of states (i.e., world state and multi-agent system state), that associates states with the (achieved) value of the progress metric in these states. In addition, in order to allow determination of whether the completion value $a_{min} \in A$ is reachable given the current state, we normally require the agent to have a *progress upper bound function* $\hat{\phi} : S \times M \rightarrow A$ that takes a state $s \in S$, and the *means* $m \in M$ that will be used for pursuing the goal, and yields (an estimation of) the maximum value in A reachable from state s with means m.

The upper bound will enable reasoning about the achievability of a goal. The function is called an *upper bound* function because we expect that in practice it will be difficult to calculate *exactly* which value in A might be reached from a certain state with a certain means. It is more practical to calculate an upper bound on the attainable value. For example, for time remaining for the forest paths yet to be searched, it may not be possible to precisely compute how many more people will be found—due for instance to the uneven progress along the trails, the movement of the civilians, and the fading daylight—but a reasonable upper estimate is the total number of people thought to be in the vicinity.

Given such an upper bound (for the current state with the means that are to be used to achieve the goal), the agent knows that it will not be possible to fully achieve a goal if the completion value of the goal exceeds its upper bound. Note, on the contrary, that the completion value being below the upper bound is no guarantee that the goal will be fully achieved. In a more conservative approach, a lower bound may be computed expressing the minimum achievable value in A, in which case the agent *would* know that the goal is fully achievable if the completion value is below the lower bound. As a further development, a combination of upper bound and lower bound may be used in the agent's reasoning. For simplicity, in this paper we consider only the upper bound function.

In the abstract framework, we do not further detail the content of the set of possible means M. The content of M will depend on the domain and the concrete agent (programming) framework that is used. Typically, we envisage that M will contain a description of plans and/or resources that can be used to pursue the goal. Section 6 contains an example in which we use the goal-plan tree to represent means.

Goal template. The functions ϕ and $\hat{\phi}$ now allow us to define a *goal template*. The intuition is that each type of goal, such as *secureArea* or *evacuateForest*, has an associated template. On the basis of a goal template, goal instances can be created.

Definition 1 (goal template). *Consider a multi-agent system (MAS) for which the set of possible states is defined as S. Let A be a nonempty set with a partial ordering $\leq$ (the progress metric), and let M be a set representing means that can be used for achieving a goal. A goal template T is then defined as a tuple $\langle A, M, \phi : S \to A, \hat{\phi} : S \times M \to A \rangle$, where ϕ is the progress appraisal function, and $\hat{\phi}$ is the progress upper bound function.*

This notion of goal template may be simplified to consist of only A and ϕ, if $\hat{\phi}$ cannot be provided in a certain case, i.e., when no sensible upper bound can be specified for a goal. Alternatively, it may be extended in various ways. First, the goal template itself may be parameterized to account for variants of the template. For example, depending on the area that has to be secured, the number of road blocks that have to be set up will differ, and this may influence the definition of ϕ and $\hat{\phi}$. Second, one may want to define a goal template for a single goal based on different progress metrics, allowing the agent to choose a progress metric depending on circumstances. We can capture this most simply by having two separate goal templates. Formally relating these templates (for instance by making them siblings in a hierarchy of goal types) is an extension of our basic framework. For reasons of simplicity and space, we leave the pursuit of these extensions for future work.

In order to simplify definition and computation of ϕ and $\hat{\phi}$, these functions may yield *estimated* values for progress appraisal and the upper bound. In environments that are not fully observable or that are open or dynamic, the agent may not be able to compute precisely the functions. However, an agent must be mindful of the potential adverse effects of estimation. In over-estimation of $\hat{\phi}$ or under-estimation of ϕ, the agent would try to achieve a goal even though it may be impossible to fully satisfy it, or it is already completely satisfied. On the other hand, in under-estimation of $\hat{\phi}$ or over-estimation of ϕ the agent would stop too soon.

While ϕ and $\hat{\phi}$ may thus yield estimated values, intuitively the agent should estimate the progress upper bound in a state $s \in S$ with means m to be at least the current achieved satisfaction in that state. We call this *coherency* of a goal template, and formally define it as $\forall s \in S, m \in M : \hat{\phi}(s, m) \geq \phi(s)$.

To illustrate Def. 1, consider the goal *secureArea* of the example scenario. In the scenario, the main resource (leaving aside time) is the number of police officers $P = \{0, \ldots, 10\}$. We base the progress metric for the goal on the NUMBER OF SUBGOALS ACHIEVED, modulated by how well they are achieved. Namely, the progress metric models the quality of achievement of each roadblock subgoal rb_i.

Example 1. The goal template for *secureArea* is: $T_{sa} = \langle \mathbb{R}, P, \phi_{sa}, \hat{\phi}_{sa} \rangle$. Thus, the progress metric is $A = \mathbb{R}$ with its standard $\leq$ ordering. Arbitrarily, we define $\phi_{sa}(s)$ to be 20 if all subgoals have been fully achieved in s (assuming the agent can determine this in each state s), which means that road blocks have been set up and at least one police officer guards each road block, 10 if all road blocks have been set up but not all of them have at least one officer, and 0 otherwise. Let the means consist of p, the number of officers allocated. We define $\hat{\phi}_{sa}(s, p)$ to be 20 iff the plan *EstablishRoadblocks* can be executed in s and it is executed with at least 6 police officers, i.e., $p \geq 6$, 10 if $1 \leq p < 6$ and the plan can be executed successfully, and 0 otherwise. Computation of the upper bound thus requires determining whether *EstablishRoadblocks* can be executed successfully. This may be done by checking simply the precondition of the plan, or by performing planning or lookahead (compare [3,12]).

A goal template specifies the progress appraisal and progress upper bound functions. As already addressed above, the definition of a concrete goal includes the specification of the completion value for the goal to specify when it is completely satisfied. In addition, the agent should determine the means that will be allocated for pursuing the goal. The completion value and means, defined with respect to a goal template, together form a *goal instance* of this template.

Definition 2 (goal instance). *Let* $T = \langle A, M, \phi : S \to A, \hat{\phi} : S \times M \to A \rangle$ *be a goal template. A* goal instance *of* T *is specified as* $(a_{min}, m) : T$, *where* $a_{min} \in A$ *is the completion value, and* $m \in M$ *specifies the means that will be used for achieving the instance.*

Example 2. In the scenario, one goal instance of the goal template T_{sa} for *secureArea* is $g_{sa} = (20, 6) : T_{sa}$, expressing that the commander would like to achieve a progress metric value of 20 with no more than six police officers.

4.2   Achievement and Unachievability

Any goal framework needs a definition of when a goal is *achieved*. Using our notion of goal instance, we can easily define when a goal is achieved, i.e., completely satisfied, in a certain state $s \in S$, namely, when the appraised value of the progress metric in s is at least the completion value. Moreover, logic-based frameworks for goals incorporate a notion of goal consistency by nature, namely logical consistency. Goal consistency is related to goal *unachievability*, since inconsistent goals are by definition not reachable. In our framework we define a notion of unachievability on the basis of the completion value of the goal instance and the progress upper bound function.

We will assume that each progress metric $(A, \leq)$ has a bottom element $\bot_A \in A$ for which $\forall a \in A$ with $a \neq \bot_A$, we have $\bot_A < a$. The bottom element represents a 'zero' achievement level. When a goal instance g is created in a state s, it may start partially completed, i.e., $\phi(s) > \bot_A$. For example, the road block on road 1 may already be in place, when an instance of *secureArea* is created, because the road was closed for construction.

Definition 3 (goal achievement and unachievability). *Let* $T = \langle A, M, \phi : S \rightarrow A, \hat{\phi} : S \times M \rightarrow A \rangle$ *be a goal template, let* $(a_{min}, m) : T$ *be an instance of* T, *and let* $s \in S$ *be the current state. The goal instance* $(a_{min}, m) : T$ *is* completely unachieved *iff* $\phi(s) = \bot_A$, (completely) achieved *(or* satisfied) *iff* $\phi(s) \geq a_{min}$, *and* partially achieved *otherwise, i.e., iff* $\bot_A < \phi(s) < a_{min}$.[2] *The goal instance is* unachievable *using* m *(or simply* unachievable, *where the context is clear) if* $\hat{\phi}(s, m) < a_{min}$.

For example, the goal instance g_{sa} of Example 2 above is achieved if all road blocks have been set up and each remains guarded by at least one police officer (since in that case the achieved ϕ_{sa} value is 20). It not unachievable in any state $s \in S$ since six police officers are allocated for achieving the instance, whence the progress upper bound is 20, equalling the completion value. If less than six officers were allocated, the goal instance would be unachievable since then the agent could maximally attain a ϕ_{sa} value of 10.

It is important to be clear that goals which are not unachievable according to the above definition are *not* necessarily achievable. The reason is that $\hat{\phi}$ provides an upper bound on the achievable value of the progress metric, i.e., the actual reachable value may be lower. Therefore, even if the completion value is below the progress upper bound, the goal may still be unachievable. This is similar to the logic-based notion of unachievability, where a goal is by definition unachievable if it is inconsistent, but not every consistent goal is achievable.

4.3   Binary Goal Achievement

We now discuss how our framework relates to logic-based frameworks for (achievement) goals. In the latter, as noted in Section 2, the success condition of a goal is usually defined as a logical formula ψ, which is achieved in a state $s \in S$ if the agent believes ψ to hold in that state. We show how our definition for partial goal achievement can be instantiated such that it yields the usual binary definition of goal. We abstract from means M.

Definition 4 (binary goal instance). *Let* ψ *be a logical formula, for which the truth value can be determined in any MAS state* $s \in S$ *(where* $s \models \psi$ *denotes that* ψ *holds in* s). *Let* $A = \{\text{false}, \text{true}\}$ *with* true $>$ false. *Let* $M = \{\epsilon\}$ *where* ϵ *is a dummy element. Let* $\phi(s) = $ true *if* $s \models \psi$ *and* false *otherwise, and let* $\hat{\phi}(s, \epsilon) = $ true *if* $\psi \not\models \bot$ *and* false *otherwise. Let* $T_{bin(\psi)} = \langle A, M, \phi, \hat{\phi} \rangle$. *Then we define a* binary goal instance $\psi = (\text{true}, \epsilon) : T_{bin(\psi)}$.

---

[2] In this definition we take advantage of a_{min} being comparable to all elements of A.

Proposition 1 (correspondence). *The instantiation of the partial goal frame-work as specified in Def. 4, corresponds to the binary definition of goal (Section 2) with respect to achievement and consistency (no unachievability).*

Proof. We have to show that achievement and consistency hold in the binary definition of goal, iff achievement and no unachievability hold in the instantiated partial definition of goal. The goal ψ is achieved in the partial case in some state s iff $\phi(s) \geq a_{min}$, i.e., iff $\phi(s) \geq$ true, i.e., iff $\phi(s) =$ true, i.e., if $s \models \psi$. This is exactly the definition of achievement in the binary case. The goal ψ is not unachievable in the partial case iff $\hat{\phi}(s, \epsilon) \geq a_{min}$, i.e., iff $\hat{\phi}(s, \epsilon) =$ true, which is precisely the case iff ψ is consistent.   □

We envisage an instantiation of our framework with the logic-based characterization of partiality of Zhou et al. [37], where in particular the ordering relation of the progress metric will have to be defined. That is, consider a semantics of partial implication and an alphabet of atoms. Intuitively, we must specify a metric on a set such as propositions over the alphabet, that gives rise to a partial order of the propositions w.r.t. the semantics of implication. Making this instantiation precise will be future research. Indeed, the role of partial implication in connection with subgoals and plans—which we account for in our framework through the computation of metrics in the GPT—has already been noted as a research topic [37].

The instantiation of our framework with a binary goal definition illustrates that progress metrics need not be numeric. However, if the progress metric A *is* numeric, the agent can compute how far it is in achieving a goal as a ratio with the completion value. That is, if T is a goal template with progress appraisal function $\phi : S \rightarrow A$ and $g = (a_{min}, m) : T$ is a goal instance of T, and if quotients in A are defined (e.g., if $A = \mathbb{R}$), then a measure of progress of goal instance g when the agent is in state s is the ratio $\frac{\phi(s)}{a_{min}}$. This metric of % COMPLETE corresponds to the intuitive notion of progress as the percentage of the completion value attained.

5   Goal Adaptation

The previous section outlined an abstract framework for partial goal satisfaction. We have taken progress appraisal as the most basic form of reasoning that such a framework should support. In the motivating scenario, we argued that the framework should support more advanced kinds of reasoning, such as goal negotiation. In this section, we highlight a type of reasoning that we suggest underlies many of these more advanced kinds of reasoning, namely *reasoning about goal adaptation*. Given a goal instance $g = (a_{min}, m) : T$ where T is a goal template, we define *goal adaptation* as modifying a_{min} or m (or both). Note that modifying the plan for g is included in the scope of modifying m.

The reasoning question is how to determine which goals to adapt and how to adapt them. While this is a question that we cannot fully answer here, we analyze the kinds of adaptation and possible reasons for adapting. One important factor that may influence the decision on how, and particularly when, to adapt is the evolution of the agent's beliefs. This aspect is a focus of prior works [26,37]. Another important factor is the consideration of a *cost/benefit analysis*. We develop our basic framework to support this kind of reasoning.

5.1   Reasons for and Uses of Adaptation

We begin by distinguishing *internal* and *external* reasons for goal adaptation. By internal reasons for we mean those that arise from issues with respect to the goal itself, while external reasons are those that arise from other factors.

More specifically, we see unachievability as a main internal reason for goal adaptation. If a goal instance g is unachievable, it means that its completion value cannot be attained from the current state with the means that are currently allocated. The options *without* a concept of partial satisfaction are to drop/abort g, to attempt a different plan for g (if possible), to suspend g until it becomes achievable (for example, waiting for more officers to arrive), or to abort or suspend another goal in favour of g [31].

In our framework, more options are available since the goal instance can be *adapted* to make it achievable by lowering the completion value, which we call *goal weakening*, as well as by the alternative of choosing different means that do allow the achievement of the current completion value, e.g., by investing additional resources.[3] Depending on the circumstances, the latter may not always be possible. For example, if the goal is to evacuate people from their houses but it is physically not possible to get to these houses, e.g., because of flooding, it does not matter whether the officers devote more time or personnel.

Several external reasons may lead to goal adaptation. First, a goal instance g may in itself be achievable, but (collective) unachievability of other goal instances may be a reason for adapting g. That is, in practice an agent has only limited resources and it has to choose how it will invest them to achieve a set of current and future goal instances [1,32]. For example, the agent may decide that another goal instance is more important and needs resources, leading to adaptation of the means of g.

Another external reason is consideration of a new candidate goal instance g', i.e., *goal adoption*. Partial satisfaction allows an agent to consider adapting an existing goal instance, or adopting the new instance g' in a weakened form. Third, an agent might be requested by another agent to increase the completion value of a goal instance, which we call *goal strengthening*. For example, the team leader may decide that more time should be spent searching the forest.

Together, progress appraisal and goal adaptation form a basis for higher-level reasoning tasks. We have already discussed goal negotiation (Section 3), goal adoption, and avoiding and resolving goal achievement conflict. We now briefly discuss several other kinds of reasoning. First, in order to coordinate their

---

[3] Note that the latter is (at least in part) also supported by frameworks where alternative plans can be chosen to reach a goal. However, in our framework it is naturally incorporated as part of goal adaptation.

actions, agents should *communicate* about how far they are in achieving certain goals [8,20,17]. Progress appraisal provides a principled approach. Second, an agent might realize it cannot achieve a goal completely. Allowing itself to weaken a goal, it can *delegate* part of the goal to other agents. Similarly, delegation may be another option for an agent finding it has achievement difficulties. Related, third, is *reasoning about other agents* and their ability to complete tasks. For example, one agent realizing that another agent is unlikely to fully complete its task(s), irrespective of whether the other agent has acknowledged this.

5.2   Cost/Benefit Analysis

When deciding which goals to adapt and how, we suggest that a cost/benefit analysis can be an important consideration (see also, e.g., [1,25]). For example, it will usually not be sensible to stop pursuit of the goal if only a small amount of resources still have to be invested to achieve its completion value, in particular if abandoning before full completion yields zero utility. On the other hand, if an agent has obtained much utility from a goal instance g, compared to that expected when the progress metric of g reaches the completion value, and if much more effort would have to be invested to fully achieve g, it may be sensible to stop pursuit of the goal if resources are needed elsewhere. These kinds of cost/benefit analyses to obtain an optimal division of resources over goals essentially form an *optimization problem*. While it is beyond the scope of this paper to investigate how optimization techniques can be applied in this context, we do analyze how our framework supports it.

In order to do a cost/benefit analysis, one needs to know how much it would cost to achieve a certain benefit. The benefit obtained through achieving a goal can be derived in our framework by means of the progress appraisal function. If the progress metric represents benefit, such as utility, the benefit the agent will obtain when achieving a goal completely, is the difference between the completion value and the value of the progress metric in the current state. That is, for a goal instance $(a_{min}, m) : T$ where $T = \langle A, M, \phi : S \to A, \hat{\phi} : S \times M \to A \rangle$, the benefit is $\Delta a = a_{min} - \phi(s_{now})$, where s_{now} is the current state. Note that Δa can only be calculated if difference $(-)$ is defined on A.

In order to calculate the cost associated with obtaining a_{min}, we need to introduce another function $\kappa : S \times M \times S \to C$, where C is a set representing cost and $\kappa(s, m, s') = c$ means that the cost of going from state s with means m to state s' is estimated to be c. Then we can calculate the estimated minimal cost to move from the current state s_{now} to a completion state, i.e., a state s' where $\phi(s') \geq a_{min}$, with means m as $\min\{\kappa(s_{now}, m, s') \mid \phi(s') \geq a_{min}\}$. In practice, there will be a very large, possibly even infinite, number of completion states. It will therefore not be practical to calculate this function directly. Rather, we expect that the agent will estimate the costs of getting from the current state to *some* completion state, since usually only those parts of the state that have something to do with the state being a completion state are relevant for calculating costs. Projection into possible future states consists of a body of work in its own right, e.g., [24,14,12].

Above, we assumed that the progress metric A represents the benefit obtained by achieving the goal. Depending on the context, progress may also be measured in terms of costs—e.g., time—rather than benefit. In that case, we thus have that $A = C$. Then we can define κ as $\kappa(s_{now}, m, s') = \phi(s') - \phi(s_{now})$, i.e., the cost that is to be invested is simply the difference between the desired value of A (namely $\phi(s')$), since A are now the costs, and the current value of A, namely $\phi(s_{now})$. Since progress is then measured in terms of costs rather than in terms of benefits, we cannot do a cost/benefit analysis. In this case, the analysis would thus be based only on minimizing costs.

6 Towards an Embedding within a Goal Framework

In this section, we sketch how our metric-based framework for partial goal satisfaction can be applied to a concrete goal representation framework, namely the GPT as introduced earlier. This is a step towards rendering the capabilities within a cognitive agent programming framework. An attraction of the GPT is its representation of goals, subgoals, and plans—which is pertinent for reasoning about the means and the progress in execution of a goal—combined with the annotation of and aggregation of quantities on the tree nodes—which we will use for computation of metrics. Fig. 1 depicted a goal-plan tree for the evacuation scenario. The goal and action nodes correspond to goal instances in our framework; the tree structure gives the plan aspect of their means.

For the reasons just given, we posit that the concept of partially satisfied goals fits naturally into this kind of representation framework for goals. Specifically, we augment annotations of tree nodes to include metrics about goal (and, where relevant, plan) satisfaction. In the simplest case, this comprises annotating each goal node with values from its progress metric A, as we will explain. The % COMPLETE metric allows normalization of the values.

Progress appraisal. Inference over the tree structure computes and updates metrics by propagation upwards from descendant nodes, in a similar fashion as resource estimates and other information are propagated [3,28]. For example, the current value of % COMPLETE of a parent plan node may be aggregated from the values of its child goal nodes. Metrics are aggregated according to their nature and the type of the node. For example, by default, a conjunctive plan node will aggregate % COMPLETE as the arithmetic mean of the children's values, while a disjunctive plan node will aggregate it as the maximum of their values. Mechanisms for aggregation have been explored in the cited literature. Since the algorithms are already parameterizable according to the nature of the quantity (in our case, the metric) and the type of the node, we refrain from reiterating them here.

The computation is to be made *dynamically* as the current situation evolves [21,17]. We assume agents can assess the progress of leaf nodes. For instance, the police officers should believe they know when they have finished clearing a house (and the team thus achieves so achieve the utility depicted on each leaf node).

Hence, there are two types of metric values attributed onto nodes. The first type are *static*, initial, *a priori* values before execution (as depicted in Fig. 1). These static values will typically capture expected, estimated, or required values, such as the utility expected upon full satisfaction of a goal, and the resources expected to achieve this. The second type of metric values are *dynamic* estimates computed during execution, such as the utility achieved so far from a goal. For the progress metric of each goal instance g, the static value corresponds to the completion value a_{min} of g, while the dynamic value corresponds to the appraised value $\phi_g(s_{now})$.[4]

6.1   Reasoning in the Example Scenario

The response team commander is given the goal *publicSafety* by her superiors. The doctrinal plan, *SecureAndClearArea*, involves the two subgoals, *secureArea* and *evacuatePeople*; they may be achieved concurrently, although the team must be mindful that the public may (re-)enter the incident area until it is secured.

Goal templates, metrics, and goal instances. Including herself, the commander has 10 police officers in her team. We model this resource as the set $P = \{0, \ldots, 10\} \subset \mathbb{N}$. The commander must decide how to allocate her officers between the two subgoal instantiations, i.e., *secureArea*(p) and *evacuatePeople*($10 - p$), where p is the number of agents assigned to the first subgoal.

secureArea. Recall from Example 1 that the goal template for *secureArea* is $T_{sa} = \langle \mathbb{R}, P, \phi_{sa}, \hat{\phi}_{sa} \rangle$, where the progress metric for T_{sa} is the achievement of its subgoals. The UTILITY metric of T_{sa} can be seen from Fig. 1 to be $u_{sa} = 5 * (\# \text{ achieved subgoals})$. For example, if either goal rb_1 or goal rb_2 is achieved (but not both), then $u_{sa} = 5$; if both are achieved, then $u_{sa} = 10$.

Since u_{sa} is not the progress metric of the goal template *secureArea*, it does not define progress of instance of this goal template. Nonetheless, u_{sa} may be of interest to the police team as a measure of progress, even though this metric does not *define* the progress (according to police doctrine) nor therefore the completion of the goal.

publicSafety. By contrast to *secureArea*, the progress metric of the initial goal *publicSafety* in the scenario is defined in terms of utility. Its goal template is $T_{ps} = \langle \mathbb{R}, P, u_\Sigma, \hat{u}_\Sigma \rangle$ where u_Σ specifies the cumulative utility from the subgoals in the current plan for a goal instance of T_{ps}. This progress metric is computed in the obvious manner by recursively transversing the subtree below the goal instance, summing up the current utility estimates for each goal node. Likewise, the progress upper bound function, $\hat{u}_\Sigma$, can be computed by a recursive descent

---

[4] An agent may be capable of directly computing the value of a metric at a (non-leaf) node. In that case, if the reasoning is consistent and the static values on leaf notes are reliable estimates, then the directly-computed and aggregated values should agree. Where they do not, the agent may resolve the conflict according to which of the two computations it believes is most reliable.

through the GPT. An *a priori* estimate can be computed, based on the upper bounds of the static, *a priori* utility attributions on leaf nodes [32,3,28]. For example, an *a priori* upper bound on using the plan *EstablishRoadblocks*, relaxing resource considerations, is $4 + 4 + \max(2,5) = 13$. Tighter bounds can be obtained by considering resource limitations and the resulting goal interaction and plan scheduling [32,28], should the agent so choose.

evacuatePeople. The goal template for *evacuatePeople* is: $T_{ep} = \langle \mathbb{R}, P, u_\Sigma, \hat{u}_\Sigma \rangle$. Note the same progress metric is specified for this template as for *publicSafety*.

Goal adoption. The police commander and her team are tasked with the initial goal *publicSafety*; its goal instance is $(40, 10) : T_{ps}$.[5] The team of 10, including the commander, has too few officers to meet the expected requirements for the full completion of the three roadblock actions (rb_i) and the two house-clearance actions (h_i), let alone the forest. That is, the goal instance is unachievable (i.e., $\hat{u}_\Sigma < a_{min}$), as can be seen to be the case by examination of the GPT.

Negotiation, delegation, and requesting help. At first, the commander considers allocating six officers for *secureArea* and weakening the *evacuatePeople* goal by omitting the *evacuateForest* subgoal. This is unacceptable to incident control. After further negotiation, control agrees to send urgently a second team to perform rb_1. The commander thus allocates four officers for *secureArea*. Hence, the goal instances are $(20, 4) : T_{sa}$ and $(25, 6) : T_{ep}$.[6] Two officers will search each house; when done, they will join the forest search. The commander selects *rb3a* over *rb3b* because it is expected to be quicker to achieve. As officers complete the roadblocks, those who do not need to remain on guard are instructed to join the officers searching the forest. The team will gain what utility it can from performing actions *t1*, *t2*, and *t3* in that order.

Thus, with the second team fulfilling rb_1, then the plan *EstablishRoadblocks* for goal *secureArea* can be achieved, and so a progress metric value of 20 will be attained. When all three forest tracks have (eventually) been searched, then plan *SearchAndEvacuate* for goal *evacuateForest* will render a progress metric value of 10 for *evacuateForest*, leading to a progress metric value of $8 + 7 + 10$ for goal *evacuatePeople*. This forward projection from the current state thus indicates that both goals are fully achievable by the augmented team.

Appraisal and sharing information. As the evacuation proceeds, updated metric values are computed on the leaf nodes of the GPT and aggregated to parent nodes. This provides a situational assessment for the commander. Searching

---

[5] The completion value is 40 because full completion of the instance of *secureArea* will have utility $5 * 3 = 15$, and full completion of the instance of *evacuatePeople* will have utility at least 25, based on the static GPT annotations.

[6] For T_{sa}, the completion value is defined as 20 (Example 1). For T_{ep}, the completion value is the sum of the utility of the children, i.e., $8 + 7 + (4 + 3 + 3)$ according to the static GPT annotations, as noted earlier.

house 2 is taking longer than anticipated, because a forced entry proves necessary. Should the two officers continue with $h2$, or join those searching the forest?
Utility of 4 is estimated achieved from $h2$ after 25 minutes have elapsed. The
original estimate of UTILITY for completion of the goal was 7; but this was only
an *a priori* estimate based on typical experience. The commander appraises that
the rate of achieving utility for the goal is outweighed by the resources employed
for it, and so calls off the officers from house 2.

This extract from the scenario illustrates the more sophisticated reasoning
enabled by and founded on a metric-based notion of partial goal satisfaction
that is embedded into a concrete computational framework for the metrics.

7   Conclusion and Next Steps

The contribution of this line of work stems from the recognition of the need for
a concept of partial goal satisfaction in cognitive agent frameworks, manifest
in terms of the proposal of an abstract framework for partial goal satisfaction
that identifies the main necessary ingredients for reasoning based on partial goal
satisfaction. Our objective is a representation of partial satisfaction integrated
into a reasoning framework, and allowing for a quantitative instantiation, in
order that cognitive agent programming frameworks might be enhanced. The
benefit of the topic and our approach is more sophisticated reasoning about
goals, impacting reasoning about selection, adoption, and pursuit; goal progress
appraisal; goal interaction; and inter-agent communication and collaboration.

Although we have indicated how our framework may be concretized in the
context of GPTs, more work is needed to flesh out the details and investigate
how advanced types of reasoning can be built on top of this basis and integrated
into a programming framework. The modifications necessary to the semantics of
an agent programming language such as GOAL [10] must be established. GOAL,
like several other agent programming languages, has a logic-based definition of
goals, and it has reasoning rules to determine which actions to execute, based on
the agent's beliefs and goals. Modifying the language to include the possibility
to reason about partial goal satisfaction will likely involve providing a new notion of goal, analogous to the one proposed in this paper. The progress appraisal
function can be defined on the agent's belief base. Defining the progress upper
bound function and possibly cost and benefit functions will be more involved;
annotations of the program text analogous to the suggested annotations of the
GPT may be useful to compute these functions. It will also have to be investigated how action selection is influenced by this new notion of goal, i.e., whether
the existing mechanism can in essence be used, or whether other mechanisms are
required. Finally, it will have to be investigated whether more advanced types of
reasoning such as goal negotiation can be programmed in GOAL, or whether additional reasoning mechanisms have to be introduced. In particular, cost/benefit
analyses seem to require such additional mechanisms.

Alongside embedding our framework in a cognitive agent programming language, to be investigated is how the various functions of our framework can be

defined in real-world cases. The importance of approximate reasoning is highlighted, as we anticipate the challenges of defining functions that will yield, for instance, exact and tight progress upper bounds. Existing work on, e.g., reasoning about resources is expected to be useful in this context [32,25]. Moreover, while our framework provides the basis for reasoning about goal adaptation, we have not sought to provide (optimization) algorithms that allow the agent to decide how to adapt, weighing costs and benefits. This is an important area for future research, with just one relevant aspect being how to estimate cost and benefit projection into the future. Lastly, possible extensions to the framework are ripe for investigation, such as a logical instantiation with reasoning between goal outcomes, following Zhou et al. [37], inclusion of parameters in goal templates, and relation of templates in a hierarchy.

Acknowledgments. We thank David Martin and the participants of the Pro-MAS'10 workshop for discussions, and the reviewers for their comments.

References

1. Bratman, M.E., Israel, D.J., Pollack, M.E.: Plans and resource-bounded practical reasoning. Computational Intelligence 14, 349–355 (1988)
2. Braubach, L., Pokahr, A.: Representing Long-Term and Interest BDI Goals. In: Braubach, L., Briot, J.-P., Thangarajah, J. (eds.) ProMAS 2009. LNCS, vol. 5919, pp. 201–218. Springer, Heidelberg (2010)
3. Clement, B.J., Durfee, E.H., Barrett, A.C.: Abstract reasoning for planning and coordination. JAIR 28, 453–515 (2007)
4. Dastani, M.: 2APL: A practical agent programming language. JAAMAS 16(3), 214–248 (2008)
5. Do, M.B., Benton, J., van den Briel, M., Kambhampati, S.: Planning with goal utility dependencies. In: Proc. of IJCAI 2007 (2007)
6. Feltovich, P.J., Bradshaw, J.M., Clancey, W.J., Johnson, M., Bunch, L.: Progress Appraisal as a Challenging Element of Coordination in Human and Machine Joint Activity. In: Artikis, A., O'Hare, G.M.P., Stathis, K., Vouros, G.A. (eds.) ESAW 2007. LNCS (LNAI), vol. 4995, pp. 124–141. Springer, Heidelberg (2008)
7. Grosz, B.J., Hunsberger, L.: The dynamics of intention in collaborative activity. Cognitive Systems Research 7(2-3), 259–272 (2006)
8. Grosz, B.J., Kraus, S.: Collaborative plans for complex group action. Artificial Intelligence 86(2), 269–357 (1996)
9. Haddawy, P., Hanks, S.: Representations for decision theoretic planning: Utility functions for deadline goals. In: Proc. of KR 1992 (1992)
10. Hindriks, K.V.: Programming rational agents in GOAL. In: Multi-Agent Programming: Languages, Tools and Applications. Springer, Berlin (2009)
11. Hindriks, K.V., Jonker, C.M., Pasman, W.: Exploring Heuristic Action Selection in Agent Programming. In: Hindriks, K.V., Pokahr, A., Sardina, S. (eds.) ProMAS 2008. LNCS, vol. 5442, pp. 24–39. Springer, Heidelberg (2009)
12. Hindriks, K.V., van der Hoek, W., van Riemsdijk, M.B.: Agent programming with temporally extended goals. In: Proc. of AAMAS 2009 (2009)
13. Holton, R.: Partial belief, partial intention. Mind 117, 27–58 (2008)

14. Hu, Y.: Temporally-expressive planning as constraint satisfaction problems. In: Proc. of ICAPS 2007 (2007)
15. Huang, Z., Bell, J.: Dynamic goal hierarchies. In: Proc. of the 1997 AAAI Spring Symp. on Qualitative Preferences in Deliberation and Practical Reasoning (1997)
16. Kamali, K., Fan, X., Yen, J.: Towards a theory for multiparty proactive communication in agent teams. Intl. J. of Cooperative Info. Systems 16(2) (2007)
17. Kamar, E., Gal, Y., Grosz, B.J.: Incorporating helpful behavior into collaborative planning. In: Proc. of AAMAS 2009 (2009)
18. Khan, S.M., Lespérance, Y.: A logical framework for prioritized goal change. In: Proc. of AAMAS 2010 (2010)
19. Klein, G., Woods, D.D., Bradshaw, J.M., Hoffman, R.R., Feltovich, P.J.: Ten challenges for making automation a "team player" in joint human-agent activity. IEEE Intelligent Systems 19(6), 91–95 (2004)
20. Lesser, V., et al.: Evolution of the GPGP/TAEMS Domain-Independent Coordination Framework. JAAMAS 9(1), 87–143 (2004)
21. Morley, D., Myers, K.L., Yorke-Smith, N.: Continuous refinement of agent resource estimates. In: Proc. of AAMAS 2006 (2006)
22. Nebel, B., Koehler, J.: Plan reuse versus plan generation: A theoretical and empirical analysis. Artificial Intelligence 76(1-2), 427–454 (1995)
23. Rao, A.S., Georgeff, M.P.: Modeling agents within a BDI-architecture. In: Proc. of KR 1991 (1991)
24. Reiter, R.: The projection problem in the situation calculus. In: Proc. of AIPS 1992 (1992)
25. Schut, M., Wooldridge, M., Parsons, S.: The theory and practice of intention reconsideration. JETAI 16(4), 261–293 (2004)
26. Shapiro, S., Brewka, G.: Dynamic interactions between goals and beliefs. In: Proc. of IJCAI 2007 (2007)
27. Shapiro, S., Lespérance, Y., Levesque, H.J.: Goal change. In: Proc. of IJCAI 2005 (2005)
28. Shaw, P.H., Farwer, B., Bordini, R.H.: Theoretical and experimental results on the goal-plan tree problem. In: Proc. of AAMAS 2008 (2008)
29. Singh, M.P.: A critical examination of use Cohen-Levesque theory of intentions. In: Proc. of ECAI 1992 (1992)
30. Smith, D.E.: Choosing objectives in over-subscription planning. In: Proc. of ICAPS 2004 (2004)
31. Thangarajah, J., Harland, J., Morley, D.N., Yorke-Smith, N.: Suspending and resuming tasks in BDI agents. In: Proc. of AAMAS 2008 (2008)
32. Thangarajah, J., Winikoff, M., Padgham, L., Fischer, K.: Avoiding resource conflicts in intelligent agents. In: Proc. of ECAI 2002 (2002)
33. van der Hoek, W., Jamroga, W., Wooldridge, M.: Towards a theory of intention revision. Synthese 155(2), 265–290 (2007)
34. van Riemsdijk, M.B., Dastani, M., Winikoff, M.: Goals in agent systems: A unifying framework. In: Proc. of AAMAS 2008 (2008)
35. Winikoff, M., Padgham, L., Harland, J., Thangarajah, J.: Declarative and procedural goals in intelligent agent systems. In: Proc. of KR 2002 (2002)
36. Zhou, Y., Chen, X.: Partial implication semantics for desirable propositions. In: Proc. of KR 2004 (2004)
37. Zhou, Y., van der Torre, L., Zhang, Y.: Partial goal satisfaction and goal change: Weak and strong partial implication, logical properties, complexity. In: Proc. of AAMAS 2008 (2008)

Part III

Programming Languages

Evaluating Agent-Oriented Programs: Towards Multi-paradigm Metrics

Howell R. Jordan and Rem Collier

Lero @ University College Dublin, Ireland

Abstract. Metrics are increasingly seen as important tools for software engineering and quantitative research, but little attention has so far been devoted to metrics for agent programming languages. This paper presents the first steps towards multi-paradigm structural metrics, which can be applied seamlessly to both agents and the object-oriented environments in which they are situated - thus enabling the designs of complete multi-agent systems to be quantitatively evaluated. Concrete paradigm-independent metrics for coupling and cohesion are proposed, and their use is demonstrated on an example Jason program, written in AgentSpeak and Java.[1]

Categories and subject descriptors: D.2.8 [**Software Engineering**]: Metrics—*Product Metrics*; I.2.5 [**Artificial Intelligence**]: Programming Languages and Software.

General terms: Measurement, Design, Languages.

Keywords: Design metrics, structural metrics, agent programming languages.

1 Introduction

Software design metrics, or structural metrics, are an important part of the professional software engineer's toolkit. Beyond their traditional roles in managerial oversight, metrics are increasingly used in iterative development processes to quickly highlight areas which may be vulnerable to defects or resistant to future change [22]. Metrics for object-oriented programming are well-established, and automated collection tools for the best-known metrics suites [10][23] are available for several popular object-oriented programming languages (OOPL).

Agent orientation is an emerging paradigm for software construction, in which software is composed of autonomous, proactive agents situated in some environment. Like other high-level software abstractions - such as components and aspects - agents complement, rather than replace, existing object technology. Agent-oriented software is often implemented using objects, for example by

---

[1] An earlier version of this paper was presented at the 8th International Workshop on PROgramming Multi-Agent Systems (PROMAS 2010).

R. Collier, J. Dix, and P. Novák (Eds.): ProMAS 2010, LNAI 6599, pp. 63–78, 2012.

building directly on the popular JADE platform [5], in which case it can be evaluated directly using existing metrics (see for example [15]).

Many researchers have argued that the benefits of agent orientation are best realised using a dedicated agent programming language (APL), thus "fixing the state of the modules to consist of components such as beliefs, capabilities, and decisions, each of which enjoys a precisely defined syntax" [33]. However, the performance cost of agents is much greater than that of passive objects, and attempting to write an industrial-strength 'pure agent' program has become a recognised pitfall of agent-oriented software development [40]. Many of the current generation of agent programming languages [7] resolve this dilemma by deferring the environment implementation [39] and any lower-level agent processing activities to object technologies such as Java.

If software designs are to be evaluated quantitatively, consistently, and comparably across the APL-OOPL divide, there is a clear need for a single metrics suite that is applicable to both domains. But let's not stop there. Inspired by recent research which integrates agents with software components [13], we expect the path towards wider adoption of agent programming languages to be through their integration with other paradigms. In this paper, we present the first steps towards a metrics suite which could, in principle, be used to evaluate software designs expressed in many different text-based programming languages.

The structure of this paper is as follows. In the next section, we discuss how the application of structural metrics to agent programming languages could benefit both practice and research. Section 3 outlines some of the wide literature of related work, and section 4 introduces an example Jason program. In section 5 we propose two structural metrics for agent programming, and apply them to the motivating example. Finally, we conclude by offering some tentative advice to the creators of agent programming languages, and some suggestions for future work in this area.

2 Why Metrics?

Metrics are used in software engineering to measure the quality of a software process or product. This paper focuses on the product. A software product consists of many linked artifacts, such as code, tests, and documentation; here the focus is specifically on the product's design, and the design information contained implicitly in its source code.

2.1 Measures of Product Quality

Software product quality is typically defined as a combination of factors, characteristics, or attributes [19] [16]. The primary quality factors are often given as functionality, reliability, usability, efficiency, maintainability, and portability. These factors are usually structured as a hierarchy, whereby each primary factor is itself defined as a combination of subfactors.

The depth and complexity of this hierarchy presents a measurement challenge. For a quantity to be measurable it must first be completely defined; unfortunately, there is no universally-agreed definition of software quality. The relative influence of quality attributes is also highly sensitive to context. For example, in mission-critical applications, reliability is obviously dominant; yet in others, reliability need be no better than 'good enough', and other quality attributes assume greater importance [3]. Attempts to combine multiple metrics into a general-purpose quality measure are therefore fraught with difficulty, and most software product metrics aim to measure a single, specific quality attribute [20].

Maintainability metrics are an important general software engineering topic [27]. However, in this paper, the focus is on maintainability as an interesting potential benefit of agent oriented software engineering. Agent programming is thought to aid the design and development of complex software, chiefly by enabling the developer to take full advantage of the intentional stance [33]; but little is currently known about the effects of agent orientation on maintainability.

Maintainability consists of at least three major subfactors: algorithmic complexity, structural or design complexity, and size[2]. Efforts to define multi-paradigm size and algorithmic complexity measures are already well advanced (see section 3), and the rest of this paper will focus on structural metrics. Structural complexity is itself a compound attribute, and among its subfactors, coupling and cohesion are thought to be dominant [12].

We take the view that structural metrics essentially predict how difficult it will be to modify a system in future; and thus they indirectly predict the likelihood of bugs, both in the present and in the immediate aftermath of any future change. In object-oriented systems, this view is supported by a large body of experimental evidence [35]. If the same is true for agents, the development of structural metrics for agent programming languages will help professional software engineers to deliver agent-oriented software of higher quality.

2.2 Tools for Software Research

Aside from their importance to professional software engineers, product metrics have an important role to play in software research.

Metrics can be used as powerful tools for technology comparison, as demonstrated by Garcia et al. [15]. The research method employed in this study is based on the 'Goal Question Metric' approach [4] and can be summarised roughly as follows: implement functionally-identical solutions to a given problem using two

---

[2] The algorithms, structure, and size of a program may be very different when it is running, due to optimisations applied during compilation, and dynamic language features such as plan passing and runtime class loading. However, these changes are usually transparent to the programmer, and therefore have little effect on software maintenance except when debugging. Similarly, our maintainability perspective leads us to ignore other runtime issues such as the frequency of message exchanges, although from a performance perspective (for example in areas such as compiler and platform development) these would be important topics.

or more different technologies; then compare those solutions using a suitable metric. If suitable multi-paradigm metrics were available, this method could be employed much more widely.

Studies of the above type could also help facilitate adoption of agent technologies by industry. It is widely thought that agent technologies provide greater benefits when used in certain application areas, but little experimental data is currently available to support these opinions. We argue that, given more quantitative evidence of the maintainability of agent oriented solutions, some of the business risks of agent adoption would be mitigated.

Finally, we hope that a focus on maintainability metrics - and on the related topics of software evolution, refactoring, coupling, and cohesion - will lead to innovations in agent programming language design. In section 6, some additions to the AgentSpeak language that might improve the maintainability of AgentSpeak code are tentatively suggested, based on experiences gained in this study.

3 Related Work

Aside from the large literature on object oriented metrics [16], structural metrics have been proposed for rule-based programs [29], concurrent logic programs [41], and knowledge based systems [21]. More recently, several metrics suites for aspect-oriented programming have also been devised [25]. In contrast, we know of only one APL-specific metrics suite, for the GOAL language [37]; it is based on usage counts of language constructs, and is therefore specialised to its target language.

Multi-paradigm metrics is a comparatively recent field of study. An automated method for measuring the relative information content of any two digital artifacts, based on Kolmogorov complexity, is proposed by Arbuckle [2]. The Normalised Compression Distance (NCD) metric estimates the difference in information content between successive versions A and B of the same program, and thus could provide insight into the retrospective maintainability of A.

Sipos et al. have proposed a multi-paradigm metric for algorithmic (as opposed to structural) complexity [34]. This metric is directly related to the number of independent paths through a given program, and high values therefore have negative implications for program testability. Given the importance of testing (and automated testing in particular) to refactoring and software evolution, we believe this metric is complimentary to ours.

Allen et al. model a program as a hypergraph, from which metrics for program size, algorithmic complexity, and coupling, can be derived [1]. Each metric is defined in detail using arguments from information theory; but no paradigm-independent method for extracting the hypergraph model from source code is offered. The hypergraph model is also insensitive to the strength and directionality of connections between nodes.

The PIMETA approach [8] leads to multi-paradigm structural metrics like ours, but it is restricted by several practical difficulties. PIMETA requires a detailed meta-model to be instantiated for each evaluation, and as the authors note, for many real programs the resulting models are large and difficult to visualise. No precise definition of coupling between PIMETA abstractions is offered, with coupling apparently defined on a case-by-case basis; it is therefore not clear how the meta-model instantiation process might be automated.

The 'separation of concerns' metrics suite of Sant'Anna et al. [32] is also, in part, applicable to agent programming languages. Though it is intended for use in the component-based and aspect-oriented paradigms, some of its metrics (Concern Diffusion over Architectural Components, Component-level Interlacing Between Concerns, Afferent Coupling Between Components, Efferent Coupling Between Components, and Lack of Concern-based Cohesion) could also be applied to agents. However the automated collection of these measures would be problematic, since the concepts of 'architectural concerns' and 'coupling between components' are not precisely defined. The remaining metrics in the suite make use of abstractions not defined for agents, such as distinct interfaces and operations.

4   Motivating Example

In this section, the need for multi-paradigm software maintainability metrics is illustrated with a simple example. The example is based on a grid environment of 16×8 squares, implemented in Java, and inspired by the 'vacuum world' of Russell and Norvig [31, p.133]. The grid is populated by four cleaning robots, and initially contains 32 pieces of 'dust'. The environment interface allows each vacuum cleaner to move north, south, east, and west; to sense its immediate surroundings with a small field of vision; and to clean its current square. The simulation is further enriched by 8 fixed obstacles, and realistic robot movement. Within this environment, the robots must clean the grid of dust, as quickly as possible.

Without excluding other technologies, the problem points towards an agent-oriented solution: the environment is dynamic, with partial, local visibility; and its four independent robots suggest at least four concurrent processes. In this example, the agent-oriented code to control the robots is written in Jason, an implementation of the AgentSpeak agent programming language.

Complete source code for the example can be downloaded from http://www.agentfactory.com.

4.1   Solution Architecture

The example solution consists of two types of agent: 'vacAgent' and 'bossAgent'. Four instances of vacAgent directly control each of the four vacuum robots. Only one bossAgent is instantiated, and is not situated in the environment; instead, it receives reports from the other agents about the world's state, from which it builds a mental map of the environment, and directs the exploration and cleaning activities of the vacAgents. For simplicity, the environment is considered as a third-party library with a stable interface - in other words, the actuators and perceptors are not part of the system under discussion, and are guaranteed not to change. Each vacAgent relies on object-oriented 'internal actions' to implement some of its functionality, as shown in Figure 1.

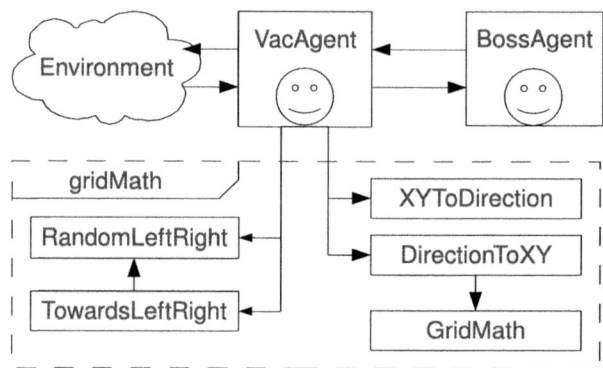

Fig. 1. Outline architecture of an example Jason program, showing AgentSpeak agents with Java internal actions

4.2   Preliminary Evaluation

The example is just one of many possible designs that would solve the given problem. The rest of this paper is motivated by asking the question: how maintainable is the example design? Existing object-oriented metrics could of course be applied to the internal actions; but these metrics would not capture any information about the design of the agents themselves, the links between those agents, or the links between agents and their internal actions.

The design could also be evaluated using one of the paradigm-independent techniques discussed in section 3. However, these structural metrics must be collected manually, which is impractical for large designs and rapid iterative development processes, and likely to result in errors. To address these shortcomings, we aim to develop a metrics suite for agent programs which operates directly on source code and is amenable to automation.

5   Paradigm-Independent Metrics

It is highly desirable that any new metrics should be validated experimentally [20], which is beyond the scope of the current study. Consequently, this paper proposes no original metrics; instead, the well-validated Coupling Between Object Classes (CBO) and Lack of Cohesion Of Methods (LCOM) measures [10] are generalized, returning to the earlier notion of 'coupling between abstractions' [24] and its cohesiveness equivalent. The generalization process described in this section is outlined as follows:

1. Generalize from OO classes, fields, and methods, to abstractions and elements, based on mereological principles [36].
2. Devise an automatable method for discovering the graph of dependencies between elements, using a simple theory of software change.
3. Derive paradigm-independent equivalents of CBO and LCOM as functions of the element dependency graph.

The terminology of Buckley et al. [9] is used throughout this section when discussing software change.

5.1 Software as Aggregation Hierarchies

Many programming languages facilitate high-level design, understanding, and reuse by means of abstraction, supported by dedicated language constructs. During the development process, these abstractions are realized as program source code, then processed (for example, by compiling) to form an executable; the term 'element' is adopted here to mean a named, realized abstraction[3]. For example, the abstractions supported in Jason include Java classes, Java methods, and AgentSpeak agents; and the standard Java platform provides many ready-made elements such as java.util.ArrayList and java.lang.System.out.println.

Elements are often composed of other elements to form an aggregation hierarchy, and a mereological approach is therefore appropriate [36]. Let E denote the set of all elements in the system under discussion s; E is the universe of discourse in the treatment that follows. In analogy with conventional mereological notation, let the binary predicate M represent direct aggregation between two elements; $Mxy \implies$ element x *is an immediate member of* element y. M has the following properties:

$$\neg Mxx \qquad (M \text{ irreflexive}) \qquad (1)$$

$$Mxy \implies \nexists z(Mxz \wedge Mzy) \qquad (M \text{ nontransitive}) \qquad (2)$$

$$Mxy \implies \neg Myx \qquad (M \text{ antisymmetric}) \qquad (3)$$

M describes relations between adjacent layers of a formal, stratified hierarchy such as a software system. However, M is inconvenient when describing relations between non-adjacent layers. To this end, a more general aggregation relation P can be defined, based on M, but compatible with ground mereology [38];

---

[3] A 'name' can be defined as a string, chosen by the programmer, that has no semantic effect on the program's functionality. Anonymously-realized abstractions, such as Java inner classes, are not 'elements' in the current model; as will be shown in section 5.2, this is a necessary model feature. If necessary, qualifying annotations can be used to distinguish between different elements with the same name, for example if a Java method is overloaded; the format of these annotations should be chosen to suit the current language, and is not prescribed here.

$Pxy \implies$ element x *is a part of* element y. P is a transitive closure of M, and has the following properties:

$$Mxy \implies Pxy \tag{4}$$

$$Pxx \qquad (P \text{ reflexive}) \tag{5}$$

$$Pxy \wedge Pyz \implies Pxz \qquad (P \text{ transitive}) \tag{6}$$

Since every element in E forms some part of s, $\forall e \in E(Pes)$.

Closely following Vaishnavi et al. [36], classes, methods, and fields can now be generalized to mereological 'levels', using the above theory base. First, define an 'atomic' element as one which aggregates no other elements, and V_0 as the set of atomic elements in E. Then recursively partition E into levels $V_0..V_n$, such that all the members of each level share similar aggregation responsibilities:

$$V_0 \equiv \{x : \nexists y(Myx)\} \tag{7}$$

$$V_n \equiv \{x \notin \bigcup V_0..V_{n-1} : \exists y \in V_{n-1}(Myx)\} \tag{8}$$

Applying this model to a system s yields a stratified aggregation hierarchy, which is an acyclic digraph $\mathcal{M} = (E, M)$ with s as root; from $\mathcal{M}$, an analogous graph $\mathcal{P} = (E, P)$ can also be derived using equations (4) and (6). A sample of the graph $\mathcal{M}$ and its associated levels, for the example Jason program, is shown in figure 2; for convenience the element names are prefixed to indicate their source language (Java j or AgentSpeak as) and abstraction type (package k, class c,

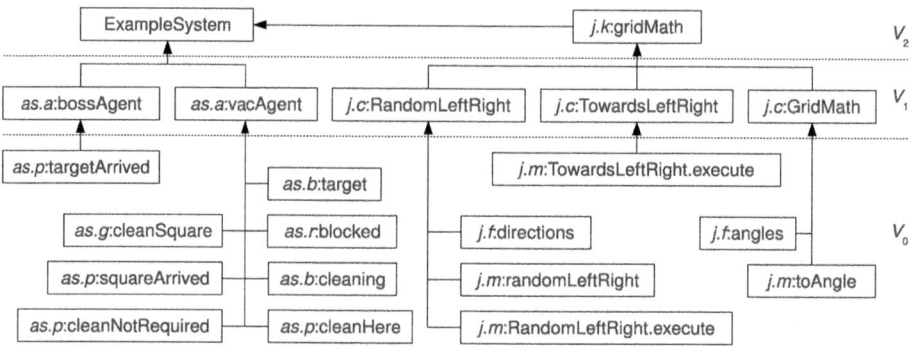

Fig. 2. Part of the element aggregation graph $\mathcal{M}$, for an example Jason program. An arrow from x to y indicates that Mxy. Note that all the information required for this graph was found in, and could easily be automatically extracted from, the program's source code.

field f, method m, agent a, rule r, belief b, goal g, or plan p). The assignment of all agents and classes to the same level accords with the widely-held view that agents are specializations of objects [33].

An interesting practical issue was encountered while compiling this aggregation graph. AgentSpeak agents can pass beliefs, goals, and plans to other agents, without prior declaration; in the example, two of the vacAgent's possible beliefs ('cleaning' and 'target') are given to it by the bossAgent. This lack of explicit declaration makes it difficult to manually determine the full set of an agent's possible beliefs.

5.2   Discovering Dependencies by Refactoring

Changes to software artifacts sometimes have widespread ripple effects, or 'change impacts', on other parts of the program. Successful software will probably undergo many changes during its lifetime; ideally, a suite of structural maintainability metrics would predict, given an existing software design, how much effort and risk will be incurred in making those changes. While acknowledging that changes to software may be radical and unanticipated, this paper focuses on incremental, evolutionary changes to existing source code, such as the modification of existing program features.

The difficulty of evolving existing code might ideally be estimated by performing example code changes, that are considered representative of the most likely feature modifications. However, for all but the most trivial programs, the list of plausible feature modifications would be vast. Even if program behaviour modifications are excluded, the list of all possible refactorings [14] is considered infinite [28].

Instead of attempting to define a set of representative changes, we propose that useful insight into the scope of any change impacts, and hence the 'evolvability' of a code segment, could be gained by repeatedly applying a very simple refactoring. Keeping our goal of paradigm-independence in mind, we suggest that just one refactoring is applicable to all conceivable text-based programming languages: the 'rename' refactoring [14, p.273]. This refactoring has the appealing property that it is a semantics-preserving change with no structural effects, which leads to two benefits: for most programming languages it can be easily automated; and the number of distinct modifications required to accommodate a rename refactoring could be said to represent the minimum ripple effect of modifications to that element.

Let D denote a binary predicate representing an explicit structural dependency between two program elements; $Dxy \implies$ element x *directly depends on* element y. The following general method can be used to discover the dependencies present within a program s:

1. Create a backup copy of the program code s.
2. For each element e in E:
   (a) Rename e, carefully avoiding new names which are used elsewhere in the program, or have special meaning in the current programming language.

(b) By text replacement only, modify the minimum set X_e of other elements, $X_e \subseteq E$, so that the program's original external behaviour is exactly restored.

(c) Record the dependency represented by each modified element[4]: $\forall x \in X_e (Dxe)$.

(d) Revert all changes to s, by restoring from the backup copy.

Applying this method yields a dependency graph $\mathcal{D} = (E, D)$, where D is the union of all the discovered dependency relations; a sample of the graph $\mathcal{D}$ for the example Jason program is shown in figure 3.

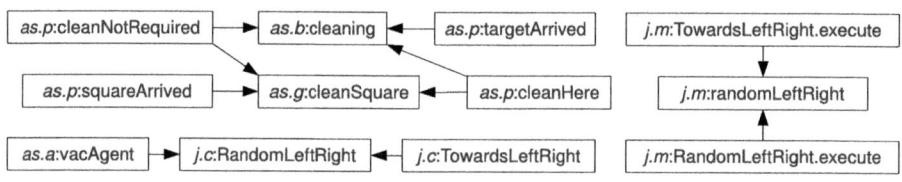

Fig. 3. Part of the element dependency graph $\mathcal{D}$, for an example Jason program. An arrow from x to y indicates that Dxy.

Figure 3 illustrates dependencies

1. within a single agent;
2. within an agent and between two agents;
3. between an internal action and the agent that uses it;
4. within an internal action and between two internal actions.

Of particular interest is the result of the rename operation on the RandomLeft-Right class. Two plans within the vacAgent refer to this internal action, and therefore required modification; however, as those plans were not named, they did not meet our definition of an element, and the resulting dependencies were therefore credited to the vacAgent itself. This illustrates a simple benefit of naming AgentSpeak plans: naming allows the location of modification points to be more precisely specified. The TowardsLeftRight class depends on RandomLeft-Right by use of the 'extends' Java keyword; thus the object-specific concept of inheritance has been captured in a paradigm-independent way.

5.3   Coupling Between Elements (CBE)

Background. The definition of CBO states that "an object is coupled to another object if one of them acts on the other". Action is defined as the methods of one class accessing or modifying the methods or instance variables of the other. CBO for a class is then a count of the number of *other* classes to which that class is coupled, implying that a class cannot be coupled to itself [10].

---

[4] An adjacency matrix is ideal for keeping track of dependencies as they are discovered.

Definition. CBO can be generalized to CBE as follows. An element $x \in V_1$ is coupled to another element $y \in V_1$, $y \neq x$, if any direct dependencies $Dij \vee Dji$ exist between any of their parts $Pix \wedge Pjy$. CBE for x is then a count of the number of other elements in V_1 to which x is coupled:

$$\text{CBE}(x) = \begin{cases} |\ \{y \in V_1/x : \exists i, j(Pix \wedge Pjy \wedge (Dij \vee Dji))\}\ | & x \in V_1 \\ \text{undefined} & x \notin V_1 \end{cases}$$
(9)

Domain and range. CBE maps from level 1 elements to the natural numbers:

$$\text{CBE} : V_1 \rightarrow \{n \in \mathbb{N} : n < |V_1|\}$$
(10)

Software engineering viewpoint. $\text{CBE}(x)$ estimates the ripple effects of modifying x, combined with the sensitivity of x to changes elsewhere in the software system. A low value, $\text{CBE}(x) \simeq 1$, generally indicates a maintainable design, while a high value, $\text{CBE}(x) \gg 1$, predicts future maintenance difficulties. $\text{CBE}(x) = 0$ implies that x has no explicit dependencies to or from the rest of the system; therefore either $|V_1| = 1$, or x is isolated.

5.4 Lack of Cohesion of Elements (LCE)

Background. The intent of LCOM is to measure the similarity of methods in a class, by comparing the sets of instance variables used by each method. However, the two published definitions of LCOM differ significantly [23]: the first is a count of the number of disjoint instance variable sets, the second is based on counts of pairwise comparisons of instance variable sets. Neither version is sensitive to dependencies between methods, thus a method which does not directly use the instance variables of its class, but instead accesses them by invoking other local methods, is counted as incohesive. The second definition also has another unappealing property: the pairwise combinations of methods in a class varies as $m(m-1)/2$, where m is the number of methods, causing this variant to scale exponentially as incohesive methods are added. We therefore choose the first version as the basis of LCE.

Definition. Let L denote a binary predicate representing transitive, undirected local dependency between two elements; $Lxy \implies$ element x *has local dependencies with* element y. Formally we define L as follows:

$$(Dxy \vee Dyx) \wedge (\exists z(Mxz \wedge Myz)) \implies Lxy$$
(11)

$$Lxx \qquad (L \text{ reflexive})$$
(12)

$$Lxy \wedge Lyz \implies Lxz \qquad (L \text{ transitive})$$
(13)

LCE for an element x is then a count of the number of sets S, where each S is the largest possible set such that all elements of S are locally interdependent members of x:

$$\text{LCE}(x) = | \{ S : \forall i, j \in S(Lij \wedge Mix \wedge Mjx \wedge \nexists k \notin S(Mkx \wedge Lik)) \} | \quad (14)$$

Domain and range. LCE maps from elements to the natural numbers:

$$\text{LCE} : E \rightarrow \{ n \in \mathbb{N} : n < |E| \} \quad (15)$$

Software engineering viewpoint. $\text{LCE}(x) = 1$ when all the members of x are locally interdependent; in other words, all members of x use each other in some way, and x is maximally cohesive. $\text{LCE}(x) > 1$ suggests a possible design problem: x could easily be divided into $\text{LCE}(x)$ separate elements. From equations 12 and 7, $\text{LCE}(x) = 0 \implies x \in V_0$, and therefore x has no structure which is representable in the current model.

5.5   Results

The values of CBE and LCE for all the level 1 elements (classes and agents) in the example Jason program are shown in table 1.

Table 1. Values of the paradigm-independent metrics *CBE* and *LCE* for level 1 elements in an example Jason program. CBE is an estimate of the connectedness of the given element. LCE is an estimate of the number of unrelated parts present in the given element. For both metrics, values closer to 1 are usually better.

Level 1 element	CBE	LCE
vacAgent	5	3
bossAgent	1	2
GridMath	1	3
RandomLeftRight	2	1
TowardsLeftRight	2	1
DirectionToXY	2	1
XYToDirection	1	1

The full benefit of metrics is difficult to demonstrate using only a small example; metrics are most useful when comparing similar programs, or evaluating parts of a large software design. However, the results for CBE closely match the connections shown in figure 1, thus illustrating how important architectural features can be captured quantitatively with this metric. Had no architectural descriptions been available, this information would have been invaluable.

The results for LCE are also of interest. GridMath has an LCE value of three, indicating that its three methods have little in common, and it could easily be split into three separate classes. Likewise, the LCE value for bossAgent reveals that it has two separate responsibilities, one for target allocation and the other for location tracking. In the case of vacAgent, its apparently separate parts are all connected via common control of an entity in the environment, illustrating that metric values should always be interpreted carefully.

6 Conclusions

Metrics are increasingly seen as valuable tools which help researchers to compare technologies, and software engineers to understand where future problems may arise. Agent programs written in languages such as Jason are often inherently multi-paradigm, with substantial functionality deferred to object-oriented elements. In order to evaluate and compare such programs, a multi-paradigm metrics suite is needed.

In this paper, paradigm-independent coupling and cohesion metrics CBE and LCE were proposed, and their application demonstrated on an example Jason program. The theoretical validity of these metrics as predictors of maintainability rests on the hypothesis that the 'rename' refactoring is representative of general software maintenance - which is currently unproven. However, the Chidamber and Kemerer (CK) metrics CBO and LCOM, from which they are generalized, are both well-validated and theoretically grounded. Validation of CBE and LCE would require a large dataset of Jason programs, and access to Jason programming experts, neither of which was available at the time of writing; independent experimental validation is therefore left for future work.

While deriving the proposed metrics, a number of issues relating to AgentSpeak programming were uncovered. The need to discover and locate dependencies in software is not limited to toolmakers; human programmers must do the same when trying to comprehend any unfamiliar code. We therefore make the following suggestions:

1. Plan naming is optional in AgentSpeak. We advocate that plans should be named where possible, arguing that it helps to precisely locate dependencies and other code issues.
2. Explicit declaration of beliefs and goals in AgentSpeak would make it easier to determine an agent's possible mental states. A similar feature is already provided in the Agent Factory AFAPL2 agent programming language by an 'ontology' construct [11].

Though our perspective is one of maintainability measurement rather than agent decomposition and re-use, these suggestions are compatible with recent work on agent programming language modularity [26] [17].

Our next steps will be to automate the collection of the CBE and LCE metrics, and validate their use experimentally. To evaluate the generality of the 'multi-paradigm' claim, the applicability of the underlying model to other programming languages should also be investigated. A preliminary examination of the structure and syntax of GOAL [18] programs suggests that the model is compatible, and that its application might raise some interesting issues. The abstractions available in GOAL include predicates, terms, actions, and macros, but the realizations of these abstractions are typically short, with many elements being completely defined within one line of code. Thus GOAL programs tend to contain more elements than their AgentSpeak equivalents, which could lead to dramatic differences in CBE and LCE values when comparing the two languages.

The CBE and LCE metrics reflect only a small proportion of the dependency information gathered. Could any other useful predictors of maintainability be devised from it? A large body of literature exists on the relative contributions of different dependency types to coupling and cohesion [16]. A second debate concerns the issue of whether metrics for software maintainability should be applied at a coarse [30] or fine [6] level of granularity. We speculate that the relative locations of dependencies may also be important; intuitively, two multiply-interdependent abstractions will require less future maintenance effort if those dependencies are closely co-located. New multi-paradigm metrics based on our dependency data could shed light on these issues. If links between these metrics and real-world maintainability can be established, this may in turn lead to new recommendations for multi-paradigm programming practices and language design.

Instead of devising new metrics, one interesting alternative would be to provide a flexible means of visualising and summarising the raw dependency data. Such a tool could allow engineers and researchers to focus on the dependency types appropriate to the current context, and aggregate results at an abstraction level of their choosing.

Acknowledgements. We would like to thank Jim Buckley, Mike Hinchey, Rebecca Yates, and the anonymous reviewers, who made many insightful suggestions. This work was supported, in part, by Science Foundation Ireland grant 03/CE2/I303_1 to Lero - the Irish Software Engineering Research Centre.

References

1. Allen, E.B., Gottipati, S., Govindarajan, R.: Measuring size, complexity, and coupling of hypergraph abstractions of software: an information-theory approach. Software Quality Journal 15(2), 179–212 (2007)
2. Arbuckle, T.: Measure Software - and its Evolution - Using Information Content. In: Proceedings of the Joint International and Annual ERCIM Workshops on Principles of Software Evolution (IWPSE) and Software Evolution (Evol) Workshops, pp. 129–134. ACM (2009)
3. Bach, J.: Good enough quality: Beyond the buzzword. Computer 30(8), 96–98 (1997)
4. Basili, V.R., Caldiera, G., Rombach, H.D.: The goal question metric approach. Encyclopedia of Software Engineering 1, 528–532 (1994)
5. Bellifemine, F., Caire, G., Greenwood, D.: Developing multi-agent systems with JADE. Springer, Heidelberg (2008)

6. Binkley, A.B., Schach, S.R.: Validation of the coupling dependency metric as a predictor of run-time failures and maintenance measures. In: Proceedings of the 20th International Conference on Software Engineering, pp. 452–455. IEEE Computer Society, Washington, DC (1998)
7. Bordini, R.H., Braubach, L., Dastani, M., Seghrouchni, A.E.F., Gomez-Sanz, J.J., Leite, J., O'Hare, G., Pokahr, A., Ricci, A.: A survey of programming languages and platforms for multi-agent systems. Special Issue: Hot Topics in European Agent Research II Guest Editors: Andrea Omicini 30, 33–44 (2006)
8. Bryton, S., e Abreu, F.B.: Towards Paradigm-Independent Software Assessment. In: Proc. of QUATIC 2007 (2007)
9. Buckley, J., Mens, T., Zenger, M., Rashid, A., Kniesel, G.: Towards a taxonomy of software change. Journal of Software Maintenance and Evolution 17(5), 309–332 (2005)
10. Chidamber, S.R., Kemerer, C.F.: A metrics suite for object oriented design. IEEE Transactions on Software Engineering 20(6), 476–493 (1994)
11. Collier, R.W., O'Hare, G.M.P.: Modelling and Programming with Commitment Rules in Agent Factory. In: Handbook of Research on Emerging Rule-Based Languages and Technologies: Open Solutions and Approaches (2009)
12. Darcy, D.P., Kemerer, C.F., Slaughter, S.A., Tomayko, J.E.: The structural complexity of software: an experimental test. IEEE Transactions on Software Engineering 31(11), 982–995 (2005)
13. Dragone, M., Lillis, D., Collier, R., O'Hare, G.M.P.: SoSAA: a framework for integrating components & agents. In: Proceedings of the 2009 ACM Symposium on Applied Computing, pp. 722–728. ACM, New York (2009)
14. Fowler, M.: Refactoring: improving the design of existing code. Addison-Wesley Professional (1999)
15. Garcia, A., Sant'Anna, C., Chavez, C., da Silva, V.T., de Lucena, C.J.P., von Staa, A.: Separation of Concerns in Multi-agent Systems: An Empirical Study. In: Lucena, C., Garcia, A., Romanovsky, A., Castro, J., Alencar, P.S.C. (eds.) SELMAS 2003. LNCS, vol. 2940, pp. 49–72. Springer, Heidelberg (2004)
16. Henderson-Sellers, B.: Object-oriented metrics: measures of complexity. Prentice-Hall, Inc., Upper Saddle River (1996)
17. Hindriks, K.: Modules as Policy-Based Intentions: Modular Agent Programming in GOAL. In: Dastani, M.M., El Fallah Seghrouchni, A., Ricci, A., Winikoff, M. (eds.) ProMAS 2007. LNCS (LNAI), vol. 4908, pp. 156–171. Springer, Heidelberg (2008)
18. Hindriks, K.V., de Boer, F.S., van der Hoek, W., Meyer, J.-J.C.: Agent Programming with Declarative Goals. In: Castelfranchi, C., Lespérance, Y. (eds.) ATAL 2000. LNCS (LNAI), vol. 1986, pp. 228–243. Springer, Heidelberg (2001)
19. Kitchenham, B., Pfleeger, S.L.: Software quality: The elusive target. IEEE Software 13(1), 12–21 (1996)
20. Kitchenham, B., Pfleeger, S.L., Fenton, N.: Towards a framework for software measurement validation. IEEE Transactions on Software Engineering 21(12), 929–944 (1995)
21. Kramer, S., Kaindl, H.: Coupling and cohesion metrics for knowledge-based systems using frames and rules. ACM Transactions on Software Engineering and Methodology (TOSEM) 13(3), 332–358 (2004)
22. Lanza, M., Marinescu, R., Ducasse, S.: Object-oriented metrics in practice: using software metrics to characterize, evaluate, and improve the design of object-oriented systems. Springer-Verlag New York Inc., New York (2006)

23. Li, W.: Another metric suite for object-oriented programming. The Journal of Systems & Software 44(2), 155–162 (1998)
24. Lieberherr, K., Holland, I., Riel, A.: Object-oriented programming: an objective sense of style. ACM SIGPLAN Notices 23(11), 323–334 (1988)
25. Lopez-Herrejon, R.E., Apel, S.: Measuring and Characterizing Crosscutting in Aspect-Based Programs: Basic Metrics and Case Studies. In: Dwyer, M.B., Lopes, A. (eds.) FASE 2007. LNCS, vol. 4422, pp. 423–437. Springer, Heidelberg (2007)
26. Madden, N., Logan, B.: Modularity and Compositionality in Jason. In: Braubach, L., Briot, J.-P., Thangarajah, J. (eds.) ProMAS 2009. LNCS, vol. 5919, pp. 237–253. Springer, Heidelberg (2010)
27. Mens, T., Demeyer, S.: Future trends in software evolution metrics. In: Proceedings of the 4th International Workshop on Principles of Software Evolution, pp. 83–86. ACM, New York (2001)
28. Mens, T., Van Eetvelde, N., Demeyer, S., Janssens, D.: Formalizing refactorings with graph transformations. Journal of Software Maintenance and Evolution 17(4), 247–276 (2005)
29. O'Neal, M.B., Edwards, W.R.: Complexity measures for rule-based programs. IEEE Transactions on Knowledge and Data Engineering 6(5), 669–680 (1994)
30. Ramil, J.F., Lehman, M.M.: Metrics of software evolution as effort predictors - a case study. In: Proc. Int. Conf. Software Maintenance, pp. 163–172 (2000)
31. Russell, S.J., Norvig, P.: Artificial intelligence: a modern approach. Prentice Hall (2009)
32. SantAnna, C., Figueiredo, E., Garcia, A., Lucena, C.: On the Modularity Assessment of Software Architectures: Do my architectural concerns count? In: Proc. International Workshop on Aspects in Architecture Descriptions (AARCH 2007), AOSD, vol. 7, Citeseer (2007)
33. Shoham, Y.: Agent-oriented programming. Artificial intelligence 60(1), 51–92 (1993)
34. Sipos, A., Pataki, N., Porkoláb, Z.: On Multiparadigm Software Complexity Metrics. In: MaCS 2006 6th Joint Conference on Mathematics and Computer Science, p. 85 (2006)
35. Subramanyam, R., Krishnan, M.S.: Empirical analysis of CK metrics for object-oriented design complexity: implications for software defects. IEEE Transactions on Software Engineering 29(4), 297–310 (2003)
36. Vaishnavi, V.K., Purao, S., Liegle, J.: Object-oriented product metrics: A generic framework. Information Sciences 177(2), 587–606 (2007)
37. van Riemsdijk, M.B., Hindriks, K.V.: An Empirical Study of Agent Programs: A Dynamic Blocks World Case Study in GOAL. In: Yang, J.-J., Yokoo, M., Ito, T., Jin, Z., Scerri, P. (eds.) PRIMA 2009. LNCS, vol. 5925, pp. 200–215. Springer, Heidelberg (2009)
38. Varzi, A.: Mereology. Stanford Encyclopedia of Philosophy (2009), http://plato.stanford.edu/entries/mereology/ (cited January 17, 2011)
39. Weyns, D., Omicini, A., Odell, J.: Environment as a first class abstraction in multiagent systems. Autonomous Agents and Multi-Agent Systems 14(1), 5–30 (2007)
40. Wooldridge, M., Jennings, N.R.: Pitfalls of agent-oriented development. In: Proceedings of the Second International Conference on Autonomous Agents, pp. 385–391. ACM, New York (1998)
41. Zhao, J., Cheng, J., Ushijima, K.: A Metrics Suite for Concurrent Logic Programs. In: Proc. 2nd Euromicro Working Conference on Software Maintenance and Reengineering, pp. 172–178, Citeseer (1998)

Atomic Intentions in Jason$^+$

Daniel Kiss, Neil Madden, and Brian Logan

School of Computer Science
University of Nottingham, UK
bsl@cs.nott.ac.uk

Abstract. We consider interactions between *atomic intentions* and plan failures in the *Jason* BDI-based agent programming language. Atomic intentions allow the agent developer to control the execution of intentions in situations where a sequence of actions must be executed 'atomically' in order to ensure the success of a plan. However, while atomic intentions in *Jason* enforce mutual exclusion, they are not atomic operations in the sense understood in conventional programming or in databases, and failure of an atomic plan can leave the agent's belief and plan bases in an inconsistent state. In this paper we present a new approach to atomic intentions which provides a transactional 'all-or-nothing' semantics, and describe its implementation in a new version of *Jason*, *Jason*$^+$. We argue that *Jason*$^+$ offers a more predictable semantics for atomic plans in the face of plan failure and can reduce the load on the agent developer by automating simple cases of failure handing, leading to the development of more robust agent programs.

1 Introduction

Jason [1] is a Java-based interpreter for an extended version of AgentSpeak(L). AgentSpeak(L) is a high-level agent-oriented programming language [2] which incorporates ideas from the BDI (belief-desire-intention) model of agency. Since it was first introduced in [3], *Jason* has evolved into a rich platform for the development of multi-agent systems. It has many sophisticated features to facilitate the development of complex agent-based systems, including control over the scheduling of intentions, support for plan exchange between agents, and facilities for handling plan failures. In this paper, we investigate some of the interactions between these features (which are also found in other BDI-based agent programming languages), and highlight some of the potential problems that can arise from their interaction.

We focus on a key feature of *Jason*, *atomic intentions*, and how these interact with *Jason*'s facilities for handling plan failures. Atomic intentions allow the agent developer to control the execution of intentions in situations where a sequence of actions must be executed 'atomically' in order to ensure the success of a plan. However, while atomic intentions enforce mutual exclusion, they are not atomic operations in the sense understood in conventional programming or in databases. In particular, we show that failure of an atomic plan can leave the agent's belief and plan bases in an inconsistent state, and further that the existing failure handling mechanisms implemented in *Jason* make it hard to recover from such failures.

To overcome these problems we have developed *Jason*$^+$, an extension of the *Jason* agent programming language which adopts a *transactional* approach to atomic plans.

R. Collier, J. Dix, and P. Novák (Eds.): ProMAS 2010, LNAI 6599, pp. 79–95, 2012.

If an action in a *Jason*$^+$ atomic plan fails, the whole atomic plan fails and the agent's belief and plan bases and event list are left in the state they were before the execution of the atomic plan. However if an atomic plan succeeds, all updates to the agent's belief and plan bases made by the atomic plan are visible to any subsequent actions in the intention containing the atomic plan and to actions in other intentions, and all events generated by the atomic plan are added to the event list. *Jason*$^+$ also implements a version of the module system described in [4] which is used to encapsulate dynamically loaded plans. With the exception of minor changes required by the module system, the syntax of *Jason*$^+$ is backwards compatible with the current release of *Jason*. We believe that the extensions implemented in *Jason*$^+$ offer a more predictable semantics for atomic plans in the face of plan failure and can reduce the load on the agent developer by automating simple cases of failure handing, leading to the development of more robust agent programs.[1]

The remainder of this paper is structured as follows. In the next section we briefly summarise the syntax and semantics of *Jason*. In section 3 we motivate the need for atomic intentions, and highlight some of the problems of the current implementation of atomic intentions in *Jason*. In section 4 we present a new approach to atomic intentions which provides a transactional 'all-or-nothing' semantics, and describe its implementation in a new version of *Jason*, *Jason*$^+$. In section 5 we briefly discuss how our approach could be generalised to other BDI-based agent programming languages, and outline plans for future work.

2   *Jason*

Jason is loosely based on the logic programming paradigm, but with an operational semantics based on plan execution in response to events and beliefs rather than SLD resolution as in Prolog.

A *Jason* agent is specified in terms of beliefs, goals and plans. An agent's beliefs represent its information about its environment, e.g., sensory input, information about other agents, etc. Beliefs are represented as ground atomic formulas. For example, the agent may believe that John is a customer: `customer(John)`. A goal is a state the agent wishes to bring about or a query to be evaluated. An achievement goal, written $!g(t_1, \ldots, t_n)$ where $t_i, \ldots, t_n$ are terms, specifies that the agent wishes to achieve a state in which $g(t_1, \ldots, t_n)$ is a true belief. A test goal, written $?g(t_1, \ldots, t_n)$, specifies that the agent wishes to determine if $g(t_1, \ldots, t_n)$ is a true belief. For example, an agent may have a goal `!order(widget, 10)` to process a purchase order for 10 widgets. (As in Prolog, constants are written in lower case and variables in upper case, and all negations must be ground when evaluated.) *Jason* extends AgentSpeak(L) with support for more complex beliefs, default and strong negation, and arbitrary internal actions implemented in Java. The belief base of AgentSpeak(L) consists simply of a set of ground literals, whereas *Jason* supports a sizeable subset of Prolog for the belief base, including universally-quantified rules (Horn clauses).

Changes in the agent's beliefs or the acquisition of new achievement goals give rise to *events*. An addition event, denoted by $+$, indicates the addition of a belief or an

---

[1] *Jason*$^+$ is available at `http://code.google.com/p/jasonp`.

achievement goal. A deletion event, denoted by −, indicates the retraction of a belief or goal. *Plans* specify sequences of actions and subgoals an agent can use to achieve its goals or respond to events (changes in its beliefs and goals). The head of a plan consists of a triggering event which specifies the kind of event the plan can be used to respond to, and a belief context which specifies the beliefs that must be true for the plan to be applicable. The body of a plan specifies a sequence of actions and (sub)goals to respond to the triggering event. Actions are the basic operations an agent can perform to change its environment (or its internal state) in order to achieve its goals. Plans may also contain achievement and test (sub)goals. Achievement subgoals allow an agent to choose a course of action as part of a larger plan on the basis of its current beliefs. An achievement subgoal $!g(t_1, \ldots, t_n)$ gives rise to a internal goal addition event $+!g(t_1, \ldots, t_n)$ which may in turn trigger subplans at the next execution cycle. Test goals are evaluated against the agent's belief base, possibly binding variables in the plan.[2] For example, an agent which forms part of an e-Commerce application might use the simple plan shown if Figure 1 to processes orders.

```
/* Initial stock */
stock(widget, 1).

@processOrder
+!order(Item, Num)[source(Customer)] <-
    ?stock(Item, Stock);             /* test plan */
    Num <= Stock;                    /* test plan */
    -+stock(Item, Stock - Num);      /* modify stock */
    +purchased(Customer, Item, Num);
    !dispatch(Customer, Item, Num).
```

Fig. 1. Example *Jason* plan

The current stock level of items is stored as a ground fact in the belief base. The plan checks that there is sufficient stock to process the order, updates the agent's beliefs to reflect the reduced stock level and record the customer's order and then generates a subgoal to dispatch the order to the customer.

At each reasoning cycle, *Jason* first processes any events and updates the agent's belief base. The interpreter then selects a single event to process and matches it against the plan library to select one or more plans to handle the event. Of these plans, a single plan is then selected to become an intention. Finally, one of the currently active intentions is selected and the next step in that intention is executed, before the cycle repeats.

Jason has been extended in a variety of ways, for example, to support decision theoretic scheduling of intentions [5]. Of particular interest here is the support provided in core *Jason* for cooperative plan exchange as described in [6,7]. In the cooperative BDI paradigm, agents can retrieve plans from other agents. Such plans can be dynamically loaded into the agent's plan base to extend its capabilities at run time. For example, the

---

[2] In the interests of brevity, we have slightly simplified the presentation of *Jason* syntax and semantics.

Jason interpreter can be configured to invoke the user-defined `selectOption` function when the set of relevant and applicable plans for an event is empty. Internal actions are also provided to allow plans to be added and removed from the agent's plan base at run time. These facilities can be used to implement the kind of plan exchange described in [7].

3   Atomic Intentions

The basic *Jason* execution strategy allows an agent to pursue multiple goals at the same time, e.g., an agent can respond to an urgent, short-duration task while engaged in a long-term task, and such flexibility is a key characteristic of an agent-oriented approach to software development. However it can increase the risk that actions in different plans will interfere with each other. For example, if an agent has an intention containing a "go right" action and another intention containing a "go left" action, their interleaved execution may result in the agent returning to its original location. (The default *Jason* intention selection function implements a form of 'round robin' scheduling: each intention is selected in turn and a single step of that intention is executed, resulting in fully-interleaved execution of plans.) More generally, the successful execution of an action in a plan (and ultimately achievement of the agent's goals) typically requires that pre-conditions established by actions earlier in the plan continue to hold when the action is eventually executed. This can be difficult or impossible to guarantee with unconstrained interleaving of agent plans. For example, the example *Jason* plan shown if Figure 1 may result in incorrect behaviour. If two orders for a widget arrive at about the same time, an agent using the default *Jason* intention selection function may attempt to dispatch the same widget to both customers. Such race conditions are well known in multi-threaded conventional programs, and it is not surprising that agent programming languages that support the parallel execution of intentions should face similar challenges.

It is therefore important that the agent developer can control which intentions are selected for execution. For example, there may be situations where a sequence of actions must be executed 'atomically' in order to ensure the success of a plan. *Jason* allows such control to be exercised in two ways: by over-riding the default intention selection function and by use of `atomic` plan annotations (both are optional). In what follows, we focus on `atomic` annotations, as these provide built-in support for atomic execution of intentions.

3.1   Atomic Plans in Jason

An `atomic` plan annotation indicates that a plan should be executed 'atomically'. If an intention containing a plan with an `atomic` annotation is selected for execution by the agent's intention selection function, it will continue to be selected for execution in subsequent execution cycles until the plan completes. In effect, an `atomic` annotation over-rides the normal operation of the event and intention selection functions during the execution of the atomic plan, and guarantees that the execution of actions in other intentions will not be interleaved with the steps of an atomic plan. (Note that unlike mutual exclusion in conventional programming languages, e.g., `synchronized` methods in

Java, an atomic plan in *Jason* is mutually exclusive with *all* other intentions, not just those containing atomic plans.) For example, adding an `atomic` annotation to the example order processing plan above ensures that all of its actions are run to completion before another intention is selected, and so avoid the possibility of attempting to dispatch the same item twice.

```
@processOrder[atomic]
+!order(Item, Num)[source(Customer)] <-
    ?stock(Item, Stock);                 /* test plan */
    Num <= Stock;                        /* test plan */
    -+stock(Item, Stock - Num);          /* modify stock */
    +purchased(Customer, Item, Num);
    !dispatch(Customer, Item, Num).
```

Fig. 2. Example *Jason* atomic plan

While `atomic` annotations are essential for many applications, they have to be used with care to maintain the reactivity of the agent, as the agent is unable to respond to external events during the execution of an atomic plan. However of greater interest here is the way in which atomic annotations interact with plan failure. While the `atomic` annotation ensures mutual exclusion (no other intention can interfere with the execution of an atomic plan), atomic plans in *Jason* are not atomic operations in the sense understood in conventional programming or in databases. In conventional programming, an 'atomic' action is effectively uninterruptible—any intermediate states which arise during the execution of an atomic operation are not visible to other processes even if the operation fails. In contrast, intermediate, possibly inconsistent, states resulting from the execution of a *Jason* atomic plan may be visible to other intentions if the plan fails.

3.2 Failure of Atomic Plans

In the open environments characteristic of MAS applications, it is impossible to guarantee that an agent's actions will always be successful. Of the six types of formulas which can appear in *Jason* plans (internal and external actions, achievement and test goals, expressions and mental notes), five can fail. Only mental notes are guaranteed to succeed. When a step in a plan fails, the plan itself is said to have failed. For example, the example plan in Figure 2 can fail either because there is insufficient stock to process the order, or if attempting to achieve the `dispatch` goal fails.

Jason provides support for dealing with plan failures in the form of *failure handling plans*. Failure handling plans allow the developer to 'clean up' following a plan failure, e.g., by specifying that the agent should perform additional actions to 'undo' the effects of internal or external actions performed prior to the failure of a plan. When a plan π in an intention i fails, the *Jason* interpreter searches for a goal g in i that has a relevant failure handling plan. If one is found, the intention is suspended and a goal deletion event $-!g$ is added to the event list. If no failure handling plan is found, the intention containing π is dropped. Execution of the agent then continues. If a goal deletion event was generated it may be selected at a future cycle and trigger a failure handling plan. If the failure handling plan is applicable in the current context, it is pushed onto the intention i, on top of the failed plan π, and i is unsuspended. This allows the failure handling to plan to inspect the current state of the failed plan (using *Jason* internal actions) and take appropriate recovery steps depending on which external actions were executed prior to failure. For example if the order processing plan fails because there is insufficient stock to process the order, a failure handling plan could send a message to the customer to this effect, and perhaps suggest a similar alternative item that is in stock.

In the case of plans with an `atomic` annotation, this basic scheme is extended in two ways. First, if the plan which gives rise to a goal deletion event $-!g$ has an `atomic` annotation, the intention retains the atomic property and will be scheduled at the next reasoning cycle. Second, the event selection function is over-ridden (including any user customisations) to ensure that the goal deletion event $-!g$ is processed at the next cycle. In effect, the failure handling plan extends the critical section created by the failed atomic plan π, allowing recovery actions to be performed before any other intention is scheduled.

While this scheme allows (atomic) recovery from the failure of an atomic plan, it suffers from a number of disadvantages. First, and most obviously, it requires that the agent developer anticipate possible failures and write appropriate failure handling plans. For external and internal actions which have complex side effects that must be undone for recovery to be possible this is inevitable. However undoing changes made to the agent's belief and plan base as a result of plan execution should not require programmer intervention if the plan fails. Such automated reversion of the belief and plan bases is currently not supported in *Jason*.

Perhaps more surprising, given the current architecture of *Jason*, it can be difficult for the agent developer to cleanly undo the effects of belief or plan base changes in a failure handling plan. For example, if the `dispatch` goal in the `processOrder` plan cannot be achieved, e.g., because it is impossible to deliver the item to the customer's delivery address, or because delivery is handled by an external organisation/agent which rejects the delivery request, the changes to the agent's beliefs to reflect the reduced level of stock and the customer's purchase of the item should be reverted. However, simply reverting the belief changes in a failure handling plan does not remove any belief change events resulting from belief changes made by the failed plan. Moreover, belief deletions and additions made by a failure handling plan result in additional belief change events which may in turn give rise to additional intentions when the atomic failure handling plan finishes execution. (Even using the internal actions provided by Jason which directly manipulate the agent's Java state, there is no obvious way to avoid this.) As a result, if an `atomic` plan fails, any intermediate, potentially inconsistent, belief changes are visible to other intentions. Such belief changes may in turn give rise to new intentions, and attempting to restore consistency to the belief base may compound the problem by generating yet more intentions.

Similarly in Coo-AgentSpeak(L) [7], the `acquisitionPolicy`, which determines whether a retrieved plan is added to or replaces any existing plan for the plan's triggering event, is applied immediately on successful completion of the retrieved plan.

If such changes to the plan base occur within the scope of an atomic plan, there is no easy way that they can be undone, as there is no record of the previous state of the plan base.

The cause of these problems is a failure to ensure that changes to the agent's belief and plan bases and event list are only visible to the rest of the agent if the plan succeeds.

4 A New Approach to Atomic Intentions

We argue that changes to an agent's state resulting from execution of an atomic plan should have a transactional 'all or nothing' semantics. If an action in an atomic plan fails, the whole atomic plan should fail and the agent's belief and plan bases and event list should be in the state they were before the execution of the atomic plan. However if an action in an atomic plan succeeds, any updates to the agent's belief and plan bases resulting from the action should be visible to subsequent actions in the atomic plan. If all the steps in an atomic plan succeed, all updates to the agent's belief and plan bases made by the atomic plan should be visible to any subsequent actions in the intention containing the atomic plan and to actions in other intentions, and all events generated by the atomic plan should be added to the event list. We believe that automating failure handling in this way can significantly reduce the load on the agent developer when writing atomic plans, particularly as the facilities available in *Jason* for reverting changes to the agent's belief and plan bases and event list are difficult to use and/or incomplete.

In the remainder of the paper we describe the changes we made to *Jason* to support such a transactional model of atomic plans in *Jason$^+$*. The syntax of plans in *Jason$^+$* is backwards compatible with the current release of *Jason*: in particular, the syntax of the existing `atomic` annotation is unchanged, only its semantics differs. We stress that the automated support provided by *Jason$^+$* for handling plan failure in atomic plans is restricted to changes to the agent's belief base, plan library and event queue. As noted above, in general, it is difficult or impossible to automatically revert actions performed in the environment or arbitrary changes to the agent's state (e.g., through sequences of 'compensation actions' applied in reverse order). Any effects of external and internal actions that must be undone on plan failure must be anticipated by the programmer and coded as failure handling plans as at present.

4.1 Delta State

To provide a transactional semantics for atomic plans, we must be able to restore the state of the agent that existed at the beginning of the execution of an intention containing an `atomic` plan in case the plan fails, and to commit the changes in the case in which the intention succeeds. This corresponds to the *atomicity* property of the traditional database 'ACID' guarantees (*isolation* is not an issue, as atomic intentions in *Jason* execute with mutual exclusion with respect to all other intentions; *consistency* is the concern of the belief update function; and *durability* can be achieved using the *Jason* persistent belief base).

A number of approaches can be taken to achieve atomicity. One approach would be to make a copy of the whole state of the agent (belief-base, plan-library and event queue) at the beginning of the execution of an atomic plan. Changes to the agent's state by actions within the atomic plan are made as normal. If the atomic plan succeeds, the copy of the agent's state is discarded. Conversely, if the plan fails, the state of the agent is restored from the copy. An alternative is to instead store a log of the belief updates performed by the atomic intention, and then revert them (and only them) on plan failure.[3] Depending on the size of the belief base and the number of belief updates made by an atomic plan, recording only the belief update actions may require less space than keeping a copy of the belief base. However care is required to ensure correct behaviour. For example, it is important to ensure that any belief change events resulting from the execution of an atomic plan are removed from the event queue on plan failure. A further variation would be to create a copy of the belief base, plan library and event queue at the start of the intention (as in the first approach), and make changes only to the copy. On success, these changes can be merged back into the main belief base, or otherwise discarded. This provides very strong atomicity and isolation guarantees (corresponding to full 'snapshot' isolation), but clearly comes at a high price in terms of memory overhead and complexity.

These difficulties can be overcome by maintaining a *delta state* of the agent to store uncommitted changes, and by querying the combination of the normal and delta state during the execution of an `atomic` plan. The delta state consists of three components: a *delta belief base*, a *delta plan base*, and a *delta event list*. We describe each of these in turn below.

4.2   Delta Belief Base

The delta belief base records changes to the belief base of the agent made by actions in an `atomic` plan. The delta belief base is initially empty. When a new atomic plan starts executing, the agent registers that it should use the delta belief-base instead of the normal belief-base to apply changes to its beliefs resulting from the atomic plan. If the atomic plan completes successfully, the delta belief base is merged with the normal belief-base of the agent and then cleared. If the atomic plan fails, the contents of the delta belief base are discarded, leaving the normal belief-base untouched.

The delta belief base consists of a list of belief additions (the *add list*) and a list of belief deletions (the *delete list*). If a new belief is added as a mental note in an `atomic` plan, it is simply appended to the add list of the delta belief base. Similarly, if an existing belief is deleted it is appended to the delete list. If an existing belief is modified, e.g., through the addition, deletion or modification of an annotation, the existing belief is appended to the delete list and and the modified version is appended to the add list of the delta belief base. The add and delete lists treat updates in the same way as the normal belief base, i.e., addition and deletion are done according to the normal rules of *Jason*. For example, if b(a)[p] is in the add list, then adding the belief b(a)[q]

---

[3] Simply recording (but not applying) changes to the agent's state made by an atomic plan can result in unacceptable performance for belief queries, when uncommitted updates are queried during execution of the plan.

simply adds the new annotation q to the existing belief b (a) resulting in b (a) [p,q].
Similarly for deletion: if the add list contains on b (a) [p,q,r], deleting b (a) [q]
results in b (a) [p,r], but if the add list contains b (a) [q], deleting b (a) [p,q]
results in the complete removal of b (a) [q] from the add list.

To determine whether a literal is a logical consequence of the combined belief and
delta belief bases, the *Jason* logicalConsequence method is over-ridden to iterate
over both the belief base and the delta belief base. Whenever a query is made on the
belief base, the beliefs in the delta belief base add list are first checked, and then those
beliefs in the belief base which do not occur in the delete list of the delta belief base.
The situation is complicated by the fact that, as in Prolog, the order of beliefs in the
belief base is significant. For example, newly added beliefs are returned before any
existing beliefs with the same functor, and a belief deletion containing a variable, such
as -b (X), deletes only the first matching belief: any other beliefs matching b (X)
remain in the belief base. It is therefore important that the order in which beliefs are
returned from the merge of the belief base and delta belief base is the same as if the
updates had been applied to the belief base. To ensure this, beliefs which occur in both
the add and delete lists of the delta belief base (i.e., modified beliefs) are returned at the
position in the sequence occupied by the belief 'deleted' from in the belief base.

If execution of the atomic plan completes successfully, the changes in the delta belief
base are applied to the agent's belief base. As above, updates are applied in order to
ensure that the order of entries in the belief base is maintained. If the atomic plan fails,
the contents of the delta belief base are simply discarded.

Below, we sketch the *Jason*$^+$ algorithms for adding and deleting beliefs and checking
whether a belief (pattern) is present in the belief base.[4]

Algorithm 1. Add a belief b with annotation a to the belief base

> **procedure** ADD-BELIEF$((b, a))$
> > **if** $(b, a') \in$ *belief-base* $\wedge$ $(b, a') \notin$ *delete-list* **then**
> > > *delete-list* $\leftarrow$ *delete-list* $\cup \{(b, a')\}$
> > > *add-list* $\leftarrow$ *add-list* $\cup \{copy((b, a'))\}$
> > *add-list* $\leftarrow$ *add-list* $+ (b, a)$

Algorithm 1 first checks if the new belief is in the original belief base and has not
already been deleted. If so, it marks the original belief as deleted, and adds a copy of the
original belief to the add list. It then merges the new belief into the add list (indicated by
$+$). This ensures that a belief is either in the add list or among the non-deleted beliefs
of the original belief-base, but not both.

Algorithm 2 first checks the add list (as new elements are checked first) for a matching belief, and if a matching belief is found (indicated by $=_m$) applies deletion according to *Jason*'s belief update rules (which either results in the removal of an annotation
or the complete removal of the belief). The search has to be sequential as we are looking
for a pattern and not an exact belief. If no belief matching the pattern is found in the

---

[4] Note that, in the interests of brevity, we do not show how the order of beliefs is maintained and
also omit some optimisations.

Algorithm 2. Delete the first belief matching the belief pattern p with annotation a from the belief base

> **procedure** DELETE-BELIEF((p, a))
>   **for all** $(b, a') \in$ *add-list* **do**
>   **if** $b =_m p$ **then**
>   *add-list* $\leftarrow$ *add-list* $-$ (b, a)
>   **return**
>   **for all** $(b, a') \in$ *belief-base* **do**
>   **if** $b =_m p \land (b, a') \notin$ *delete-list* **then**
>   *delete-list* $\leftarrow$ *delete-list* $\cup \{(b, a')\}$
>   *add-list* $\leftarrow$ *add-list* $\cup \{copy((b, a'))\}$
>   *add-list* $\leftarrow$ *add-list* $-$ (b, a)
>   **return**

add list, it looks for a matching belief amongst the non-deleted elements of the original belief base. If a matching belief is found, then, as in Algorithm 1 we mark the belief as deleted, put a copy in the add list, and then apply deletion according to *Jason*'s belief update rules.

Algorithm 3. Return the first belief matching the belief pattern p with annotation a in the belief base

> **function** GET-BELIEF((p, a))
>   **for all** $(b, a') \in$ *add-list* **do**
>   **if** $b =_m p \land a' =_m a$ **then**
>   **return** (b, a')
>   **for all** $(b, a') \in$ *belief-base* **do**
>   **if** $b =_m p \land a' =_m a \land (b, a') \notin$ *delete-list* **then**
>   **return** (b, a')
>   **return** *not-found*

Algorithm 3 first checks the add list for a belief matching the pattern. If none is found in the add list, it looks for it amongst the non-deleted elements of the original belief base. Again, the search has to be sequential as we are looking for a pattern and not an exact belief.

4.3 Delta Plan Base

To support retrieval of external plans at run time, e.g., from another agent via plan exchange or from a library of plans, *Jason*$^+$ also incorporates a delta plan base. The delta plan base functions in an analogous way to the delta belief base. When an intention containing an `atomic` plan is initially selected, the delta plan base is initialised and the agent registers that it should use the delta plan base to apply changes instead of the normal plan base. Plans which are dynamically loaded or modified as a result of actions in the atomic plan are held in the delta plan base. If the atomic plan succeeds, these plan changes are permanently merged with the agent's plan base and the delta plan base cleared. However if the atomic plan fails, the contents of the delta plan base are discarded.

Jason$^+$ implements a version of the module system described in [4]. Changes to the agent's plan base therefore involve the addition of new modules (containing one or more plans) and/or the modification of plans in an existing module. Below, we briefly describe the functionality of the module system necessary to understand the delta plan base.

Jason$^+$ Modules

A *Jason*$^+$ *module* is an encapsulated subset of the functionality of an agent consisting of:

1. a local belief base, containing any beliefs that are private to the module;
2. a plan library, implementing the functionality of the module;
3. a local event queue for belief and goal update events that are local to the module;
4. a list of exported belief and goal predicates;
5. a unique identifier (URI) and a 'short' name for the module;

Each module defines an XML-like namespace [8] identified by a URI which acts as a prefix for all beliefs and goals defined in the module. Agents can therefore be composed from existing modules without the risk of name clashes.

Modules control the visibility of predicates they define by *exporting*. Each module contains zero or more `export` directives, which specify the predicate symbols that are visible outside the module. Each export directive is of the form

```
{export predicateNameA/arity, predicateNameB/arity, ...}
```

where `predicateNameA/arity`, `predicateNameB/arity` etc. are the functor names and arities of the predicates exported from the module. In the case of predicates of no arguments, the `/0` can be omitted. Also, for convenience, the wildcard character `?` can be used in place of both the predicate name and arity, and will match any predicate name and arity respectively. For example `{export foo/?}` will export all predicates with the functor `foo` of any arity. Predicates which are not exported from a module are considered implementation details of the module and are not visible outside the module. Each module therefore effectively defines its own local belief base containing its non-exported beliefs, and any belief additions or revisions of non-exported beliefs by plans in a module are applied to its private belief base. For example, a module encapsulating the order processing plan shown in Figure 2 might export the `purchased/3` predicate, but not `stock/2`. The encapsulation provided by modules also applies to events arising from belief and goal addition and deletion (so-called 'internal events'). Each module effectively has a private event queue, and events arising from changes to non-exported beliefs or goals are added only to that module's event queue. Events arising from changes to the agent's main belief or goal base (i.e., from exported beliefs or goals) are visible to all modules, as in the current *Jason* implementation.

Agents (and modules) access the functionality of a module by *importing* the module. Each *Jason*$^+$ source file may contain zero or more `import` directives. Each import directive specifies the URI of a module and a local or 'short' name that can be used within the source file in place of the full URI.[5] The URI specifies the location of the file containing the source code of the module, and in the current implementation can be a relative or absolute path on the local file system, or a URL. The URI forms the module's fully qualified name, which is prefixed to every term in the module when the code in the module is parsed. The short name expands into the full URI reference for the imported module, and can be used to conveniently refer to the exported beliefs and goals of an imported module in the code of the importing module.[6] For example, the import directive

```
{import order = http://example.com/orderProc.aslm}
```

imports the module with URI `http://example.com/orderProc.aslm` and defines the short name `order`, allowing predicates exported by the module to be referred to using, e.g., `order::purchased(Customer, Item, Num)` (which expands to `http://example.com/orderProc.aslm::purchased(Customer, Item, Num)`). Goals defined in the module can be accessed in a similar fashion, e.g., `!order::invoice(Customer, Item, Num)`. A null short name is taken to refer to predicates defined in the agent itself. For example, the term `::customer(X)` in code for a module refers to the belief `customer(X)` defined in the agent. The standard *Jason* internal actions (e.g., `.send`), reserved terms used in annotations (e.g., `source`), operators, strings, numbers and the literals `true` and `false` are not prefixed with the module URI and are visible in all modules.

Each module may therefore access the beliefs, goals and events defined in the agent. Plans within a module can respond to events that occur either within that module, events exported from an imported module, or evens in the agent event queue. Likewise, the context of a plan can refer to belief predicates that are private to the module in which that plan is defined, beliefs exported from an imported module, or beliefs defined in the agent. As noted above, only those predicates which are exported by a module can be accessed by a module that imports it: attempting to access a predicate which is not exported (using either the short or fully qualified name of the module as a prefix) results in a parse error. Multiple modules can import the same module, but the import directive ensures that the module is only loaded once. Each agent therefore contains a single copy of an imported module. References to a module are shared between all modules that import it. Different modules can therefore communicate with each other through the exported beliefs and goals of a shared module or the beliefs and goals defined in the agent itself. For example, the order processing plan(s) and their associated beliefs may be encapsulated in a `http://example.com/orderProc.aslm` module which exports the `order/3` and `purchased/3` predicates and imports a module containing plans which handle dispatch of purchased items which in turn exports the `dispatch/3` predicate (see Figure 3).

---

[5] The URI parameter is optional. If it is omitted, it defaults to a file with the same name as the short name plus the the standard `.aslm` extension in the same directory as the agent.

[6] Short names are also used by the *Jason*[+] mind inspector when displaying code during debugging.

```
{export order/3, purchased/3}
{import delivery = http://example.com/dispatchProc.aslm}

/* Initial stock */
stock(widget, 1).

@processOrder[atomic]
+!order(Item, Num)[source(Customer)] : stock(Item, Stock) <-
    Num <= Stock;
    -+stock(Item, Stock - Num);
    +purchased(Customer, Item, Num);
    !delivery::dispatch(Customer, Item, Num).
```

Fig. 3. Example *Jason$^+$* module

Dynamically Importing Modules

Plans (modules) may be dynamically loaded at run time using the `.import` internal action. The `.import` action takes as argument the URI of the module to be loaded, and, optionally, a short name to be used for debugging. The specified file or URL is located, read and parsed. After the module's source file is successfully parsed and prefixed with the module's unique identifier, the contents of the module (beliefs, goals and plans) are dynamically added to the agent's belief and plan bases, and the appropriate events generated. Once the import finishes, execution of the plan continues. If an `.import` action fails, e.g., if the file could not be located or read, the import is aborted and a *Jason$^+$* action execution failure is generated. This allows failure handling plans to dynamically handle module load failures.

The `.import` action can be used directly in plans or its underlying Java implementation can be used to redefine the `selectOption` function as in Coo-AgentSpeak(L) [7]. Using modules for plan retrieval and exchange eliminates the risk of namespace clashes inherent in the Coo-AgentSpeak(L) model, leading to more robust multiagent systems. Exchanging URIs rather than providing the source of plans in `TellHow` messages, is a departure from the Coo-AgentSpeak(L) model. However we would argue that it is consistent with a more "modular" approach to agent design, which makes greater use of pre-existing library code.

Dynamic Importing and the Delta Plan Base

Dynamically loading modules or modifying plans in an `atomic` plan makes use of the delta belief and plan bases and the delta event list:

1. each of the initial beliefs listed in the module are added to the agent's delta belief-base and a belief addition event is added to the delta event list for each belief;
2. a new goal achievement event is generated as new focus for each of the initial goals listed in the module and added to the delta event list; and
3. each plan defined in the module is added to the agent's delta plan base.

As with the delta belief base, the delta plan base consists of a list of plan additions (the *add list*) and a list of plan deletions (the *delete list*). New plans are simply appended to the add list in the same way as plans are added to the normal plan base. The addition of a plan with the same label as that of an existing plan in the plan base is interpreted as a modification of that plan. The plan currently in the agent's plan base is copied to the delete list of the delta plan base and the modified version of the plan (including any modified plan annotations) is appended to the add list. Any subsequent modification of the plan replaces the version of the plan in the add list. If a plan in the agent's plan base is deleted (e.g., using the internal action `.remove_plan`), it is added to the delete list. The deletion of a plan which was added during the execution of an `atomic` plan removes the deleted plan from the add list. Deleting a modified plan causes the modified version to be removed from the add list and the original, unmodified, plan to be removed from the delete list.

Plan retrieval is handled in a similar way to queries of the belief and delta belief bases. First the plan base is checked for applicable plans, ignoring any plans which appear in the delete list of the delta plan base, and then the add list of the delta plan base is checked for applicable plans. As with beliefs, care is required to ensure that the order in which plans are returned is the same as would be the case if the updates had actually been applied to the agent's plan base. Plans which occur in both the add and delete lists of the delta plan base (i.e., modified plans) are returned at the position in the sequence occupied by the plan 'deleted' from in the plan base.

The delta plan base supports the same $Jason^+$ transition system events as the delta belief base. If the atomic plan completes successfully, the delta plan base is merged with the normal plan base and then cleared. To merge the contents of the delta plan base with the normal plan base, the delete list is used to achieve the same ordering of plans that would have been produced during the execution of a non-atomic intention. Those plans in the normal plan base which have been modified are replaced with the copy stored in the add list of the delta plan base. At the same time, plans which have been removed are also deleted from the normal plan base. Any newly added plans are then inserted either at the beginning or the end of the plan base, as appropriate. If execution of an atomic plan containing an `.import` (or `.remove_plan`) action fails, either while executing the imported plan or subsequently, the contents of the delta plan base are discarded. Note that this partially pre-empts the role of the `acquisitionPolicy` in [6,7] as implemented in Coo-AgentSpeak(L). It could be argued that we should not discard a retrieved plan if failure was not attributable to that plan. However the approach adopted here is consistent with our transactional view of atomic intentions. If the atomic plan succeeds, then the `acquisitionPolicy` is applied, which may result in the retrieved plan being permanently added to the agent's plan base, or discarded.

4.4   Delta Event List

The delta event list contains internal belief change events generated by updates to the delta belief base. The delta event list also contains all internal goal change events generated by the atomic plan which could result in the creation of a new intention (denoted by !!*g* achievement goals in *Jason*). Goal addition events corresponding to subgoals of the atomic plan are added to the event list in the normal way.

If execution of the atomic plan completes successfully, the changes in the delta event list are applied to the agent's event list. If the atomic plan fails, the contents of the delta event list are simply discarded.

5   Conclusion

Most BDI-based agent programming languages support parallel execution of intentions, either as their default execution strategy, or as an option. Several languages also provide some form of 'atomic' construct. For example, in addition to the `atomic` plan annotation in *Jason* [1] considered here, 2APL [9] has a 'non-interleaving operator' which prohibits arbitrary interleaving of plans. Likewise, some form of 'failure handling' facility can be found in most mature BDI-based agent languages and platforms. For example, 2APL [9,10] provides plan revision rules which can be applied to revise plans whose executions have failed, JACK [11] and SPARK [12] provide failure methods and/or meta-procedures which are triggered when plan execution fails, and in [13,14] features are proposed for aborting and suspending tasks in the context of the CAN abstract agent programming language. Taken independently, such features can simplify the development of more robust agents. However, to the best of our knowledge, how these features (should) interact has received little attention in the literature.

In this paper we have presented *Jason$^+$*, an extension to the *Jason* agent programming language which adopts a transactional approach to atomic plans. If an action in a *Jason$^+$* atomic plan fails, the whole atomic plan fails and the agent's belief and plan bases and event list are left in the state they were before the execution of the atomic plan. However if an atomic plan succeeds, all updates to the agent's belief and plan bases made by the atomic plan are visible to any subsequent actions in the intention containing the atomic plan and to actions in other intentions, and all events generated by the atomic plan are added to the event list. *Jason$^+$*, also implements a version of the module system described in [4] which is used to encapsulate retrieved plans. With the exception of minor changes required by the module system, the syntax of *Jason$^+$* is backwards compatible with the current release of *Jason*.

We have argued that the extensions implemented in *Jason$^+$* offer a more predictable semantics for atomic plans in the face of plan failure and can reduce the load on the agent developer by automating simple cases of failure handing, leading to the development of more robust agent programs. In many applications, atomic plans tend to be short and generate only a relatively small number of belief and plan updates. In such cases, the impact of the extensions on the performance of the *Jason* interpreter is minimal. For simple atomic plans consisting of fewer than 10 non-recursive actions, the run time memory usage of *Jason$^+$* is approximately 0.25% greater on average than for an equivalent implementation in *Jason*, and the CPU overhead is approximately 1.5% on average.[7]

While our approach has been developed in the context of *Jason*, we believe that the transactional approach to atomic intentions adopted by *Jason$^+$* can be usefully applied to other BDI-based agent programming languages. More generally, our work raises interesting questions about the ways in which universal programming problems such

---

[7] The tests were run on a 2.33 GHz PC with 6 GB of memory.

as atomicity, synchronisation and modularity should be addressed in a BDI context. For example, to what extent should the parallel execution of intentions share state? We believe deeper consideration of these issues offers a fruitful avenue for future research, and is necessary for BDI-based agent programming languages to develop into robust software development platforms.

In the current implementation of *Jason*$^+$, nested atomic actions (when an `atomic` plan spawns another `atomic` plan via sub-goal) reuse the existing delta state. This is reasonable in situations where the failure of a sub-plan ultimately results in the failure of the parent/root atomic intention. However in many cases it is possible to recover from the failure of a sub-plan, and in future work we plan to extend our current approach to allow nesting of delta belief bases. Another, related area of future work, is to extend our approach to atomic intentions in *Jason*$^+$ to allow support for *transactional* plans and intentions. For example, this could be implemented by associating a different delta belief and plan base with each intention that contains a plan with a `trans` annotation. In those cases where external actions in plans do not interfere, we believe such an approach would provide the advantages of the cleaner approach to plan failure found in *Jason*$^+$ atomic plans while avoiding the problem of lack of responsiveness inherent in the use of the `atomic` construct.

Acknowledgements. We would like to thank Rafael Bordini and Jomi Fred Hübner for helpful discussions on the current implementation of *Jason*.

References

1. Bordini, R.H., Hübner, J.F., Wooldridge, M.: Programming Multi-Agent Systems in AgentSpeak using Jason. John Wiley & Sons Ltd. (2007)
2. Rao, A.S.: AgentSpeak(L): BDI Agents Speak Out in a Logical Computable Language. In: Perram, J., Van de Velde, W. (eds.) MAAMAW 1996. LNCS, vol. 1038, pp. 42–55. Springer, Heidelberg (1996)
3. Bordini, R.H., Hübner, J.F., Vieira, R.: Jason and the Golden Fleece of Agent-Oriented Programming. In: Bordini, R.H., Dastani, M., Dix, J., El Fallah Seghrouchni, A. (eds.) Multi-Agent Programming: Languages, Platforms and Applications. Springer, Heidelberg (2005)
4. Madden, N., Logan, B.: Modularity and Compositionality in Jason. In: Braubach, L., Briot, J.-P., Thangarajah, J. (eds.) ProMAS 2009. LNCS (LNAI), vol. 5919, pp. 237–253. Springer, Heidelberg (2010)
5. Bordini, R., Bazzan, A.L.C., de Jannone, R.O., Basso, D.M., Vicari, R.M., Lesser, V.R.: AgentSpeak(XL): efficient intention selection in BDI agents via decision-theoretic task scheduling. In: Proceedings of the First International Conference on Autonomous Agents and Multiagent Systems (AAMAS 2002), pp. 1294–1302. ACM Press, New York (2002)
6. Ancona, D., Mascardi, V.: Coo-BDI: Extending the BDI Model with Cooperativity. In: Leite, J., Omicini, A., Sterling, L., Torroni, P. (eds.) DALT 2003. LNCS (LNAI), vol. 2990, pp. 109–134. Springer, Heidelberg (2004), doi:10.1007/978-3-540-25932-9_7
7. Ancona, D., Mascardi, V., Hubner, J.F., Bordini, R.H.: Coo-AgentSpeak: Cooperation in AgentSpeak through plan exchange. In: Proceedings of the Third International Joint Conference on Autonomous Agents and Multiagent Systems (AAMAS 2004), pp. 696–705. IEEE Computer Society, Washington, DC (2004)

8. Bray, T., Hollander, D., Layman, A., Tobin, R.: Namespaces in XML 1.0, 2nd edn. Technical report, W3C (2006),
   http://www.w3.org/TR/2006/REC-xml-names-20060816
9. Dastani, M.: 2APL: a practical agent programming language. Autonomous Agents and Multi-Agent Systems 16, 214–248 (2008)
10. Dastani, M., Meyer, J.J.C.: A Practical Agent Programming Language. In: Dastani, M.M., El Fallah Seghrouchni, A., Ricci, A., Winikoff, M. (eds.) ProMAS 2007. LNCS (LNAI), vol. 4908, pp. 107–123. Springer, Heidelberg (2008)
11. Busetta, P., Rönnquist, R., Hodgson, A., Lucas, A.: JACK intelligent agents - components for intelligent agents in Java. AgentLink Newsletter (2), 2–5 (1992)
12. Morley, D., Myers, K.: The SPARK agent framework. In: Proceedings of the Third International Joint Conference on Autonomous Agents and Multiagent Systems (AAMAS 2004), pp. 714–721. IEEE Computer Society, Washington, DC (2004)
13. Thangarajah, J., Harland, J., Morley, D., Yorke-Smith, N.: Aborting tasks in BDI agents. In: Proceedings of the Sixth International Joint Conference on Autonomous Agents and Multi Agent Systems (AAMAS 2007), Honolulu, HI, pp. 8–15 (May 2007)
14. Thangarajah, J., Harland, J., Morley, D., Yorke-Smith, N.: Suspending and resuming tasks in BDI agents. In: Proceedings of the Seventh International Conference on Autonomous Agents and Multi Agent Systems (AAMAS 2008), Estoril, Portugal, pp. 405–412 (May 2008)

Software Support for Organised Adaptation

Hugo Carr[1], Alexander Artikis[2,1], and Jeremy Pitt[1]

[1] Electrical & Electronic Engineering Department,
Imperial College London, SW7 2BT
[2] Institute of Informatics and Telecommunications,
National Centre for Scientific Research "Demokritos", Athens 15310

Abstract. Emergence is a powerful mechanism for coordination of hundreds of uniform agents with limited reasoning capacity. These structures are in contrast to open systems of heterogeneous agents in which a population's conception of global goals and the plan of how to achieve said goals may differ between agents. To reconcile these conflicts, agents require a means of contextualising past and proposed system change in terms of their local model of utility. Metric spaces allow designers to map system change to a set of functions describing different aspects of adaptation (temporal delay, physical cost etc.), giving agents the means to self-organise through compromise and introspection with respect to a set of conventional rules, as opposed to linear adherence to local computations with respect to physical rules or environmental constraints. In this paper we present a new multi-agent programming environment, PreSage-$\mathcal{MS}$, a rapid prototyping and animation tool designed to facilitate experiments in organised adaptation of metric spaces of 'sophisticated' agent teams.

Keywords: Agent-oriented programming, organised adaptation, dynamic specification, temporal logic.

1 Introduction

Emergent systems and evolutionary computing (eg. swarm intelligence [13] and stigmergy [11]) often operate on teams comprising hundreds of agents with hard-wired internal specifications. Such arrangements are in contrast to open systems comprising smaller populations of heterogeneous agents between which local perceptions of global goals may differ. To resolve such conflicts, these systems benefit from more sophisticated soft-wired participants with complex interactive abilities (e.g. BDI agents [12]), allowing agents to engage with one another and converge on optimal system policy. This discursive model can be complemented with metric spaces [2], allowing agents to contextualise past and present policy adaptation, and giving them the means to arrive at a global goal compromise or Nash equilibrium through *organised adaptation.*

Organised adaptation, as opposed to emergent behaviour, is the conscious, deliberate and targeted adaptation of a specification and/or configuration of a

R. Collier, J. Dix, and P. Novák (Eds.): ProMAS 2010, LNAI 6599, pp. 96–115, 2012.
© Springer-Verlag Berlin Heidelberg 2012

multi-agent system, in response to systemic requirements or environmental conditions. Emergent behaviour produces unintended or unknown global outcomes derived from hard-wired local computations, with respect to the environment and/or physical rules. Instead, we are concerned with the introspective application of soft-wired local computations, with respect to the environment, physical rules and conventional rules (what some philosophers of language would call 'constitutive rules'), to produce intended and coordinated global outcomes.

The complexity of modern software systems demands that organised adaptation be an on-line mechanism, that proceeds without human intervention or supervision (cf. autonomic computing [14]); in other words, to make the mechanics for organised adaptation available to software agents at run-time. In this paper we present a new multi-agent programming environment, **Pre**Sage-$\mathcal{MS}$, which converges the multi-agent programming environment **Pre**Sage [16] with the analytic tool of [1]. The result is a rapid prototyping and animation tool designed to facilitate experiments with organised adaptation of dynamic specifications at run-time, for 'sophisticated' agents (i.e. agents with complex reasoning capability wrt. adaptation, goals, other agents, etc.).

In this paper, we present the **Pre**Sage-$\mathcal{MS}$ system architecture and functionality, and give a walkthrough of system design. Accordingly, this paper is organised as follows. The next section outlines how a dynamic specification can be defined, and pre-existing tools for evaluating such specifications. Section 3 describes the architecture of, and functionality supported by, the new system. A walkthrough of experimental design in **Pre**Sage-$\mathcal{MS}$ is given in Section 4. We conclude with a discussion of the current, related and future work; in particular we discuss the role of institutional agents in the migration from design-time tools for human users to run-time services for software agents.

2   Background Work

In this section, we present the background to the current work. First we discuss dynamic protocol specifications, then we present two existing software tools used for experimenting with different aspects of dynamic protocols. This is the basis for the system description of **Pre**Sage-$\mathcal{MS}$ in Section 3, which is a convergence and enhancement of both these tools.

2.1   Dynamic Protocol Specification

Consider the two following examples:

Example 1: Resource-sharing protocol: There is a set of agents S, a subset of which occupies the role of *subjects* who are entitled to access a resource, and a designated agent in S occupying the role of *chair*. The subjects are empowered to request access to the resource, the chair is empowered to grant or revoke access. The protocol stipulates that one or more subjects request access to the resource, the chair grants access to only one; that agent uses the resource until it is released it or access is revoked, and the cycle repeats.

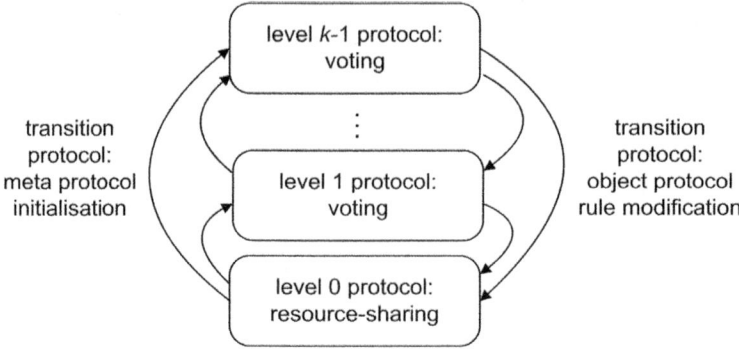

Fig. 1. A k-level Infrastructure for Dynamic Specifications

Example 2: Voting protocol: There is a set of agents S, a subset of which occupy the role of *voters* who are entitled to vote, and a designated agent in S occupying the role of *returning officer*, who declares the result of a vote. The protocol stipulates that the officer calls for a ballot on a specific motion, the voters cast their votes (express their preference), the officer counts the votes and declares the result according to the standing rules.

In both examples, there are values which may be changed, even during their animation. Consider these protocols in terms of a normative specification, in the first example, agents may occupy different sets of roles, the rules by which access is granted, the period until the chair has permission to revoke access, etc., may all be changed. Similarly, in the second example, role assignment again is mutable, and there are many parameters to a vote: single or multiple winner, standing rules for winner determination (plurality, run-off, borda count, etc.), votes required to be quorate, and so on. In the context of open systems, adaptation of the normative rules in these examples cannot be treated as a system-wide factorisation of code, since the way in which participants comply with specification changes isn't known in advance.

One key aspect of organised adaptation is the implementation of dynamic specifications, which allow agents to alter the rules of a protocol P, even during the protocol execution. P is considered an 'object' protocol, if at any point in time the participants may start a 'meta' protocol in order to decide whether the object protocol rules should be modified to P' (say). Moreover, the participants of the meta-protocol may initiate a meta-meta-protocol to decide whether to modify the rules of the meta-protocol, and so on. Figure 1 shows an infrastructure for dynamic resource-sharing protocols, that is, the object protocol is a resource-sharing protocol, and every $\{meta^+\}$-protocol is (some type of) a voting protocol. We briefly demonstrate an Event Calculus implementation of meta-argumentation in Section 4.2, in which an object protocol is assigned a set of degrees of freedom which are adapted according to the consensus of the system population.

Apart from object and meta protocols, the infrastructure for dynamic specifications includes 'transition' protocols (again, see Figure 1) that is, procedures that express, among other things, the conditions under which an agent may validly initiate a meta-protocol, the roles that each meta-protocol participant will occupy, and the ways in which an object protocol is modified as a result of the meta-protocol interactions.

2.2 System Support for Adaptive Specifications

Adaptive Behaviour. Pre Sage is a simulation platform for agent animation and rapid prototyping of societies of agents. It offers a multi agent systems programmer a flexible and generic set of Java classes, interfaces and tools with which key aspects of agent societies can be designed and simulated.

To develop a prototype in **Pre**Sage, it is necessary to define agent participant types: this can be done by extending the abstract class supplied with standard environment (to guarantee compatibility with the simulation calls and provide core functionality like message handling etc.) or by defining a new class. The **Pre**Sage environment is in fact neutral with respect to the internal architecture of its agents: thus agents can be of arbitrary complexity. Agents can then either be animated (i.e. a 'sophisticated' agent with complex reasoning capability is actually embedded in an artificial environment) or simulated (complex behaviour is approximated by simulation rather than actually computed).

Then the network properties and physical world are defined, using or extending the given base classes. Finally, additional plugins can be written for visualisation, connection to other components (e.g. a database for logging results, etc.), or generation of exogeneous events.

We have used **Pre**Sage for initial experiments in organised adaptation. We set up a simple iterated 'tragedy of the commons' scenario, with partial knowledge, no central control, and self-interested agents, and allowed the agents two votes: one for whom to allocate resources, and one to decide how many votes should be received in order to be allocated resources. The idea was that co-operative agents should manage the system by voting 'fairly'. Initial experiments showed that 'responsible' agents performed better than selfish or cautious ones (indeed approximated the outcomes achieved with a 'benevolent dictator') [6], and that social networking (gossiping) algorithms can be used on an individual and group basis to protect the system from self-interested behaviour [7].

Metric Space Analysis. Given an adaptable specification, the protocol rules and parameters that may be modified at run-time are called *Degrees of Freedom* (*DoF*). Each DoF can take one value from a specific set of possible values; we map each of the possible values onto a rank order. A specification with m DoFs can then be represented as an m-tuple, where each tuple element defines the rank order of the value for the corresponding DoF. The set S of all possible tuples is given by all the possible instantiations of every DoF with the rank order of each of its possible values. Clearly there are:

$$|v_1| \times |v_2| \times \ldots \times |v_m|$$

members of this set, where $|v_i|$ is the maximum rank value of the ith DoF $v_i(1 \leq i \leq m)$ can take. This set is the basis of a *metric space* $\mathcal{M} =< S, d >$ if we define a metric d on the set which defines a 'distance' between any pair of set members (subject to the usual constraints [18]).

We can use this representation of an m-dimensional specification as a metric space by measuring the 'distance' between members of the set, or rather, *specification points* in the metric space. A designer can then define an adaptable specification with its degrees of freedom, and additional constraints on run-time modification. For example, the designer could specify a 'desired' specification point, and proposed modifications could be evaluated on the 'distances' of the proposed specification point from the 'current' point and the 'desired point. The designer could also specify that some points are 'forbidden', if for example they were normatively inconsistent [2].

The metric space representation was the basis of automated support for design-time analysis of a dynamic protocol specification, that is, an off-line, static analysis of a protocol that could be adapted at run-time [18]. This tool allowed the designer to analyse a narrative of events (actions taken by agents to modify the specification) and determine, at each time point, the distance to the desired specification point for a range of different metrics (euclidean, manhattan, weighted manhattan, etc.) This allowed the designer to evaluate comparatively the effects of different metrics on different instances of a dynamic specification.

3   PreSage-$\mathcal{MS}$

Both of the tools described in the previous section are useful for investigating certain aspects of organised adaptation but are ultimately limited. PreSage allowed mixed agent strategies and populations, but the agents did not have an explicit representation of metric spaces; while the second tool is restricted to a retrospective, design-time analysis of a given narrative of events. Ultimately, we want to perform an introspective, run-time analysis *as the narrative unfolds*. Therefore, we have developed a new system, **PreSage-$\mathcal{MS}$**, which retains and integrates the agent-level granularity of **Pre**Sage with the metric space analysis of [2], but extends both by equipping the agents themselves with the functionality to represent and reason about metric spaces and specification points.

In this section, we present the architecture and functionality of the **Pre**Sage-$\mathcal{MS}$ programming environment.

3.1   PreSage-$\mathcal{MS}$ Architecture

The core **Pre**Sage System is conceptually composed of three layers: the base simulation layer, the services layer, and the instances layer.

The base simulation layer performs parameter initialisation, manages the simulation execution, and provides generic functions to higher level modules and classes. **Pre**Sage uses a multi-agent discrete-time-driven simulation model. In this model, each loop of the simulator control thread equates to a time-slice of the simulated multi-agent system. In each time-slice, the agent participants are given a turn to perform physical and communicative actions, the state of the network(s) and physical world is updated, scripted events are executed, and plugins perform their specified operations.

The services layer provides the skeleton models that designers use to implement a simulation. The agents and their environment are implemented through the provided interfaces, simulating network(s), and a physical world. The managers handle scripted events and other user plugins as well as providing a dedicated Event Calculus tool to improve latency in rule unification.

The third layer comprises the user-specified instances of these components.

PreSage-$\mathcal{MS}$ extends **PreSage** by implementing the Event Calculus (EC) [15] as a universal language for communication and specification. Using the EC, the agents can establish a narrative of speech acts, whose consequences can be calculated as a normative state; ie. the set of permissions, powers and obligations of agents according to which roles they occupy. These norms can be derived by unifying the narrative with the object and meta-level rules can also be written in the EC.

To integrate the EC with **PreSage**, we have implemented a new manager at the interface level which handles the EC requests and keeps track of the EC fluents. A fluent is a value which varies over time, so the EC manager keeps track of its current value to prevent unnecessary queries to the temporal calculus engine. This manager uses JPL, an interface to Prolog from Java, by keeping a Prolog implementation of the EC and the implementation specific rules.

At the instance level, we have included

- An environment in which agents may navigate a centrally managed metric space
- An extendable agent which can send and interpret EC messages
- An EC plugin which displays the object and meta level protocol read by the EC manager, and the fluents which 'hold' at the current time point.
- A metric space plugin which allows a system designer to rank the DoF values and alter the metric space of the system
- An environmental state plugin which gives a designer the opportunity to map a set of analogue inputs to a finite set of system states.

The plugins act as run-time services for participants, providing live information about the EC fluents, the metric space and the state of the environment.

The final architecture of **PreSage-**$\mathcal{MS}$ is illustrated in Figure 2. Next, we will look at the functionality of the **PreSage** extensions in more detail.

3.2   Agents and Environment

Simulation design in **PreSage-**$\mathcal{MS}$ has been divided into the environment, and the agents which act therein. At its simplest, an environment may act only as a communication link between the agents, but it is often convenient to keep a central representation of the object and meta-level rules. For example, when designing systems which have dynamic specifications, it is usually desirable to have

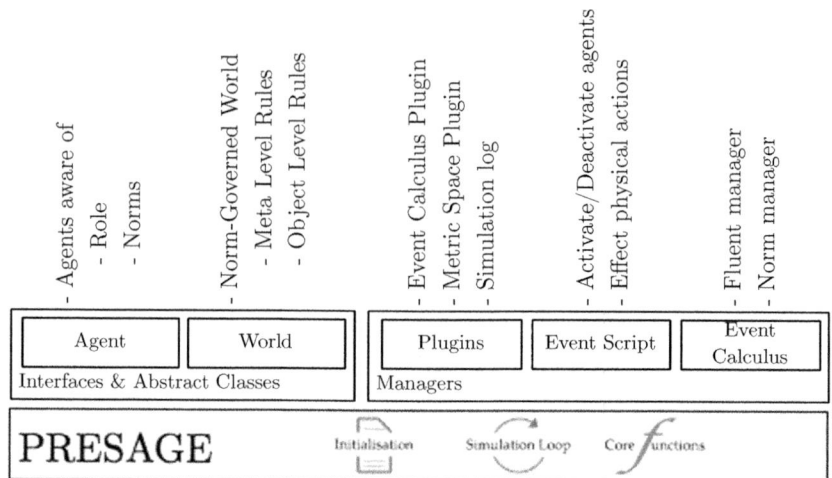

Fig. 2. Architecture of the **Pre**Sage-$\mathcal{MS}$ system

an environment which includes the system's specification space and a register for global system values. This serves as a central reference for newly registered agents, and ensures that there is no confusion about where in the metric space the system lies.

Environments in **Pre**Sage-$\mathcal{MS}$ go further than the basic message passing paradigm and handle actions made by agents by broadcasting the appropriate speech act to the agents affected. These speech acts are similarly sent to the Event Calculus manager to update the narrative (ie. the action history). The EC Manager maintains the metric space and object level rules in Prolog, and with a minimal number of queries, sends back the new set of norms effected by the speech act. In order for agents in **Pre**Sage-$\mathcal{MS}$ can understand messages from the environment, we have tools for parsing event calculus messages and a set of fluent and norm handlers which are invoked when an update message relating to a fluent or norm is received from the environment.

3.3   Event Calculus Manager

The event calculus manager acts as a buffer between **Pre**Sage-$\mathcal{MS}$ and the declarative implementation of the Event Calculus (Figure 3). The EC derives the norms at a timepoint T by unifying the history of speech acts with the predicates describing the rules of the system. However, as the action history increases the computation time becomes prohibitively slow. The EC manager has therefore been optimised to reduce the number of queries to the Prolog knowledgebase by implementing a caching mechanism to bound the size of the action history.

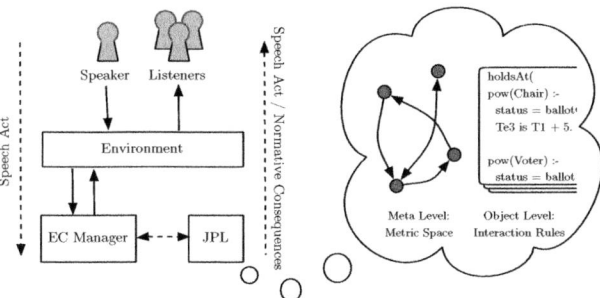

Fig. 3. The relationship between the Agents of a system, the environment and the event calculus specification of the object and meta-level rules. Calls to the Prolog implementation of the event calculus, through the JPL library, are minimised by the EC Manager.

We have included an interface to the event calculus manager, which monitors the current states of the event calculus fluents and norms. This front end receives updates from the manager with respect to speech acts and their consequences. Agents who for whatever reason are not able to receive messages from the environment, can register with this service to check that their local representation of system norms is consistent. Designers may also use this inspector to view the history of all fluent and norm changes throughout the life cycle of the system.

3.4   Metric Space Plugin

The metric space plugin in Figure 4 represents an extension of the analytic tool in [1]. The plugin implements much of the same functionality as the original, but includes a graphical visualisation of the metric space based on a selected metric; run-time services to supply participants metric space specific information in real time; and a generalisation of the ranking process for DoF values.

As demonstrated in section 2.2, DoFs can be ranked using a one dimensional number for each of the DoF values. We have generalised this model by ranking each value with a more general fixed size vector.

In a specification of m DoFs, each DoF still takes one value from specific set of possible values but we map each of the possible values onto the domain $\mathbb{R}^{n_k}$ where $0 \leq k < m$. Rank order no longer exists, as the relationship between the DoF values becomes more sophisticated and vectors cannot be compared in terms of higher versus lower. However, a metric space is still formed provided that the metrics used within the vectors are the same as those for the space which they form.

The metric space visualisation draws a graph of specification points based on a selected metric (Euclidean, Manhattan etc.) and threshold distance. This threshold represents the furthest distance value that an edge can take between two specification points, and may be used to represent several things. For example, it may relate to the furthest distance that an agent may travel away from the current point. This may be due to the cost of adaptation being too high, or an attempt to limit the volatility of the system by making incremental changes. This results in an agent having to choose the shortest path along the edges of the graph to reach a desired specification point.

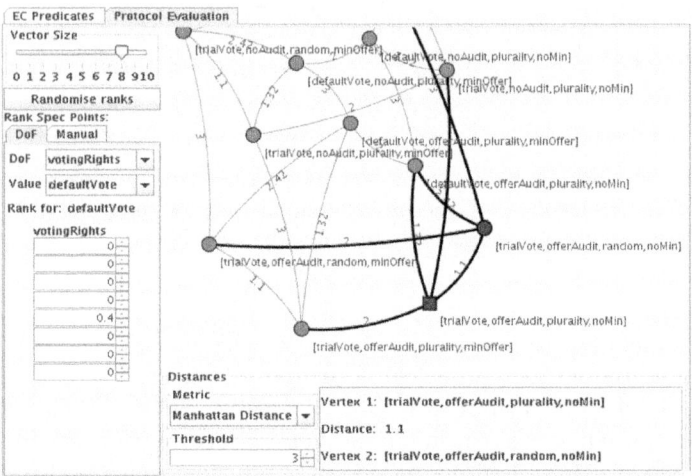

Fig. 4. Interface to the metric space: The degrees of freedom of the metric space are resized and ranked in the lefthand column. The bottom panel selects which metric the system is using to form the space, and the graph is drawn according to the threshold value which represents the maximum value that an edge may take.

3.5   Environmental State Plugin

The Environmental State Plugin has been written to allow designers to minimise the frequency of adaptation by mapping the analogue global inputs onto a set of finite states. A system is then able to remain at a specification point until an environmental state change occurs. Once such a change has been triggered the system may start to decide whether this fluctuation warrants an adaptation. For example, if there is a cost associated with the adaptation it is prudent to ensure that a state change is not the result of noise and represents a permanent system shift; if not the system will be frequently retracting potentially expensive updates to the specification.

The Environmental State Plugin interacts with the environment by periodically taking a measure of the global inputs of a system; as defined by the system designer. These analogue global inputs are divided along a number line over which a cross-product may be performed to form the set of states. It is then based on these environmental states that the system can be trained with the utilities of each specification point. It is the utility of a point under a perceived environmental state that will drive adaptation and act as the vehicle a designer uses to motivate policy change.

4 PreSage Experimental Design

System designers operate **PreSage-$\mathcal{MS}$** in three inter-related stages: Agent design, protocol design and metric space design. On completion of these stages, experiments exploring the metric space can be designed.

A system lifecycle begins offline with the Java and Prolog implementation of the agents and protocol. The designer goes on to choose how the agents are to reason about the DoFs by formulating a metric space which represents a set of measurements agents may use to compare different specifications. The metric can be defined in conjunction with further permissions, powers and obligations which constrain how the system may adapt.

To demonstrate the experimental design in **PreSage-$\mathcal{MS}$** we have provided a walkthrough of the resource allocation example outlined in section 2 with four object level DoFs and a static meta level protocol. Based on this architecture we outline a set of experiments which we intend to address investigating *when* agents should adapt.

4.1 Agent Design

The agent design process results in a test population which recreates the conditions of an open system. Agents, along with their EC handlers, are designed offline in Java with extendable **PreSage-$\mathcal{MS}$** interfaces. They must then be endowed with the capacities required to approximate independent decision making. At the most basic level agents require a complete set of norm and fluent handlers for the parts of the protocol which they are involved in. For example in the resource allocation scenario we have a set of basic speech acts which all agents must be able to interpret (openSession, callForProposals, propose). A propose handler must be able to read the proposal made by an agent and store the offer and request for use during the voting protocol:

```
protected class ProposeHappensHandler extends HappensHandler {
    public void handle(ProposeHappens happens) {
        String[] arguments = happens.getArguments();
        requests.put(arguments[0], new Integer(arguments[1]));
        offers.put(arguments[0], new Integer(arguments[2]));
        totalRequests+=Integer.parseInt(arguments[1]);
    }
}
```

Agents require the means to reason about the dynamic protocol, this may require specific knowledge about the protocol. There are however, general ways of navigating a specification space which can be used in conjunction with machine learning techniques and heuristics to find optimal points.

4.2   Protocol Design

The logical implementation of the resource allocation protocol is developed offline in Prolog using the programming environment included in the Event Calculus plugin.

Consider the voting protocol (Section 2.1), which begins with participants
offering resources to be centrally pooled and allocated by the chair of the session.
These offers may or may not be verified for authenticity before allocating the
resources according to either a vote between the participants of the system, or
a random selection by the chair. It is important at this stage of design that the
protocol is implemented in such a way that ensures a linear computational cost
is incurred. **PreSage-**$\mathcal{MS}$ offers a basic caching instrument in which the Event
Calculus fluents representing the actions of the system are retracted from the
knowledgebase when no longer needed (See Figures 5 and 6).

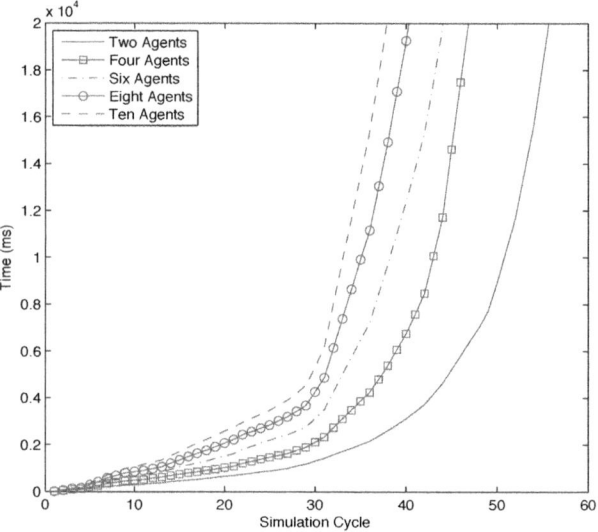

Fig. 5. A graph showing, for an increasing number of agents, the execution time of the
system in terms of the simulation cycles without the caching optimisation outlined in
PreSage-$\mathcal{MS}$

To form a dynamic protocol, we extend the static Event Calculus specification
of the voting protocol with four degrees of freedom:

  - *MinimumRequired* - Places a limit on the least amount of resources that an
    agent must offer each time cycle in order to participate in the allocation.
  - *OfferAudit* - Whether we verify the authenticity of the resource offers made
    by participants before the distribution. This is important if there is an ele-
    ment of agents which misrepresent their contributions.

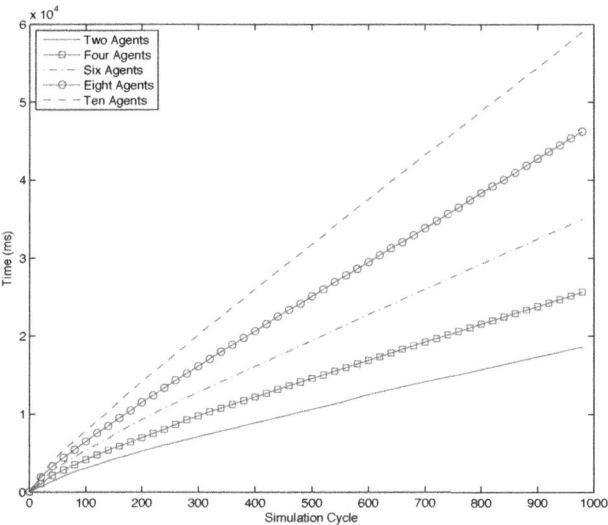

Fig. 6. A graph showing, for an increasing number of agents, the execution time of the system in terms of the simulation cycles with the caching optimisation outlined in PreSage-$\mathcal{MS}$

- *AllocationMethod* - Whether we submit the allocation to a plurality vote, or if the chair simply assigns resources randomly to participants.
- *VotingRights* - This DoF is only valid if a vote occurs in the first place and refers to how long agents must have been members of the system, before they are granted voting rights.

$$dofs = \{votingRights, allocationMethod, minRequired, offerAudit\}$$

$$votingRights = \{trialVote, defaultVote\},$$
$$offerAudit = \{auditOffers, noAudit\},$$
$$allocationMethod = \{plurality, random\},$$
$$minRequired = \{minOffer, noMin\}.$$

By selecting a value for each DoF, we form a complete specification instance which is referred to as a specification point (SP). Here each DoF can take one of two values, resulting in sixteen possible SPs. If we consider the specification as a state transition system, these points represent all possible states and the adaptations correspond to the transitions between them.

These DoFs must be defined in conjunction with the event calculus implementation of the object level protocol. We present the predicates from the resource allocation example representing how the *allocationMethod* degree of freedom is implemented. The following can be translated directly into Prolog and represents the part of the protocol where the chair is permitted to distribute the pooled resources. $R1a$ refers to a plurality distribution, $R1b$ random allocation. The conditions in bold refer to which of the DoF values is currently active, to ensure that the correct rule is used.

$R1a : holdsAt(permission(Chair, distribute(Chair, Agent)) = true, T) : -$
 $\quad holdsAt(roleof(Chair, chair) = true, T),$
 $\quad selectPluralityResult(Result),$
 $\quad holdsAt(ballot = closed),$
 $\quad \boldsymbol{holdsAt(dof(votingProtocol) = plurality, T)}.$

$R1b : holdsAt(permission(Chair, distribute(Chair, Agent)) = true, T) : -$
 $\quad holdsAt(roleof(Chair, chair) = true, T),$
 $\quad selectRandom(Result),$
 $\quad holdsAt(ballot = closed),$
 $\quad \boldsymbol{holdsAt(dof(votingProtocol) = random, T)}.$

The meta level protocol is defined alongside the object protocol in the EC and can be invoked at any time by the agents to initiate a discussion about which DoFs to change in the next session. Note that we have not included any DoFs at this level as we would need another discussion protocol at the meta-meta level to adapt it.

4.3   Metric Space Design

Once the DoFs and their respective values have been set for the protocol a system designer can move from the Event Calculus Plugin to the Metric Space Plugin where the DoF values can be formed into a specification space. Given the set of specification points T determined by the number and value-ranges of the DoFs, a metric space on this set is defined by a distance function d such for any $x, y, z \in T$, d obeys symmetry $(d(x, y) = d(y, x))$, identity of indiscernibles $(d(x, y) = 0 \leftrightarrow x = y)$, and the triangle inequality $(d(x, z) \leq d(x, y) + d(y, z))$, from which it follows that for all x and y, $d(x, y) \geq 0$.

To use the **PreSage-$\mathcal{MS}$** plug-in, the programmer must assign the DoF values, and encode the function d. The topology of the space is therefore determined by the values and d, which are dependent on what the distance between specification points actually represents. If, for example, the distance was a simple similarity measure, we could assign DoF values as follows:

$$AllocationMethod : \{plurality, random\} \rightarrow \{0, 1\}$$
$$VotingRights : \{defaultVote, trialVote\} \rightarrow \{0, 1\}$$
$$AuditOffers : \{offerAudit, noAudit\} \rightarrow \{0, 1\}$$
$$MinimumRequired : \{minOffer, noMin\} \rightarrow \{0, 1\}$$

and a metric d_1 simply implemented as the hamming distance between points represented as strings in $(0|1)^4$, or the Manhattan distance between cells in a Karnaugh map of the points.

Alternatively, we could define the metric space to represent the *cost* of implementing a (move to a) new specification point. If, in order to change to the new SP, a DoF value must be changed, we define a cost to remove the current value and a further cost to install the new value. Each value must therefore have a cost of installation orthogonal to the cost of removal (resp. installation) of the alternative DoF value. To preserve symmetry, let us assume the cost to install a value to be the same as that to remove it.

Then we could assign values as follows (based on an estimate of the number of lines of code and predicates that have to be changed from the previous section):

$$AllocationMethod : \{plurality, random\} \rightarrow \{(0.5, 0), (0, 0.6)\}$$
$$VotingRights : \{defaultVote, trialVote\} \rightarrow \{(0.4, 0), (0, 0.9165)\}$$
$$AuditOffers : \{offerAudit, noAudit\} \rightarrow \{(1, 0), (0, 2)\}$$
$$MinimumRequired : \{minOffer, noMin\} \rightarrow \{(1, 0), (0, 1)\}$$

The two specification points in Figure 4 can therefore be encoded as follows:

$$(random, offerAudit, trialVote, noMin)$$
$$(\overbrace{0, \quad 0.6,} \quad \overbrace{1, \quad 0,} \quad \overbrace{0, 0.9165,} \quad \overbrace{0, \quad 1})$$
$$(plurality, offerAudit, trialVote, noMin)$$
$$(\overbrace{0.5, \quad 0,} \quad \overbrace{1, \quad 0,} \quad \overbrace{0, 0.9165,} \quad \overbrace{0, \quad 1})$$

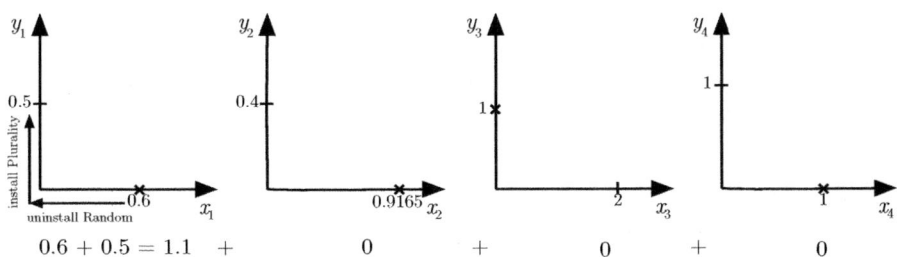

Fig. 7. The distance between the specification points *(trialVote, offerAudit, random, noMin)* and *(trialVote, offerAudit, plurality, noMin)*. Note that we are only changing the allocationMethod degree of freedom from random to plurality.

Then we need to define a metric d_2 on this space which is the summation of the manhattan distances moved in each of the four dimensions (illustrated in Figure 7). Since we have assigned a cost of 0.5 to implement or remove a plurality allocation method and a cost of 0.6 to implement or remove a random allocation method, then to move from one method to the other the complete removal and installation cost is $0.5 + 0.6 = 1.1$. Similarly to change the voting rights DoF costs $0.4 + 0.9165 = 1.3165$.

Figure 4 shows the formulated metric space given this configuration. The distance between the current specification point (the square node) and the selected circular node in bold is 1.1. This is because the current specification point uses a plurality allocation method and the other vertex is identical except for the random allocation method.

4.4   Experimental Design and Example

Once the protocol specifications are given and the metric space functions defined, a programmer can experiment with effect of the metric on this space for organised adaptation under different agent populations. Given the experimental arrangement described in this paper, we intend to investigate *when a system should adapt*. Agents performing adaptation must be capable of trading off the costs of adaptation versus the expected benefit. This requires that agents can take two measurements: the average utility per timecycle of a specification point under a particular environmental state and an estimate of the amount of time the system will remain in that state. If the cost to adapt consistently outweighs the incentives then the participants must know to refrain from adaptation.

To begin this process we must first limit the environmental measurements to a finite state space using the environmental state plugin. For the resource allocation scenario we have chosen four environmental states, based on the supply and demand of resources and the proportion of agents in the system behaving selfishly:

Env1: Supply $>$ Demand, 25% agents behaving selfishly
Env2: Supply $<$ Demand, 25% agents behaving selfishly
Env3: Supply $>$ Demand, 50% agents behaving selfishly
Env4: Supply $<$ Demand, 50% agents behaving selfishly

We can then run non-adaptive simulations for each environmental state under each of the twelve specification points to get the expected utilities:

$$
\begin{array}{c}
 \quad sp1 \quad\ sp2 \quad \cdots \quad sp16 \\
\begin{array}{c} env1 \\ env2 \\ env3 \\ env4 \end{array}
\left(\begin{array}{cccc}
\mu_{1,1} & \mu_{1,2} & \cdots & \mu_{1,16} \\
\mu_{2,1} & \mu_{2,2} & \cdots & \mu_{2,16} \\
\mu_{3,1} & \mu_{3,2} & \cdots & \mu_{3,16} \\
\mu_{4,1} & \mu_{4,2} & \cdots & \mu_{4,16}
\end{array} \right)
\end{array}
$$

If we assume that the utility is only dependent on the current state we can calculate the total expected benefit by estimating the time the system will remain in an environmental state. For the preliminary experiments we can take a simple geometric distribution of rate λ to predict the number of timecycles between state changes. The expected utility of $sp1$ in under $env1$ then becomes:

$$E_{env1}(sp1) = \frac{\mu_{1,1}}{\lambda}$$

Given these values we can form a decision function based by subtracting the cost to change specification points from the total expected utility. This cost may be calculated from the second metric space formulated in section 4.3. It is based on this decision function that we can look at how different metrics contribute towards better cost benefit ratios.

Consider a system in which there is a small amount of noise in the environmental readings. If a system detects an environmental state change the adaptation process may result in an expensive and unnecessary shift to a new specification point. One means of limiting the cost associated with this noise is to enforce a threshold such that a system can only choose specification points which are within a given radius of the current point.

Figure 8 outlines the results of a preliminary examination of a thresholded metric in a closed system given different noise probabilities. When the system has no noise a high threshold performs better allowing the system to move to the optimal point immediately; a low threshold in contrast adapts over the course of several iterations and incurs a higher cost. When a small amount of noise is introduced however (probability of noise in a timecycle = 0.05) the results are reversed. This can be attributed to a reduced noise cost as the system does not immediately make a potentially expensive adaptation, only to have to retract it in the following timecycle.

5   Discussion and Related Research

PreSage-$\mathcal{MS}$ is proving useful for experimenting with dynamic specifications in terms of the three parameters: agent internals, protocol and DoF specification, and metric space design. However, it has also thrown into relief a number of inter-linked issues concerning organised adaption, namely:

- the role of institutional agents and the migration from design-time tools to run-time services;
- the animation of organised and organisational adaptation in linear time; and
- the relationship between formal models of norm change and compliance pervasion amongst the affected population of agents.

We briefly consider these issues here.

Open systems, following Hewitt [10], assume independently developed subsystems without global objects or objectives, but with a commonly understood communication language. However, it is possible to relax the assumption that there are no global objects, and consider the status of the EC plug-in and the Metric Space plug-in. These plug-ins are providing computationally-intensive services; they are also computing a global state (the set of norms and normative

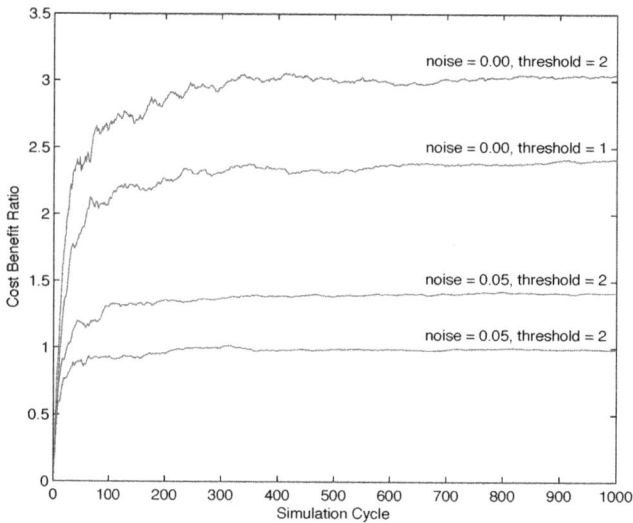

Fig. 8. A graph showing the benefit to cost ratio for different noise probabilities of a metric space in which movement is constrained by a maximum threshold distance

positions, and the current/desired specification points). In these cases, we may wrap such services in institutional agents of the kind envisaged by Lopez et al [4]. As such, this move represents a step in the migration from design-time tools for human users to run-time services for software agents.

Sophisticated teams of agents ruled by a declarative representation of global law do not always execute in linear time (as shown in Section 4.2). **Pre**Sage-$\mathcal{MS}$ attempts to address this by including a basic caching function, but this can only be applied to a subset of dynamic protocols wherein historical actions may be ignored past a certain point. Dynamic protocols of organisational adaptation however, may fall outside of this definition, for example in non-trivial societies of institutional agents.

Consider systems comprising 'large' teams of sophisticated agents: the question then is whether it is possible (necessary, desirable) to have a single flat hierarchy, or whether some kind of structure is required, e.g. [9]. In organisational adaptation, it is needed to extend a dynamic specification to the creation, modification and deletion of roles, and the creation, remit, modification and deletion of sub-structures (in the way that human institutions are often structured into departments, committees, etc.) This opens up an inquiry into the scale and effective size of 'sophisticated' agent teams, and whether some form of Dunbar's number can be derived for agents (i.e. a computational rather than a cognitive limit on the size of a stable group).

Many other issues are raised by stable groups in organisational adaptation, which includes the impact of an underlying social network on the 'observable' institutional structure (cf. [3]). This includes: how an arbitrary collection of agents can self-organise into an organisational structure; how an arbitrary collection of agents can self-organise its social network (which is structurally distinct from the organisational structure); and, what is the interplay between the explicit formal organisation and the implicit social network.

6 Further Work

PreSage-$\mathcal{MS}$ divides the motivation to adapt into two sub-questions: *Where* to move in the specification space and *When* to move there. Choosing where to move to in a specification space takes into consideration the expected utility of the point weighed against the cost to perform the adaptation. In order to verify the preliminary Matlab investigation outlined in Figure 8 we intend to implement the threshold metric of Section 4.4 in PreSage-MS and run a series of simulations subject to varying noise levels to demonstrate the effect of different metric thresholds.

One key limitation of metric spaces is that given the implementation of the system, the costs associated with adaptation may not conform to the constraints of the geometry, e.g. the adaptive cost is not always symmetric between two specifications. To address this, we intend to look at more general representation of policy change in which cost of adaptation depends not only on the ordered pair of specification points, but environmental state change as well. Using this, we intend to construct a framework upon which agents can calculate the expected utility of an adaptation strategy, without having to verify the result empirically.

The consideration of social networks as a parameter influencing adaption raises further concerns with respect to the relationship between formal models of norm change and compliance pervasion amongst the affected population of agents. There is a growing body of work on formal models of explicit norm change in legal systems [8]. A particular question for future research is how to use **PreSage-$\mathcal{MS}$** to experiment with modifiable legal systems and synthetic micro-populations of agents and the interaction between the two: i.e. how does ('top down') norm change impact population behaviour, and how does population behaviour influence ('bottom up') changes to norms.

Quality of Service (QoS) in distributed systems of agents is of particular concern in mission critical applications (eg. Wade [5] and Multimedia Network Support Platforms [17]), in the sense of predicting the system trajectory and guaranteeing that a system remains within an 'adaptive envelope'. As a future avenue of research, we intend to look at to what extent QoS can be maintained in open systems, in which a subset of participants may be non-compliant and guarantees are worth only as much as the trust that is placed in them.

7 Summary and Conclusions

The system represents a novel design framework for open systems performing organisational adaptation. The rules and protocols are entirely specified in the Event Calculus providing foreign agents with a transparent description of how the system functions and as such can decide whether their interests will be served. Metric Spaces are used in conjunction with a variety of plugins to manage which aspects of the system may be adapted in order to prevent an adaptation which could irreparably harm the system. It is in this way that we ensure the level of control required by a system designer while at the same time maintaining a publicly accessible specification.

PreSage-$\mathcal{MS}$ is an extended agent programming environment which offers a flexible and open solution to implementing organised adaptation in multi agent systems using dynamic specifications. We intend to explore the question of *when to adapt* in the context of a self adapting resource allocation scenario in which the agents stockpile and allocate a shared resource. Periodically the system will need to adapt to deal with invasions by a selfish population who try to divert the flow of resources to themselves. We intend to explore adaptation strategies in specification spaces, which trade off the cost of making an adaptation versus the benefit of moving to a different specification point.

Acknowledgements. The first author is supported by a UK EPSRC studentship. The authors are grateful for the reviewers' comments on earlier versions of this paper.

References

1. Apostolou, M., Artikis, A.: Evaluating dynamic protocols for open agent systems. In: AAMAS 2009: Proceedings of The 8th International Conference on Autonomous Agents and Multiagent Systems, pp. 1419–1420 (May 2009)
2. Artikis, A.: Dynamic protocols for open agent systems. In: AAMAS 2009: Proceedings of the 8th International Conference on Autonomous Agents and Multiagent Systems, pp. 97–104 (2009)
3. Ashworth, M., Carley, K.: Who you know vs. what you know: The impact of social position and knowledge on team performance. Journal of Mathematical Sociology 30, 43–75 (2006)
4. Bou, E., López-Sánchez, M., Rodríguez-Aguilar, J.A.: Adaptation of Autonomic Electronic Institutions Through Norms and Institutional Agents. In: O'Hare, G.M.P., Ricci, A., O'Grady, M.J., Dikenelli, O. (eds.) ESAW 2006. LNCS (LNAI), vol. 4457, pp. 300–319. Springer, Heidelberg (2007)
5. Caire, G., Gotta, D., Banzi, M.: Wade: a software platform to develop mission critical applications exploiting agents and workflows. In: AAMAS 2008: Proceedings of the 7th International Joint Conference on Autonomous Agents and Multiagent Systems: Industrial Track, pp. 29–36 (2008)
6. Carr, H., Pitt, J.: Adaptation of voting rules in agent societies. In: OA-MAS@AAMAS 2008: Proceedings from the AAMAS Workshop on Organised Adaptation in Multi-Agent Systems, pp. 36–53 (2008)
7. Carr, H., Pitt, J., Artikis, A.: Peer Pressure as a Driver of Adaptation in Agent Societies. In: Artikis, A., Picard, G., Vercouter, L. (eds.) ESAW 2008. LNCS, vol. 5485, pp. 191–207. Springer, Heidelberg (2009)

8. Governatori, G., Rotolo, A., Riveret, R., Palmirani, M., Sartor, G.: Variants of temporal defeasible logics for modelling norm modifications. In: ICAIL 2007: Proceedings of the 11th International Conference on Artificial Intelligence and Law, pp. 155–159 (June 2007)

9. Guessoum, Z., Ziane, M., Faci, N.: Monitoring and organizational-level adaptation of multi-agent systems. In: AAMAS 2004: Proceedings of the Third International Joint Conference on Autonomous Agents and Multiagent Systems, vol. 2, pp. 514–521 (July 2004)

10. Hewitt, C.: Offices are open systems. ACM TOIS: ACM Transactions on Information Systems 4(3), 271–287 (1986)

11. Holland, O., Melhuish, C.: Stigmergy, self-organization, and sorting in collective robotics. Artificial Life 5(2), 173–202 (1999)

12. Jarvis, B., Jarvis, D., Jain, L.: Teams in multi-agent systems. International Federation for Information Processing (Springer) 228, 1–10 (2007)

13. Kennedy, J., Eberhart, R.C., Shi, Y.: Swarm Intelligence. Springer, Heidelberg (2001)

14. Kephart, J.: Research challenges of autonomic computing. In: ICSE 2005: Proceedings of the 27th International Conference on Software Engineering, pp. 15–22 (May 2005)

15. Kowalski, R., Sergot, M.: A logic-based calculus of events. New Generation Computing 4(1), 67–95 (1986)

16. Neville, B., Pitt, J.: PRESAGE: A Programming Environment for the Simulation of Agent Societies. In: Hindriks, K.V., Pokahr, A., Sardina, S. (eds.) ProMAS 2008. LNCS, vol. 5442, pp. 88–103. Springer, Heidelberg (2009)

17. Pitt, J., Venkataram, P., Mamdani, A.: Qos management in manets using norm-governed agent societies

18. Searcóid, M.Ó.: Metric Spaces. Springer, Heidelberg (2006)

Part IV

Environments

Action and Perception
in Agent Programming Languages:
From Exogenous to Endogenous Environments

Alessandro Ricci, Andrea Santi, and Michele Piunti

DEIS, Alma Mater Studiorum – Università di Bologna
via Venezia 52, 47023 Cesena, Italy
{a.ricci,a.santi,michele.piunti}@unibo.it

Abstract. The action and perception models adopted by state-of-the-art agent programming languages – in the context of Multi-Agent System (MAS) programming – have been conceived mainly to work with *exogenous* environments, i.e. physical or computational environments completely external to the MAS and then out of MAS design and programming. In this paper we discuss the limits of adopting such models when *endogenous environments* are considered, i.e. computational environments – often referred also as *application environments* – that are designed and programmed by MAS developers as a first-class abstraction to encapsulate functionalities useful for agent individual and cooperative activities. In the paper we describe an action and perception model for agent programming languages specifically conceived to be effective for endogenous environments and we discuss its evaluation using CArtAgO environment technology. On the agent side, we focus our attention on programming languages based on the BDI (Belief-Desire-Intention) model, taking Jason, 2APL and GOAL as reference case studies.

Keywords: Environment programming, Action and perception, Agent Programming Languages, CArtAgO.

1 Introduction

A large body of Multi-Agent System (MAS) literature has remarked the role that the notion of *environment* can play as *first-class abstraction* to design and develop MAS [22]. The environment in this case – also referred as *application* environment, or *virtual/software* environment – is exploited as a suitable place where to encapsulate functionalities and mechanisms that agents can exploit at runtime to do their tasks, in particular to support their communication, coordination and organisation [13,12,22]. By adopting such a perspective, the environment becomes an orthogonal design and *programming* dimension for MAS developers with respect to the agent one [15]. Accordingly, several models, architectures and technologies have been proposed for environment design and engineering, either general-purpose or to solve specific application problems [23,24]. Among the others, the CArtAgO framework [15,16,17] – which will be considered

R. Collier, J. Dix, and P. Novák (Eds.): ProMAS 2010, LNAI 6599, pp. 119–138, 2012.

in this paper – introduced a general-purpose computational and programming model for engineering environments based on the notion of *artifact*, as defined by the A&A meta-model [11].

Even if orthogonal to the agent dimension, artifact-based environments and CArtAgO have been conceived especially for being integrated with agent programming languages (APL) and frameworks based on high-level model of agency such as the BDI (Belief-Desire-Intention) one. Examples of APL based on the BDI model are Jason [1], 2APL [3], GOAL [7], AF-APL [18]. These agent programming languages have already an explicit notion of environment, which is the classical one as defined in Artificial Intelligence literature [19]: the environment is the external context – either physical or computational/software – where agents and MAS are situated, source of the agents' percepts and target of agents' actions. In this case the environment is not part of MAS design and development, it is not a first-class abstraction meant to be exploited to encapsulate functionalities. In order to avoid ambiguities, in this paper we refer to this notion of environment as *exogenous*, while we use the term *endogenous* to refer to the former ones (i.e. application/computational/virtual/software environments)[1]. Almost every APL includes some kind of API to define the *interface* to exogenous environments, and often provides also an API – typically Object-Oriented – to develop *simulated* environments conceived for doing tests.

Given this context, in this paper we focus on some issues that arise when situating intelligent/BDI agents within endogenous environments. For conceptual and practical reasons, we want to frame agents interaction within endogenous environment still in terms of *actions* and *perceptions*, like it happens for exogenous environments. However, in this paper we show that the classic action and perception models/architectures adopted in state-of-the-art APL – devised for dealing with exogenous environments – are not fully adequate to work with endogenous environments. We show that this has a negative impact on agent programming, in particular on the development of software agents and multi-agent programs that need to work with endogenous environments. In Section 2 we describe such weaknesses in details, focussing in particular on agent programming languages based on the BDI model—even if the remarks provided in the section would apply more generally to any APL or framework based on the classic abstract architecture for intelligent agents [25].

Then, in Section 3 we introduce an action/perception model that extends the classic one adopted by APL so as to fully exploit the features provided by endogenous environments. To evaluate the model, we implemented it in the CArtAgO framework and in the bridge integrating CArtAgO with Jason: in Section 4 we describe the model at work with some examples involving Jason agents working inside artifact-based environments.

Several works in agent environment literature tackle the problem of defining proper action models for endogenous environments – a brief account of these is reported in related works (Section 5). However, to authors' knowledge this is the first work to focus on how such models can be effectively integrated with agent

---

[1] Endogenous because they are actually part of the MAS, not external.

programming languages, in particular with those based on BDI-like models, and, in particular, on finding out the most suitable action and perception model to make endogenous environments exploitation by intelligent agents (and agent programmers) straightforward and effective.

2   Action and Perception in Agent Programming Languages

In this section we analyze and discuss the action and perception model and related architectures adopted in current agent programming languages, focussing in particular on those based on BDI-like model. Jason, 2APL and GOAL are taken as reference case studies, since *(a)* they provide a good spectrum of the different approaches that can be adopted to implement the BDI conceptual model, *(b)* they provide an explicit programming interface to the environment.

By referring to existing formalisations, these languages follow the abstract reference architecture for intelligent agents and the agent reasoning cycle reported by Wooldridge in [25]. Essentially, it can be sumarised as a *sense-plan-act* (SPA) cycle where the agent repeatedly *(i)* observes the environment and updates its beliefs, *(ii)* uses practical reasoning to deliberate what intention achieve and how, and *(iii)* executes a step of a proper plan for fulfilling the selected intention. The environment (software or hardware) here is fully exogenous.

Moving from formal models to concrete architectures and implementations, current APL adopt richer approaches and semantics, which are explicitly oriented toward the integration with some kind of programmable environments, to be developed to create simulated environments, typically using an Object-Oriented language such as Java. A comprehensive survey of the environment interface models adopted by mainstream APL and the API for interacting with them can be found in the Environment Interface Standard (EIS) initiative [9]: here we focus on the semantics underlying the action and perception model.

2.1   The Action Model

In the abstract architecture, the action chosen by agent's action selection function is dispatched to effectors which will eventually execute it (act stage, or *execute* command in the practical reasoning cycle) and the reasoning cycle can start again (sense stage). Actions are considered as options in agents repertoire which can be translated by moves enabled by the environment. The success or failure of the action executed by effectors is meant to be determined by an agent by analyzing the percepts that will eventually be observed from the environment. From the execution model point of view, action execution is modelled then as an atomic *event*, which corresponds to dispatching the action to effectors. This semantics is the basic one adopted by almost all APLs formal models. Not surprisingly, concrete implementations of APLs adopt more complex solutions than the one just presented. Examples follow.

In AgentSpeak(L) and Jason operational semantics [1], action execution is modelled by a transition inserting the action selected by previous stages of the agent cycle into a particular set of actions, i.e. a set of actions to be performed in the environment. The formal model does not provide any further information: the selected action is scheduled to be executed – sooner or later – by other components (i.e. effectors) of the agent architecture [1]. Actually, in the concrete architecture and implementation of the Jason interpreter[2], the action execution model is more articulated and expressive than the one described in the operational semantics. Action execution is done by calling a special method of the Java class representing the environment—the action to be performed is a parameter of this method. As a key aspect, the method is executed *asynchronously* with respect to the agent cycle: current agent intention – i.e. the plan in execution – is *suspended* until the action execution is terminated, so the agent can carry on other plans and react to percepts. So, in practice, the action execution model is not atomic. The environment method can return – as action feedback – a boolean value, indicating if the requested action has been executed at all. A false value means it was not, so the plan fails. A true value means that the action has been executed (accepted), however it does not mean that the expected changes will necessarily take place ([1], p. 50).

Also GOAL adopts the basic action semantics found in the abstract practical reasoning agent cycle, so executing the actions atomically and establishing their outcomes only by sensing the environment. Analogously to Jason, action execution is done by calling a special execute-action method of the Java class representing the environment, with the action to be performed as a parameter of this method. As reported in [9], in GOAL invoking the execute-action method might have three outcomes: either the return value true indicating success, false indicating that the action has not been recognised, or an exception indicating that the action has failed. In this case the meaning of *success* is more subtle: it triggers the application of the action post-conditions that can be specified in the agent program, to update the belief base. In the examples described in [7] – the blocks-world in particular – such updates seem to refer not simply to an action (e.g. move) that has been recognised by the environment, but to an action whose execution has been fully executed with success and the environment has been changed accordingly. This action semantics appears a natural choice when exogenous environments are considered. However, it is not the most effective semantics when considering endogenous environments. In the following we describe two main drawbacks.

The first one is that, both conceptually and formally, by treating actions as events[3], it is not possible to implement concurrent actions – where for *concurrent* here we mean actions whose execution overlaps in time – so having a temporal extension. For endogenous environments this is a quite strong limitation, since concurrent actions make it possible to naturally implement effective

---

[2] http://jason.sourceforge.net

[3] here we consider a strict notion of event, as something happening at a specific point in time, with no duration.

synchronisation and coordination mechanisms. As a main example, let's consider the use of endogenous environments to implement the *tuple space* coordination model [5], providing *out, in, rd* primitives as defined by the Linda language – respectively inserting a tuple in the space, associatively removing/reading a tuple from the space. The key synchronisation mechanism is that the execution of *in* or *rd* suspends the invoking process until a tuple matching the specified template is found or has been inserted by an *out* in the space. In an agent perspective, we would model such primitives directly as actions that the environment provides to agent to coordinate, in which the execution of an *in* suspends current agent plan – not the agent execution itself, which must go on with the execution cycle – until, for instance, a tuple is inserted by another agent executing an *out*. By treating actions as events, this is not possible and one is forced to change the semantics of the *in* action, for instance assuming that the successful execution of the action represents just the act of making the request, not the fact that a tuple has been removed.

The second related drawback concerns, more generally, the success/failure semantics of actions. Endogenous environments are explicitly designed and programmed by MAS developers to support agent activities; so, it is natural to devise a stronger semantics for action execution where – for instance – action success, and so the success of the execute-action method if we consider the environment interface model adopted by Jason[4] and GOAL, means not only that the action has been accepted or recognised by the environment, but that it has completed and its effects and changes took place. This makes the exploitation of endogenous environment more straightforward and agent programs simpler and more efficient. As a simple example, let us consider an endogenous environment providing to agents functionalities to work with the local file system, so, for instance, a *make-directory* action with the obvious meaning: it would be natural to define the action success/failure semantics such that the successful execution of the action by the environment would imply that the specified directory has been created. By strictly adopting the classic action model, this is not possible: in principle, to know that the action succeeded an agent (programmer) would need to check for percepts reporting a state of the environment in which the new directory is available. This is burdensome, both from a programming point of view and for the runtime performance of the agent program.

Among the languages, 2APL apparently adopts a stronger semantics for action success and failure with respect to the classical one, not only at the implementation level but also in the formal model, explicitly assuming to work with computational environments, represented by Java objects. In the formal model, an external action is modeled as an atomic transition involving changes in the configuration of both the agent and the environment [3]. Action execution is done by calling methods of the Java class(es) representing the environment(s), which directly implement the actions behaviour. Following [9], executing an action-method in 2APL can have two outcomes: either a return-value (an object)

---

[4] Actually Jason makes it possible to implement a different semantics by customizing some part of the agent architecture.

```
// agent code (Tom)

Goals:
  do_job

PG-rules:
  do_job <- true |
  {  @TestEnv(compute(100000), Res );
     @TestEnv(log(Res));
     dropgoal(do_job)
  }

PC-rules:
  event( my_ev(Num), simple2APLEnv)
                        <- true |
  {
    @TestEnv(log(Num))
  }
```

```
public class TestEnv extends Environment {

  public APLNum compute(String agent, APLNum howLong)
  {
    long sum = 0;
    int burn= howLong.toInt();
    for (int i = 0; i < burn; i++){
      for (int j = 0; j < 100000; j++){
        sum+=i*j;
      }
    }
    return ( new APLNum( sum ) );
  }

  public void update(String user, APLNum n)
  {
    int nEvents = n.toInt();
    for(int i=0; i < nEvents; i++){
      APLNum evNum = new APLNum(i);
      APLFunction event = new APLFunction( "my_ev", evNum );
      throwEvent(event);
    }
  }

  public void log(String user, APLString s){
    System.out.println(s);
  }
}
```

Fig. 1. *(left)* 2APL example for an agent blocked on a long term activity. *(right)* A simple 2APL environment in Java.

indicating success is returned, that might be non-trivial (e.g. list of percepts in the case of an sense-action) or terminate with an exception indicating action-failure. In this case success means that the action completed with success—and so the effects of the action execution took place, exhibiting then a stronger semantics with respect to Jason and GOAL. However, analogously to Jason and GOAL formal model, action execution is modelled and finally implemented as an atomic transition (so an event) coupling the agent and the environment. This means that by executing an action, the agent *cycle* is blocked until the completion of the action with success or failure occurs, and this can have some drawbacks for agent reactivity.

We clarify the point with an example shown in Fig. 1, a 2APL program composed by two agents, Tom and Alice, interacting in the same environment, represented by the TestEnv Java class (only Tom's source code is shown). The actions provided by the environment – i.e. the methods implemented by the class – are compute, which is meant to execute a long-term computation returning finally a result – and update, which is meant to update the state of the environment generating percepts—that are events in the case of 2APL. To achieve its goal, the agent Tom must perform the compute action; however Tom is also interested to perceive events generated by the environment to react accordingly—in this case simply printing to output the percepts. Alice simply acts on the environment performing an update, so generating percepts that are relevant also for Tom. However Tom is not able to react to percepts generated by the environment until the compute action has completed. So if one want to save agent reactivity, it cannot perform long-term actions, or rather: every long term action must be implemented in terms of multiple sub-actions.

2.2   The Perception Model

In the abstract intelligent agent architecture [25], agent perception is modeled by a *see* function: $E \rightarrow Per$. This function encapsulates agent's ability to obtain information from the environment E in which it is situated. The output produced by this function is a percept Per, which typically contains information about the *actual state* of the environment. Percepts are then elaborated by the agent through appropriate belief-update/revision functions, to keep its mental state consistent with the actual state of the environment. This model is adopted both in Jason and GOAL.

A GOAL agent implements a simple SPA cycle in which (i) it receives percepts from the environment (containing the whole state of interest) through its perceptual interface and (ii) it updates its mental state through the percept rules included by the agent programmer to specify how the agent belief base should be updated when certain percepts are received (see [7] for more details). In Jason, at each cycle an agent perceives the actual state of the environment and updates its mental state, in particular automatically removing/updating/adding beliefs related to percepts. Actually this is the default behaviour of the belief-update and belief-revision function: the highly customizable architecture of the Jason interpreter allows for changing this semantics, customizing both the perceive stage (implementing the *see* function) and the belief update/revision stage.

So both in the case of GOAL and Jason, percepts represent *actual* information regarding the environment—typically a snapshot of the environment state which is observable to the agent. Actually, this is the natural choice when considering exogenous environments. However, it suffers of some problems that are particularly important when applying the approach to endogenous environments. A first problem concerns the possibility for an agent of *losing* (not perceiving) environment states that could be relevant for agent reasoning and course of action. This can occur because of environment dynamics, related to internal processes and also actions performed by other agents, changing asynchronously the environment multiple times between two subsequent perceive stages.

We clarify the problem with a simple example written in Jason, shown in Fig. 2. The example includes a simple endogenous environment that provides a generic *shared resource* bounded by capacity limit, i.e. the resource can be used concurrently only by a limited number of agents. Then, a set of worker agents – with a cardinality greater than the resource capacity – cyclically try to use the resource, first attempting to acquire it by means of an acquire_resource action, then using it and finally releasing it by means of a release_resource action, making it available for further usages. The single kind of percept generated by environment – max_use(N) – represent the actual number of times that the resource reaches its max capacity—so it starts from zero and is incremented each time the limit is achieved. The scenario is completed by an observer agent, whose goal is to observe the shared resource and to output a message each time max_use changes. The agent monitors the number of times the resource reached its max capacity and, also, does a check for detecting lost states, by executing the check_state_lost plan each time it perceives a new value for the max

```
// worker source code

times(100).

!run_worker.
+!run_worker : times(X) & X \== 0
   <- acquire_resource;
      !use_resource;
      release_resource;
      -+times(X-1);
      !!run_worker.

-!run_worker : true
   <- .wait(10);
      !!run_worker.
```

```
// Observer agent source code

last_occurrence(0).

@my_plan [atomic]
+max_use(Occurrence) : last_occurrence(N)
   <- .print("New max usage perceived:",
             Occurrence);
      !check_state_lost(Occurrence, N);
      -+last_occurrence(Occurrence).

+!check_state_lost(Current,Local): true
   <- X = Local + 1;
      if (Current > X){
         .print("State(s) lost! from ",
                Local," to ",Current)
      }.
```

```
// Jason Environment

public class ResEnv extends jason.environment.Environment {
   int occurenceNum = 0;
   int resourceUse = 0;
   int maxResourceUse = 3;
   ReentrantLock lock;

   public void init(String[] args) {
      ReentrantLock lock = new ReentrantLock();
   }

   public boolean synchronized executeAction(String ag,
                                              Structure act) {
      if (act.getFunctor().equals("acquire_resource")){
         if (resourceUse == maxResourceUse){
            return false;
         } else{
            resourceUse++;
            if (resourceUse == maxResourceUse){
               clearPercepts();
               occurenceNum++;
               String perc = "max_use("+occurenceNum+")";
               addPercept(Literal.parseLiteral(perc));
            }
         }
      } else if (act.getFunctor().equals("release_resource")){
         if (resourceUse == 0) {
            return false;
         } {
            else resourceUse--;
         }
      }
      informAgsEnvironmentChanged();
      return true;
   }
}
```

```
MAS Console - test_losing_states
[observer] New max usage perceived: 4
[observer] New max usage perceived: 5
[observer] New max usage perceived: 7
[observer] State(s) lost! from 5 to 7
[observer] New max usage perceived: 8
[observer] New max usage perceived: 27
[observer] State(s) lost! from 8 to 27
[observer] New max usage perceived: 28

   Clean   Stop   Continue   Debug   Sources   New agent   Kill agent
```

Fig. 2. *(left)* Jason source code of the worker and observer agents. *(right)* Java implementation of the resource environment where the workers and observer are situated. *(bottom)* A screenshot of the Jason console during a run of a MAS composed by three workers and an observer.

use – represented by the belief-update event related to max_use(N). The check_state_lost plan checks if the difference between the current observed max_use occurrence and the previous one (stored by the observer into the last_occurence belief) is greater than one unit. If so, it means that some max_use percepts have been lost and a message is printed in standard output. By running the example it is possible to verify that the observer loses states (Fig. 2 shows a screenshot) and that the frequency of the losses increases with the number of worker agents concurrently working in the same environment.

A second problem is that retrieving perceptual information at each cycle regarding the current observable state of the environment can be computationally expensive, in particular when considering non-naive environments, being either centralised or, worst, distributed. Then, given the list of percepts representing the current state, the belief update must be updated accordingly: in the case of a direct mapping between beliefs and environment state as in the case of Jason adopting the default belief-update and belief-revision semantics, this typically involves iterating both through the list of percepts and the whole belief-base to remove old beliefs and to add new ones.

Differently from Jason, 2APL models percepts as events. This in principle makes it possible to avoid the previous problem—as will be shown in next section. However in 2APL – analogously to GOAL – in order to keep track of the observable state of the environment in terms of beliefs, the programmer is forced to explicitly define the rules that specify how to change the belief-base when a percept is detected. This is an important capability when dealing with exogenous environments, but when adopting endogenous environments – in particular complex ones – this can become burdensome. Being specifically designed by MAS engineers, endogenous environments allow for stronger assumption on the relationships between percepts generated by the environment and related beliefs. Such assumption can be used then to define a mapping percepts-beliefs to be applied by default by the architecture: this allows for both avoiding the burden to the agent programmers of specifying the percept rules on the one side, and automatically keeping consistency between the actual state of the environment and the belief base on the other side.

3   An Effective Interaction Model for Endogenous Environments

In this section we describe a model for actions and perceptions to be adopted in APL so as to fully exploit the features provided by endogenous environments, solving the drawbacks shown in previous section. Here we describe the main concepts and (informal) semantics, which will be shown in practice in next section using the new version of the CArtAgO framework.

3.1   Action Side

As mentioned in the previous sections, endogenous environments allow for a stronger semantics for action success/failure, which finally simplifies agent programming and make multi-agent programs more efficient. In an endogenous environment, the success (or failure) of an action on the agent side can be directly related to the successful (or failed) completion of an operation or process executed on the environment side as a consequence of the agent action request. So, differently from exogenous environments where action success or failure can be established by an agent only by interpreting the percepts generated by the environment after the action execution, in endogenous environments action success/failure can be represented by an explicit *action completion event* generated by the environment, thereby an explicit information related to operation execution completion (with success or failure). Accordingly, from the APL point of view, the execution of an action does not mean that the action has been simply accepted or recognised by the environment, but that the related environment operation has been executed up to completion. This promotes a perspective in which the set of actions are conceived as part of a *usage contract* provided by the environment, including both the *effects* that can be assumed with action completion and the *action feedbacks*, including further information related to action success or failure. Action feedbacks are an effective way to represent results computed by the action – so information which are not suitably modelled as effects over the environment: a simple example is given by actions performing just pure calculation, providing some kind of output given an input. The notion of usage contract introduced here is similar to the notion of contract adopted in Object-Oriented programming languages to represent the set of services or features that an object is meant to provide, being an instance of a class implementing some kind of interface [10].

By assuming this semantics, agent programs become – generally speaking – simpler, more compact and efficient. Action completion events are meant to be automatically processed by the agent architecture, in order to – for instance – reactivate the suspended plan where the action was executed, without the burden for the agent programmer to manage such percepts by hand. Also, the usage contract makes it simpler for agents to reason about the state of the environment: agents can appraise step by step their course of actions and, by completing an action, an agent is sure that the effects possibly specified for the action in its specification took place.

From the action execution model point of view, this approach promotes an *action-as-a-process* semantics, where actions are not modeled as single atomic events but as processes – i.e. a sequence of events – that can be long-term, whose completion is notified by action completion events. When adopted in APL, this semantics have two main benefits: First, it makes it possible to effectively program agents that execute (long-term) actions without hampering their reactivity (see the example using 2APL in Section 2): the action-as-process semantics makes it possible then for an agent to start the execution of action and then go on perceiving, reacting to percepts that are generated by the action itself or other actions, possibly carrying on other activities by choosing other actions to execute. Second, the action-as-process semantics makes it possible to implement concurrent actions and then effective coordination mechanisms simply based on action synchronisation, designing environments which provide operations for that purpose. This because the action completion event of an action performed by a certain agent can be generated as a consequence of the execution of the action(s) of other agents in the same environment. As remarked in Section 2, this is not possible with an action-as-event semantics. The coordination semantics in this case is encapsulated in the the environment providing the operations. Recalling the example of tuple spaces and Linda, blocking actions like in or read can be implemented quite straightforwardly by adopting an action-as-process semantics. In particular, an in action can start its execution before the execution of an out action and complete after the out's completion. A concrete example about this will be given in next section, using CArtAgO.

3.2   Perception Side

On the perception side, we argue that modeling percepts as *events* – carrying on information about *changes* occurred in the endogenous environment – is more effective and efficient than modeling percepts as facts about the *actual state* of the environment itself, as in the case of exogenous environments. At a first glance this makes it possible to solve a main problem that has been described in Section 2, i.e. the possibility for agents not to perceive environment states – so loosing relevant environment configurations – due to the different update frequencies of agent perceptive activities and environment internal processes. Referring to the abstract model mentioned in Section 2, the set of percepts returned by the *see* function represents a list of changes occurred in the environment during the last agent execution cycle and which are relevant for the observing agent. Accordingly, the *next* function can update the current internal state of the agent with respect to the whole set of changes occurred inside the environment, thus eventually reconstructing all the intermediate states that the environment assumed between a couple of *see* activities.

Then, to support the automated reconstruction of such states it is useful to identify the basic set of possible kinds of event that can occur inside an endogenous environment: *(i)* an observable part of the environment has changed; *(ii)* an observable part of the environment has been added or removed; *(iii)* a signal has been generated to acknowledge agents with some information. In the latter case, signals represent observable events explicitly generated by the environment – as designed by the environment programmer – to carry on some data which can be purposefully processed by agents observing that part of the environment.

By explicitly defining a model to represent environment observable parts – for instance *observable properties*, in the case of artifact-based environments used in next section – it is possible then at the agent architecture level to automatically reconstruct a consistent snapshot of the current observable state of the environment by processing a list of events updating the previous snapshot. In the APL considered here this means introducing in the basic architecture a support for *(i)* representing the observable part of the endogenous environments as beliefs, and *(ii)* automatically updating such beliefs as soon as such events are processed. In this perspective, there is no more the need for an agent programmer to explicitly define belief updates function (such as in 2APL) or percept rules and post-condition in action specification: the belief base is automatically updated reflecting the perceived/reconstructed state of the observed environment.

Actually, due to concurrency and distribution, the correct and efficient reconstruction of the observable state of the environment from the individual agent architecture perspective is an issue, both from the theoretical and practical point of view. First, by working with multi-agent systems, we must assume that multiple agents can concurrently work in the same environment and then events generated concern concurrent processes; Second, environments can be distributed, which means that it is not feasible to consider the availability of a total order among the distributed events.

In order to cope with these two aspects, first it is useful to conceive a distributed endogenous environment as a set of non-distributed sub-environments, eventually connected, and assume that each sub-environment defines a spatial-temporal locality. For each sub-environment it is feasible then to assume that *(i)* a local logical notion of time can be defined, and *(ii)* observable events occurring the in the sub-environment can be totally ordered using logical timestamps, even if they are generated by concurrent processes. Given this assumption, agents perceive chains of events, which are totally ordered if the source is a single sub-environment, partially ordered if more sub-environments are involved. Then, some *modularisation* strategy should be considered for structuring individual sub-environments, so as to *(i)* allow multiple agents to work concurrently to different parts of the overall structure, promoting as far as possible decentralisation and parallelism; *(ii)* make it possible to easily change structure at runtime, eventually changing/extending dynamically the set of actions available, so to better support openness, adaptation, etc.

4   Evaluation Using CArtAgO

The idea presented in previous section has been implemented in the new version of CArtAgO [16], a platform for developing endogenous environments in multi-agent systems. Before discussing in detail some examples evaluating the new action/perception model, a brief description of CArtAgO follows – a complete description is outside the scope of this paper, the interested reader can find it here [15,16]. CArtAgO makes it possible to design and program endogenous distributed environments as set of *workspaces* – playing the roles of sub-environments – where agents can share and use *artifacts*, which are the basic first-class abstraction used to modularise (sub-)environments.

Artifacts are, on the one side, designed and programmed by MAS developers – a Java API is provided to this end; on the other side, they are instantiated, used, composed by agents at runtime, representing first-class resources and tools of their world. To be used, an artifact provides a usage interface containing a set of *operations* that agents can execute to get some functionality. To be perceived, an artifact can have one or multiple *observable properties*, as data items that can be perceived by agents as environment state variables, whose value can change dynamically because of operation execution. Operations are computational processes occurring inside the artifact, possibly changing the observable properties and generating *observable events*, as environment signals that can be relevant for agents using/observing the artifact.

By integrating CArtAgO with existing APL, agents written in different agent programming languages can cooperatively work inside the same workspaces, sharing and co-using the same artifacts [14]. The new action and perception model described in this paper essentially improves the way in which agents can exploit artifact-based environments. In the remainder of the section we will consider as APL Jason, whose platform[5] provides flexible API that made it possible

---

[5] Available at http://jason.sourceforge.net

to adapt quite straightforwardly the agent architecture to implement the new action and perception semantics.

4.1   The Action Model at Work

Following the new model, artifacts' operations now represent directly the repertoire of the (external) actions available to the agent situated in an artifact-based environment. So, by performing an action $act(P)$ where P are action parameters, a corresponding operation $op(P)$ provided by some artifact currently available in the workspace is executed—where act and op match. Then, the action succeeds or fails when (if) the corresponding operation has completed with success or failure. Action feedbacks eventually resulting from action execution are made available to the agent performing the action (operation) as output parameters of the action itself. Then, by executing an action the agent plan (activity) including such action is *suspended* until the corresponding operation has completed, i.e. the action has completed. In the meanwhile, the agent control cycle can go on, making it possible for the agent to get percepts and select and perform other actions. So, by adopting this semantics the use of artifact-based environments by agents becomes more agile and agent programs more concise.

As a simple example, Fig. 3 shows a Jason agent working in a workspace containing some artifacts, in particular: an instance of Calc artifact, an instance of SharedData artifact, one of Stream and one Console. Calc provides an operation compute which does a long term computation returning finally a result as feedback. SharedData has a value observable property and provides an operation, update, to update such value. Stream has an operation generate which results in the generation of a stream of observable events (signals in this case) which can be perceived by agents focussing the artifact. Finally Console (whose source code is not reported) provides an operation println to print messages on standard output.

At a first glance, the agent sees the workspace as an environment providing four kind of external actions: compute, update, generate and println, and an observable property value(X), besides the specific artifacts where the operations and observable properties are stored. Accordingly, in main_plan plan, which is triggered by a new work_todo goal, the agent interacts with the environment directly performing compute and then println to show the computed result on standard output[6]. By triggering the execution of compute – which is carried on asynchronously in the environment – my_plan is suspended until the action has completed, reporting the result as feedback (second parameter). Even if this plan is suspended, the agent is free to carry on other plans and react to percepts. In the example the agent – by executing a focus at the beginning of

---

[6] Actually, to avoid ambiguities when performing actions in the case of multiple instances of artifacts providing operations with the same names, it is possible to specify the artifact target of the action by means of proper annotations, such as the artifact_name.: the annotated action becomes compute(X,Result) [artifact_name("calc")].

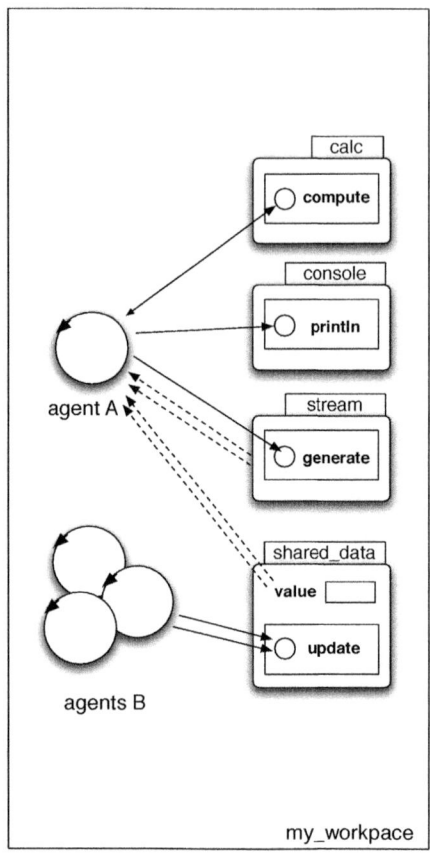

```
// agent A code

@main_plan
+!work_todo(X,Y) : true
    <- lookupArtifact("shared_data",ArtId);
       focus(ArtId);
       compute(X,Result);
       println(Result);
       +sum(0);
       focus("stream");
       generate(Y);
       ?sum(S);
       println(S).

+value(X)
    <- println(X).

+new_number(V) : sum(S)
    <- -+sum(S+V).
```

```
// artifacts code

class Calc extends Artifact {
    ...
    @OPERATION void compute(double x,
                OpFeedbackParam<Double> res){
        double result = longTermCalc(x);
        res.set(result);
    }
    private long longTermCalc(double x){...}
}

class SharedData extends Artifact {
    void init(){
        defineObsProperty("value",0);
    }
    @OPERATION void update(int v){
        getObsProperty("value").updateValue(v);
    }
}

class Stream extends Artifact {
    ...
    @OPERATION void generate(int n){
        for (int i = 0; i < n; i++){
            int v = compute_next();
            signal("new_number",v);
        }
    }
    private int compute_next(){...}
}
```

Fig. 3. A Jason agent executing some actions to exploit the functionalities of the artifacts of a workspace, reacting to percepts related to the environment observable state and events

the plan[7] – is observing the shared_data artifact, whose observable properties (value) are mapped then onto the agent belief base. So, as soon as the value of the property changes (because some other agents perform an update), the belief is automatically updated and a new belief update event is generated, triggering a plan that simply prints (by exploiting the console) the value on standard output. Finally, after using the calc artifact, the agent uses the stream artifact by doing a generate. Then, by observing the stream, the agent processes the events generated by the artifact – by updating a belief related to the sum of the values generated by the stream – before the generate action completes. After the action completion, the agent then prints on standard output the final sum.

---

[7] focus is a basic primitive of CArtAgO which makes it possible for an agent to select the parts (artifacts) of the workspace to be aware of, perceiving their observable properties and events.

```
                                            class RendezVous extends Artifact {

                                                int num;

// agent using the Rendez-Vous                  void init(int numPart){
                                                    num = numPart;
@meeting_plan                                   }
+!meet_altogether
   <- println("before meeting altogether.");    @OPERATION void meet(){
      meet;                                         num--;
      println("after meeting altogether.");         await("allReady");
                                                 }

                                                 @GUARD boolean allReady(){
                                                     return num == 0;
                                                 }
                                            }
```

Fig. 4. *(left)* Snipped of a plan of Jason agent to achieve a meeting point with other agents, exploiting a RendezVous artifact; *(right)* Source code of the RendezVous artifact

So, by mapping external actions onto artifact operations, we obtain quite compact and readable agent programs, fully preserving agent reactivity; also, we have a further important outcome about openness and dynamism: the set of external actions available to an agent is *dynamic*, it depends on the current shape of the environment – the actual set of artifacts available in workspaces – and it can be then extended or specialised by agents themselves creating new artifacts or replacing existing ones.

The effectiveness of the action model for implementing coordination mechanisms – which was a second main outcome remarked in Section 3 – should be clear from the example shown in Fig. 4. The example shows a RendezVous artifact which can be used by N agents to achieve a synchronisation point and an agent plan meeting_plan in which the artifact is used. From the agent point of view, this is done by simply performing a single meet action, which is mapped onto the related operation of the artifact. The artifact is programmed so that the operation completes with success only when N agents have executed the same operation.

4.2   Exploiting the Perception Model

By applying the new perception model, percepts received by an agent who is focussing an artifact are events that concern signals and observable properties updates: such events are used then to automatically update the beliefs in the belief-base of the agent. By adopting this model we have the guarantee that no states are lost for an agent who is observing the environment (or a part of it). Here we show this in practice by revisiting the shared resource example used in Section 2. In particular the objective of the example is the same, as well as the source code of the agents, but in this case the environment is implemented in CArtAgO by an artifact called ResourceArtifact[8]. The artifact – whose source

---

[8] The example is included in CArtAgO 2.0 distribution, available at
   http://cartago.sourceforge.net

```
// worker source code

times(100).

!run_worker.
+!run_worker : times(X) & X \== 0
   <- acquire_resource;
      !use_resource;
      release_resource;
      -+times(X-1);
      !!run_worker.

-!run_worker : true
   <- .wait(10); !!run_worker.
```

```
// Observer agent source code

last_occurrence(0).
!setup.

+!setup : true
   <- makeArtifact("res","ResArtifact",Id);
      focus(Id).

@my_plan [atomic]
+max_use(Occurrence) : last_occurrence(N)
   <- println("New max usage perceived: ",
              Occurrence);
      !check_state_lost(Occurrence, N);
      -+last_occurrence(Occurrence).

+!check_state_lost(Current,Local): true
   <- X = Local + 1;
      if (Current > X){
         .print("State(s) lost! from ",
                Local," to ",Current)
      }.
```

```
// Resource Artifact implemented in CArtAgO

public class ResArtifact extends Artifact {

   int resourceUse = 0;
   int maxResourceUse;

   void init(){
      defineObsProperty("max_use",0);
      maxResourceUse = 3;
   }

   @OPERATION void acquire_resource(){
      if(resourceUse == maxResourceUse){
         failed("error");
      } else{
         resourceUse++;
         if (resourceUse == maxResourceUse){
            ObsProperty prop = getObsProperty("max_use");
            prop.updateValue(prop.intValue() + 1);
         }
      }
   }

   @OPERATION void release_resource(){
      if(resourceUse == 0) {
         failed("error");
      } else {
         resourceUse--;
      }
   }
}
```

Fig. 5. The *resource environment* example introduced in Section 2 implemented here by means of a `ResourceArtifact`. The source code of the workers and of the observer (on the right) is almost the same.

code is reported in Fig. 5 – provides the same functionalities of the Jason environment developed in the previous example. In this case, the underlying perception model ensures that *every change to the max_use observable property is perceived by the observer agent*, which, differently from the one in Section 2, never prints to standard output any log message about the loss of states. It is worth noting that the source code of both the `worker` and the `observer` agent is almost the same used in the previous example, with minor differences, such as the explicit creation of the `ResourceArtifact` by the observer agent.

5   Related Works

The definition of action and perception models and architectures in agent-based systems has been tackled in many contexts, from cognitive science to Multi-Agent Based Simulations, with different characterisations and objectives. Here we restrict the discussion to related works in MAS programming and agent-based software engineering, which is the reference scope of the paper.

In this context, several works can be found in literature about environments for multi-agent systems (see [23,24] for comprehensive surveys), some of them explicitly focussing on action and perception. A main related work is the formal model of situated MAS proposed by Weyns and Holvoet [20], who introduced a reference architecture for designing environments in multi-agent systems [21]. This work is based and extends the *influences and reactions* action model proposed by Ferber and Müller in [4]. In that model, influences come from inside the agents and are attempts to modify the course of events in the world. Reactions, which result in state changes, are produced by the environment by combining influences of all agents, given the local state of the environment and the laws of the world. This distinction between the products of the agents behavior and the reaction of the environment provides a way to handle simultaneous activity in the MAS. The influences and reactions action model has been implemented in the MadKit multi-agent platform [6].

In the formal model of situated MAS proposed by Weyns and Holvoet, the definition of an influence includes the specification of an operation that is provided by the application environment and that can be invoked by the agents. The action model is expressive enough to model simultaneous actions and synchronisation among agents acting/perceiving in the same locality: so agents can synchronise with other agents within their perceptual range. On the perception side, the formal model includes a form of *active sensing*: an agent can actively sense the environment to obtain a percept (i.e., a representation of its vicinity), possibly specifying *foci* to select what to perceive, an agent can perform an influence in the environment (i.e., attempt to modify the state of affairs in the environment), and it can exchange messages with other agents. So many similarities hold between Weyns and Holvoet's model and the action/perception model described in Section 3 and adopted in CArtAgO: for instance, the notion of action/operation as defined in CArtAgO is quite similar to the notion of influences as defined above. Another one is the possibility for agents to select which parts of the environment to focus, even specifying filters. Besides similarities, some important differences are there. A main one concerns the kind of modularisation adopted, which – indirectly – impacts also on the action/perception model. Weyns and Holvoet adopt an *architectural* point of view, describing the architecture of the environment decomposed into layers and modules corresponding to functional blocks. No specific computational or programming model is specified to define and program environment computational behaviour. This is – instead – a main point in A&A and CArtAgO, in which modularisation is framed in terms of artifacts, as first-class designing and programming abstractions, functioning as runtime modules composing the environment. Each artifact defines a set of actions (operations) that an agent can use to work with it. Also, it defines the set of observable properties that can be perceived by agents focussing on it. So the repertoire of agents' actions and possible perception of an agent is dynamic, depending on the set of artifacts available in the environment. A second main difference concerns the integration with agent programming languages and cognitive agent architectures. Related works described above do not tackle this point – because out of their aims – and typically do not consider any specific agent architecture or programming language. Conversely, the action/perception model proposed in this paper has been formulated by considering not only the environment side, but also the agent side, so as to find out an approach which would make as straightforward and effective as possible the use of environments by intelligent agents and related programming languages.

A similar perspective is adopted in GOLEM [2], a logic-based framework which shares many features with CArtAgO. The framework allows for representing agent environments declaratively and adopting a cognitive model for programming situated agents, based on the KGP model of agency [8]. The environment is represented as a composite structure that evolves over time, including two main classes of entities – agents and *objects*, similar to artifacts – organised in *containers*, similar to workspaces. Interactions between these entities inside a container are specified in term of *events* whose occurrence is governed by a set of physical laws specifying the possible evolutions of the agent environment, including how these evolutions are perceived by agents and affect objects and other agents in the environment. A key point of the approach is the notion of *affordances*, representing the external states of objects that can be perceived by cognitive agents so as to interact with them. This notion is quite similar to the notion of artifact's usage interface and observable properties, in particular. Also this framework was inspired by the influence-reaction model by Ferber and Müller and its extensions as the work of Weyns and Holvoet, in particular influences are represented as *attempts* of events and reactions as environment notifications. Differently from previous related works, GOLEM explicitly deals with the agent and environment programming dimension, as in our case, and considers a cognitive model of agency (KGP), so the perspective is very similar to the one adopted in CArtAgO and in this work. Said this, two main differences can be remarked between GOLEM's action/perception model and ours'. The first one is that in GOLEM action execution is modelled as an event, being represented by an attempt. In our case, instead, action execution is modelled as a process, being mapped onto artifacts' operations, including a start event and a completion event. The benefits of this choice have been discussed in the paper. The second main difference concerns the perception model, in particular passive perception. In GOLEM this accounts for notifying events to interested agents' sensors, and – according to what described in [2] – no automated mapping between such events and the knowledge component of a KGP agent is provided. In our proposal, we model percepts as events as in GOLEM, and, furthermore, we map at runtime observable properties provided by the artifacts observed by an agent into agents' beliefs. As discussed in the paper, we believe that this is a key feature to improve agent programming, making agent programs more compact, readable and elegant.

Another related work is the EIS (Environment Interface Standard) initiative [9], already mentioned in the paper, whose aim is to define a standard interface to allow agents developed using different programming languages to share the same environment, typically exogenous, independently of the specific model and technology adopted for it.

Finally, this paper is naturally related to previous works on CArtAgO [16,17] and environment programming in general [15]: the new contribution with respect to such existing work is an in-depth elaboration of the specific aspect concerning the action and perception model, and the definition of a new improved approach that has been implemented in the new version of the framework.

6   Conclusion

As remarked by the EIS initiative [9], the definition of a general-purpose and standard environment interface is a relevant issue of current APL. This is even more important when developing multi-agent programs that aims at exploiting endogenous environments, as first-class abstraction to encapsulate functionalities. Accordingly, in this paper we discussed the main features of an action and perception model that effectively exploits key properties of endogenous environments, simplifying agent and environment programming.

Then, we evaluated the approach by implementing it in the new version of CArtAgO, which aims at providing a general-purpose and standard model to conceive, design and program endogenous environments in MAS. In order to achieve this objective, future works include: *(i)* the evaluation of the approach using other APL besides Jason, starting from GOAL and 2APL; *(ii)* analyzing how the semantics devised in this model and the one proposed in the EIS initiative [9] can be suitably integrated; *(iii)* a formalisation of the model and the analysis of its impact on existing agent programming language formalisations.

References

1. Bordini, R., Hübner, J.F., Wooldridge, M.: Programming Multi-Agent Systems in AgentSpeak Using Jason. John Wiley & Sons, Ltd. (2007)
2. Bromuri, S., Stathis, K.: Situating Cognitive Agents in GOLEM. In: Weyns, D., Brueckner, S.A., Demazeau, Y. (eds.) EEMMAS 2007. LNCS (LNAI), vol. 5049, pp. 115–134. Springer, Heidelberg (2008)
3. Dastani, M.: 2APL: a practical agent programming language. Autonomous Agents and Multi-Agent Systems 16(3), 214–248 (2008)
4. Ferber, J., Müller, J.-P.: Influences and reaction: a model of situated multi-agent systems. In: Proc. of the 2nd Int. Conf. on Multi-Agent Systems (ICMAS 1996). AAAI (1996)
5. Gelernter, D.: Generative communication in Linda. ACM Transactions on Programming Languages and Systems 7(1), 80–112 (1985)
6. Gutknecht, O., Ferber, J.: The MADKIT agent platform architecture. In: Agents Workshop on Infrastructure for Multi-Agent Systems, pp. 48–55 (2000)
7. Hindriks, K.V.: Programming rational agents in GOAL. In: Bordini, R.H., et al. (eds.) Multi-Agent Programming: Languages, Platforms and Applications, vol. 2, pp. 3–37. Springer, Heidelberg (2009)
8. Kakas, A.C., Mancarella, P., Sadri, F., Stathis, K., Toni, F.: The KGP model of agency. In: Proceedings of the 16th Eureopean Conference on Artificial Intelligence, ECAI 2004, pp. 33–37 (2004)
9. Behrens, T.M., Hindriks, K.V., Bordini, R.H., Braubach, L., Dastani, M., Dix, J., Hübner, J.F., Pokahr, A.: An interface for agent-environment interaction. In: Programming Multi-Agent Systems 2010 (2010) (this volume)
10. Meyer, B.: Applying "design by contract". IEEE Computer 25(10), 40–51 (1992)

11. Omicini, A., Ricci, A., Viroli, M.: Artifacts in the A&A meta-model for multi-agent systems. Autonomous Agents and Multi-Agent Systems 17(3) (December 2008)
12. Omicini, A., Ricci, A., Viroli, M., Castelfranchi, C., Tummolini, L.: Coordination artifacts: Environment-based coordination for intelligent agents. In: AAMAS 2004, vol. 1, pp. 286–293. ACM, New York (2004)
13. Platon, E., Mamei, M., Sabouret, N., Honiden, S., Parunak, H.V.D.: Mechanisms for environments in multi-agent systems: Survey and opportunities. Autonomous Agents and Multi-Agent Systems 14(1), 31–47 (2007)
14. Ricci, A., Piunti, M., Acay, L.D., Bordini, R., Hübner, J., Dastani, M.: Integrating Artifact-Based Environments with Heterogeneous Agent-Programming Platforms. In: AAMAS 2008, pp. 225–232 (2008)
15. Ricci, A., Piunti, M., Viroli, M.: Environment Programming in Multi-Agent Systems – An Artifact-Based Perspective. Autonomous Agents and Multi-Agent Systems (June 2010), doi:10.1007/s10458-010-9140-7
16. Ricci, A., Piunti, M., Viroli, M., Omicini, A.: Environment programming with cartago. In: Bordini, R., Dastani, M., Dix, J., El Fallah Seghrouchni, A. (eds.) Multi-Agent Programming: Languages, Tools and Applications. Springer, Heidelberg (2009)
17. Ricci, A., Viroli, M., Omicini, A.: CArtAgO: A Framework for Prototyping Artifact-Based Environments in MAS. In: Weyns, D., Van Dyke Parunak, H., Michel, F. (eds.) E4MAS 2006. LNCS (LNAI), vol. 4389, pp. 67–86. Springer, Heidelberg (2007)
18. Ross, R.J., Collier, R., O'Hare, G.M.P.: AF-APL – Bridging Principles and Practice in Agent Oriented Languages. In: Bordini, R.H., Dastani, M.M., Dix, J., El Fallah Seghrouchni, A. (eds.) PROMAS 2004. LNCS (LNAI), vol. 3346, pp. 66–88. Springer, Heidelberg (2005)
19. Russell, S., Norvig, P.: Artificial Intelligence – A Modern Approach. Prentice Hall (2003)
20. Weyns, D., Holvoet, T.: A formal model for situated multi-agent systems. Fundam. Inf. 63(2-3), 125–158 (2004)
21. Weyns, D., Holvoet, T.: A Reference Architecture for Situated Multiagent Systems. In: Weyns, D., Van Dyke Parunak, H., Michel, F. (eds.) E4MAS 2006. LNCS (LNAI), vol. 4389, pp. 1–40. Springer, Heidelberg (2007)
22. Weyns, D., Omicini, A., Odell, J.: Environment as a first-class abstraction in multi-agent systems. Autonomous Agents and Multi-Agent Systems 14(1), 5–30 (2007)
23. Weyns, D., Parunak, H.V.D. (eds.): Autonomous Agents and Multi-Agent Systems, vol. 14(1). Springer, Heidelberg (2007); Special Issue on Environments for multiagent systems
24. Weyns, D., Van Dyke Parunak, H., Michel, F., Holvoet, T., Ferber, J.: Environments for Multiagent Systems State-of-the-Art and Research Challenges. In: Weyns, D., Van Dyke Parunak, H., Michel, F. (eds.) E4MAS 2004. LNCS (LNAI), vol. 3374, pp. 1–47. Springer, Heidelberg (2005)
25. Wooldridge, M.: Intelligent Agents. In: An Introduction to Multi-Agent Systems. John Wiley & Sons, Ltd. (2009)

An Interface for Agent-Environment Interaction

Tristan Behrens[1], Koen V. Hindriks[2], Rafael H. Bordini[3], Lars Braubach[4],
Mehdi Dastani[5], Jürgen Dix[1,*], Jomi F. Hübner[6], and Alexander Pokahr[4]

[1] Clausthal University of Technology, Germany
{behrens,dix}@in.tu-clausthal.de
[2] Delft University of Technology, The Netherlands
k.v.hindriks@tudelft.nl
[3] Federal University of Rio Grande do Sul, Brazil
r.bordini@inf.ufrgs.br
[4] Hamburg University, Germany
{braubach,pokahr}@informatik.uni-hamburg.de
[5] Utrecht University, Utrecht, The Netherlands
mehdi@cs.uu.nl
[6] Federal University of Santa Catarina, Brazil
jomi@das.ufsc.br

Abstract. Agents act and perceive in shared environments where they
are situated. Although there are many environments for agents – rang-
ing from testbeds to commercial applications – such environments have
not been widely used because of the difficulty of interfacing agents with
those environments. A more generic approach for connecting agents to
environments would be beneficial for several reasons. It would facilitate
reuse, comparison, the development of truly heterogeneous agent systems, and increase our understanding of the issues involved in the design
of agent-environment interaction. To this end, we have *designed and developed a generic environment interface standard*. Our design has been
guided by existing agent programming platforms. These platforms are
not only suitable for developing agents but also already provide some
support for connecting agents to environments. The interface standard
itself is generic, however, and does not commit to any specific platform
features. The interface proposal has been implemented and evaluated in
a number of agent platforms. We aim at a de facto standard that might
become an actual standard in the near future.

Categories and subject descriptors: I.2.5 [**Artificial Intelligence**]:
Programming Languages and Software; I.2.11 [**Artificial Intelligence**]:
Distributed Artificial Intelligence—*Intelligent Agents*; I.6.3 [**Simulation
and Modeling**]: Applications; I.6.7 [**Simulation Support Systems**]:
Environments.

General terms: Standardization.

* This work was partly funded by the NTH School for IT Ecosystems. NTH
(Niedersächsische Technische Hochschule) is a joint university consisting of Technische Universität Braunschweig, Technische Universität Clausthal, and Leibniz Universität Hannover.

R. Collier, J. Dix, and P. Novák (Eds.): ProMAS 2010, LNAI 6599, pp. 139–158, 2012.

Keywords: Agent development techniques, tools and environments, and Case studies and implemented systems.

1   Introduction

Agents are situated in environments in which they perceive and act. From an engineering point of view, an issue that repeatedly has to be dealt with is how to connect agents to environments. Sometimes this issue is (partially) solved by the physical sensors and actuators provided (e.g. in the case of a robot). But even if sensor and actuator specifications are available, the design and implementation of the interaction between the agents and the environment still require substantial effort. This is due in part to the fact that each environment is different but also because the platforms to build agents provide different support for agent-environment interaction.

By now, there exist many interesting environments which range from specialized testbeds for agent systems to industrial applications based on agent technology. In each of these applications, the interaction between agents and environments has to be addressed. This is particularly true in application areas for agent technology such as multi-agent based simulation and the use of agents in (serious) gaming [12,20,21]. In the former, agents need to be connected to computational models of real-world scenarios whereas in the latter agents are used to control virtual characters that are part of a game. The design of agent-environment interaction raises many interesting issues such as who is in control of particular features of the system and what would be the right level of abstraction of the interface that supports the interaction. Technically, there are also many challenges as witnessed by [11] who discuss an interface for connecting agents to the game Unreal Tournament 2004. This gaming environment has been identified as a potentially interesting testbed for multi-agent systems [6]. But without a suitable, generic interface that supports flexible agent-environment interaction such a testbed is unlikely to be widely used.

The availability of many interesting environments for applying agents does not mean that they are easily accessed by agents that are built using different platforms. To the contrary, in practice, it is often the case that agent developers rebuild very similar environments such as grid-like environments from scratch (one well-known toy example is the Wumpus environment [26] of which many implementations exist). Apart from the duplicate work of developing these environments, this also means that dedicated interfaces for agent-environment interaction are built: this makes it difficult to reuse existing environments. Instead, it would be much better to work with an *environment interface standard* which provides all the required functionality for connecting agents to an environment in a standardized way. If environments were developed using such a standard, they could be exchanged freely between agent platforms that support the standard and thus would make already existing environments widely available.

In this paper, we propose an *environment interface standard* that facilitates the sharing and easy exchange of environments for agents. Such a standard will facilitate the reuse of environments between agent platforms; it will support the easy distribution of environments such as the Multi-Agent Contest [15], Unreal Tournament,and many others. There are, however, many other benefits. An environment interface standard will provide a standardized and general approach for designing agent-environment interaction: this is important for the comparison of agent platforms as it would ensure that the same interface is used by each platform. Moreover, a generic interface will support the development of truly heterogeneous MAS, consisting of agents from several platforms. From a more abstract point of view, the design of an interface standard will also increase insight and conceptual understanding of agent-environment interaction.

Our approach is to design an interface that is *as generic as possible*, and that facilitates *reuse as much as possible* from existing interfaces. Clearly, there is a trade-off between these two goals. Our strategy for designing a generic environment interface is (1) to start with what is currently "out there" in existing platforms, and (2) to try to merge this into a generic interface which is sufficiently close to these approaches. As agent-oriented programming platforms seem particularly suitable for developing agents, we have chosen to use four of the more well-known agent programming languages (APLs) as our starting point. The advantage of this choice is that each of these languages to some extent have already solved the problem of agent-environment interaction even though in ways more or less specific to the language. As a consequence, a second advantage is that it may be easier to adapt such platforms to the new interface standard, and we can evaluate the interface proposal by implementing it in these agent languages. The design outlined in this paper fits for current APLs and we are confident that our interface would also be suitable for other agent platforms. We have incorporated the same functionality as has been used to connect the selected APLs to environments in the past and improved upon those interfaces. Our current experience has shown that EIS eases the issue of connecting APLs to environments, when it comes both to time as well as structure, showing that standardization helped here.

The paper is organized as follows. The design of an environment interface requires a *meta model* of environments, agents, and agent platforms. In Section 2, the principles and requirements such a meta-model should satisfy are identified and the basic components of the model, their interrelations, and the functionalities provided are described. The meta model is used in Section 3 to define the proposed *environment interface standard*, the main contribution of this paper. Section 4 discusses related work and Section 5 evaluates the proposed standard.

2 Principles and Meta-model

2.1 Principles

Two of the main motivations for introducing a generic environment interface are to facilitate the easy exchange of environments between agent platforms and to gain a more thorough understanding of the issues related to agent-environment interaction. The environment interface should allow for: (1) wrapping already existing environments, (2) creating new environments by connecting already existing applications, and (3) creating new environments from scratch. To this end, in this section we discuss and present requirements such an interface should satisfy. We do so by introducing various principles the interface should adhere to. We have analyzed the agent-environment support provided by four well-known agent programming languages: 2APL [14], GOAL [17], JADEX [9], and JASON [10]. Based on the principles, we then present a meta-model for an agent-environment interface that is able to provide at least the support for agent-environment interaction already provided by existing agent platforms (Section 2.2).

In order to guide the design of the interface, and to ensure that the interface meets our objectives, we have identified a number of principles we believe a generic environment interface should meet. First, as we aim for a generic interface, the interface should impose as few restrictions on agent platforms and environments as possible. More specifically, we believe that an environment interface should *not* impose: (1) scheduling restrictions on the execution of actions (actions can be scheduled by the agent platform and/or by the environment), (2) restrictions on agent communication or organization structure (communication facilities may be provided by the agent platform as well as by the environment), (3) restrictions on what is controlled in an environment or how this control is implemented except for the fact that control is established by an agent performing actions , and (4) restrictions on how various components of the model should be implemented; for example, the interface should allow for different types of agent-environment connection (e.g. TCP/IP, RMI, JNI).

Second, as the interface is aimed at facilitating comparison of agent platforms, a strict separation of concerns is advocated: the interface should not make any assumptions about either the agent platform or the environments such platforms are connected to, except for the type of connection that is established and associated functionalities. In our meta-model, this will be represented by a clear distinction between agents and what we call controllable entities (i.e. "agents' bodies situated in the environment"). Technically, this means the environment interface must abstract from all implementation details concerning both agents as well as environment objects. Instead, the environment interface may only store identifiers to agents and entities and should administrate which agents are associated with which entities (i.e. "who controls which body"). This level of abstraction is required to ensure that no additional implementation effort is required once the agent platform has been adapted.

Finally, as a more technical requirement, the interface should support portability, i.e., the easy exchange of environments from one agent platform to another. As most agent platforms are implemented using JAVA it is at least possible to provide this kind of functionality for such platforms if certain fixed policies are adopted for initialising an environment.

2.2   Meta-model

We have identified five components that are part of the meta-model on which we base the design of the proposed environment interface. This meta-model is illustrated in Fig. 1, and includes an *environment model*, an *environment interface* that consists of an *environment management system* and an *environment interface* component, an *agent platform* and *agents*.

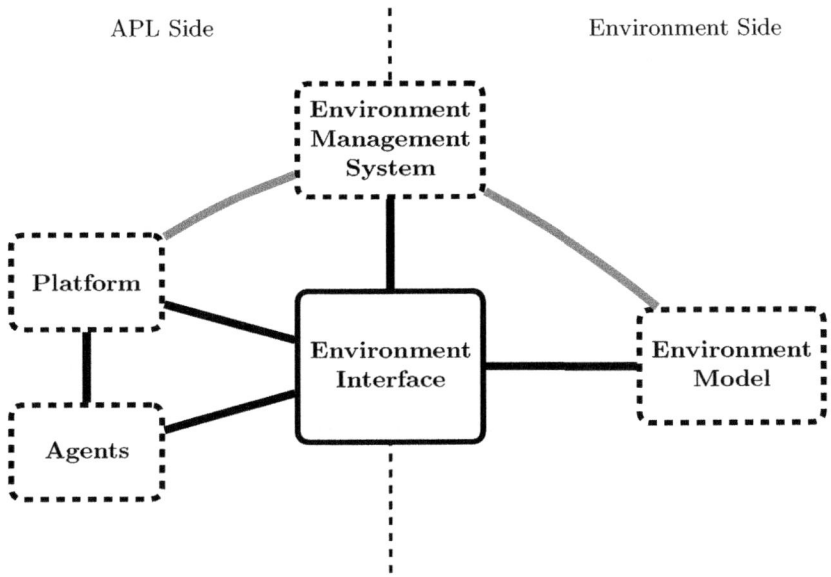

Fig. 1. The components of our environment meta-model. The platform and the agents are on the APL side. The environment management system is in between. The specific environment model is on the environment side. A specific environment model combined with the environment interface, yields a specific environment interface.

Our *environment model* assumes the presence of a specific kind of entity. [7] defines an entity as "any object or component that requires explicit representation in the model." In the context of agent-environment interaction, the entities that we are interested in may be controlled by an agent. This means that the behavior generated by the entity can be controlled by an agent if the agent is properly connected to the entity. It is the task of the interface to establish such a connection. Entities in an environment that can be so controlled are called *controllable entities*.

Controllable entities facilitate the connection between the agents running on an agent platform and an environment by providing identifiers, *effecting* capabilities, and *sensory* capabilities to agents. An agent's identifier allows the environment to send percepts or events to agents by means of the interface. Moreover, the effecting and sensory capabilities specified by controllable entities allow the environment to contextualize an agent's action repertoire, the actions' effects, and which part of the environment can be sensed, thus establishing the *situatedness* of the agents.

The objective of defining an environment interface standard is to provide a generic approach for connecting *agents* to environments. Agents may refer to almost any kind of software entity but the stance taken here is that agents are able to perform actions in the environment, sense the state of the environment and process such sensorial input, and receive and process events that are generated by the environment. We use the following very generic definition taken from [26] that includes precisely these two aspects: *An agent is anything that can be viewed as* **perceiving** *its* **environment** *through sensors and* **acting** *upon that* **environment** *through effectors.* We do not intend to restrict our proposal to any specific kind of agent program, although we are primarily motivated by existing agent-oriented programming languages.

An *agent platform* is the infrastructure that facilitates the instantiation and execution of individual agents. It is also assumed to facilitate connecting agents with environments and associating agents to controllable entities by means of the environment interface functionality. Other than that, nothing else is assumed about an agent platform.

The *environment interface* consists of two components: the *agent-environment interaction* component and the *environment management* component. The agent-environment interaction component manages the mapping and interaction between individual agents and the agent platform on one hand, and the environment and controllable entities on the other hand. The interaction between an agent platform and the agent-environment interaction component allows agents to act in an environment, sense its state, and receive events from it. We allow two ways of sensing: (1) active sensing through specific sense actions, and (2) passive sensing through a generic sense action embedded in the control cycle of the agents. Using the agent-environment interaction component, the platform can process different types of actions by calling different methods of this component and possibly wait for the return values which are subsequently passed on to the platform. The values returned can be either success/failure notifications or sense information if actions were (passive or active) sense actions. The environment interface can also interact with a platform by sending an event to a specified agent. The platform is then responsible to pass the event on to the specified agent (e.g., by adding the event to the agent's event base).

3   A Generic Environment Interface

In this section, we explain our ideas for a generic environment interface. First, we define an *interface intermediate language* that facilitates data-exchange (percepts, actions, events) between different components. Second, we assume a functional point-of-view of the interface architecture. The interface provides functions for:

1. attaching, detaching, and notifying observers (software design pattern);
2. registering and unregistering agents;

3. adding and removing entities;
4. managing the agents-entities-relation;
5. performing actions and retrieving percepts; and
6. managing the environment.

3.1 Motivating Example: Multi-Agent Contest

The Multi-Agent Programming Contest (MAPC) 2010 tournament consists of a series of simulations. In each simulation (see Fig. 2) two teams of agents compete in a grid-like world. There are virtual cowboys that can be controlled by agents. Agents have access to incomplete information, because the cowboys have a fixed sensor-range. Acting means moving a cowboy to a neighboring cell on the grid. There are no further actions. The environment contains obstacles: some cells can be blocked and thus are unreachable. The grid is also populated by virtual cows, that behave according to a simple flocking-algorithm. To win a simulation, an agent team has to herd more cows, and take them to their own corral, than the opponent team. The simulation proceeds through discrete time steps. In each step, agents can perceive, have a fixed amount of time to deliberate, and are then allowed to act. After a number of steps the simulation is finished. The tournament is run by the MASSim-server, which schedules and runs simulations.

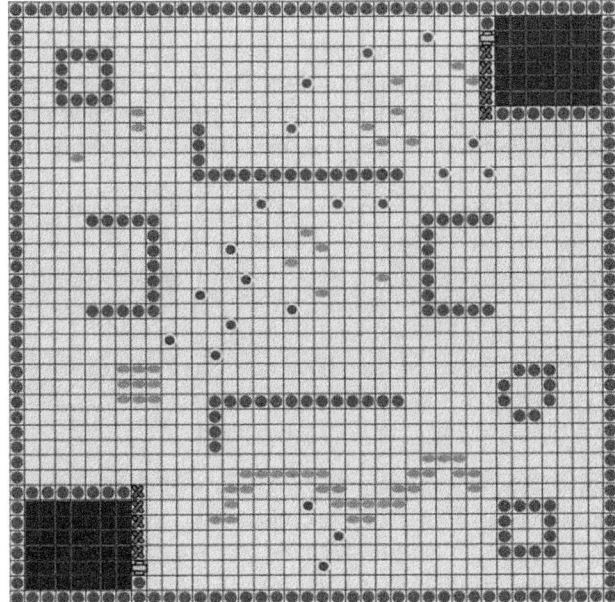

Fig. 2. A screen-shot of a simulation from MAPC 2010. Cowboys (red and blue circles) should scare cows (brown ellipses) into the corrals (red and blue rectangles). In this environment, acting is moving the cowboys, and perceiving is getting information about which objects are contained in each cowboy's square of visibility.

Agents are supposed to connect to the server as clients. Communication between clients and server is facilitated by exchanging XML-messages via the TCP/IP protocol.

We have given a very informal but adequate description of the environment-model. The environment is discrete in space (grid-world) and time (step-wise evolution). Platforms can interface with the MASSim-server by adhering to the defined communication-protocol. This has to be done for every platform, in a way specific to that platform. This is the case because, as we have observed, every platform has a specific way of connecting to environments. Every platform would have to use that connection-mechanism, parse XML-messages to evaluate the percepts, and generate XML-messages for performing actions. Now, assuming that a platform would be EIS-compatible, you only have to go through the trouble of connecting to the MASSim-server once and create a specific environment-interface.

3.2   Interface Intermediate Language

An important design decision has been to define, as part of the environment interface, a convention for representing actions and percepts. This convention is called the *interface intermediate language* (IIL), and supports the exchange of percepts and actions from/to environments. A conventional representation for actions and percepts is required to be able to meet the second principle aimed at facilitating comparison of platforms and the fourth principle that aims at easy exchange of environments and portability. To meet these principles, the interface should be agnostic to any implementation details of either agent platform or environment; this can be achieved by an abstract intermediate language. The convention proposed here, however, imposes almost no restrictions (which is in line with our first principle of generality).

The language consists of: (1) *data containers* (e.g. actions and percepts), and (2) *parameters* for those containers. Parameters are *identifiers* and *numerals* (both represent constant values), *functions* over parameters, and *lists* of parameters. Data containers are: *actions* that are performed by agents, *results* of such actions, and *percepts* that are received by agents.

Syntactically each element of the IIL is an abstract syntax-tree (AST). Fig. 3 shows the relationship of the IIL-elements. Internally, each such element is stored as a tree of Java-Objects with the following structure:

- An DataContainer is either an Action or a Percept.
- An Action consists of (1) a string name that denotes the action's name, (2) an ordered collection parameters, containing instances of Parameter, representing the parameters of the action, and (3) an integer timeStamp encoding the exact time the action-object has been created.
- An Percept consists of (1) a string name that denotes the percepts's name, (2) an ordered collection parameters, containing instances of Parameter, representing the parameters of the percept, and (3) an integer timeStamp encoding the exact time the percept-object has been created.

- A `Parameter` is either a `Numeral`, a `Identifier`, a `ParameterList`, or a `Function`.
- A `Numeral` encapsulates a number value.
- An `Identifier` encapsulates a string value.

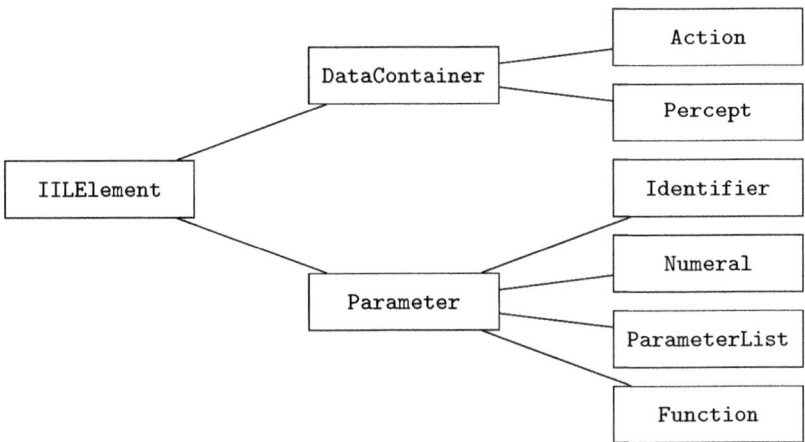

Fig. 3. The inheritance relation of the IIL-elements. Actions and percepts are data-containers. Each data-container consists of a name and an ordered collection of parameters.

For the sake of readability each IIL-element can be printed either in a prolog-like or in a XML-notation. Note however, that these string representations are not supposed to be used on either the platform-side or the environment-side. They are for reading purposes only.

Example 1 (a simple action with two atomic parameters). Assuming the existence of an entity that is capable of moving in a grid-like world, consider that this entity's action-repertoire includes an move-action that moves the entity to a position $[X, Y]$. This is the Prolog-like representation of such an action:

```
moveTo(2,3)
```

The action's name-field is `moveTo`. There are two parameters 2 and 3. Both of the `Identifier`-type.

This is the XML-representation of the action:

```
<action name="moveTo">
  <actionParameter> <number value="2"/> </actionParameter>
  <actionParameter> <number value="3"/> </actionParameter>
</action>
```

□

Example 2 (another action using functions and a list). Consider now that the same entity is capable of performing a more complex action, that is following a path consisting of a sequence of positions at a given speed..

```
followPath([pos(1,1),pos(2,1)],speed(10.0))
```

The action's first parameter [pos(1,1),pos(2,1)] is a ParameterList. The list's elements are both instances of Function. Considering pos(1,1), the function name is pos, both parameters are instances of Numeral. The second parameter of the action is a function, too.

Here is the XML-representation of the action:

```
<action name="followPath"><actionParameter>
    <parameterList>
      <function name="pos">
        <number value="1"/>
        <number value="1"/>
      </function>
      <function name="pos">
        <number value="2"/>
        <number value="1"/>
      </function>
    </parameterList>
  </actionParameter>
  <actionParameter>
    <function name="speed"><number value="10.0"/></function>
  </actionParameter>
</action>
```

□

We do not need an explicit example for percepts, because syntactically percepts and actions are almost equivalent.

At this point, we have introduced the syntax of the IIL, and elaborated on it a bit by considering some examples. Now, we have to look at the semantics. The semantics of an action and/or a percept depends on the specific environment. Again, EIS does not make any assumptions here, except for the syntactical requirements.

After some experiments, a certain but trivial problem became evident. Some environments (e.g. UT 2004) provide identifiers that might be interpreted as variables on the platform side, thus rendering every IIL-expression that contains such identifiers unusable by the platform, causing errors that are difficult to deal with. To solve the problem we need to assume that none of the IIL-expressions that are distributed by a specific environment-interface contains interpreters that might be interpreted as variables.

3.3   Functional Point-of-View

What exactly is the correspondence between an environment-interface and the components (platform, agents, etc.)? We allow for a two-way connection via *interactions* that are performed by the components and *notifications* that are performed by the environment-interface.

Interactions are facilitated by function calls to the environment-interface that can yield a return value. For notifications we employ the *observer design pattern* (call-back methods, known as *listeners* in Java). The observer pattern defines that a *subject* maintains a list of *observers*. The subject informs the observers of any state change by calling one of their methods. The observer pattern is usually employed when a state-change in one object requires changes in another one. This is the reason why we made that choice. The subject in the observer pattern usually provides functionality for *attaching* and *detaching* observers, and for *notifying* all attached observers. The observer, on the other hand, defines an *updating* interface to receive update notifications from the subject.

We allow for both interactions and notifications, because this approach is the least restrictive one. This clearly corresponds to the notions of *polling* (an agent performs an action to query the state of the environment) and *interrupts* (the environment sends percepts to the agents as in the *AgentContest* example).

Agents and Entities: We make three assumptions: (1) there is a set of agents on the agent platform side (we do not know anything about them), (2) there is a set of controllable entities on the environments side (again we do not know anything about them), and (3) agents can control entities through the environment-interface. An important design decision that we had to make is to store in the environment-interface only identifiers to the agents, identifiers to the entities, and a mapping between these two sets. The reason for that decision is, as mentioned before, that we do not assume anything about the agent platform side or the environment side. Fig. 4 shows the agents-entities relation. The agents live on the agent platform side, they are known by the environment-interface through their identifiers. The entities live on the environment-side, and they are also known by their identifiers. The agents-entities relation is stored as a mapping between both sets of identifiers. In the *AgentContest*, each cowboy is a controllable entity. Cows are entities as well but they are not controllable. Each agent can control only a single cowboy.

In general, we allow the agents-entities relation to be arbitrary. For example, we also allow for one agent to be associated with several entities. This would be useful when using the agents&artifacts meta-model [23] to provide means for agent-coordination through the environment. An artifact would be an entity that can be controlled by several agents. Agents would perceive the state of the artifact and can act so as to change it.

Attaching, Detaching, and Notifying Observers: There are two directions for exchanging data between components and environment interfaces. One is via environment observers, which inform observers about changes in the environment or the environment interface. The second is via agent observers, which send percepts to agents. In order to facilitate sending events (i.e. percepts as notifications and environment events), the interface provides functions that allow for attaching and detaching observers, and for notifying components connected

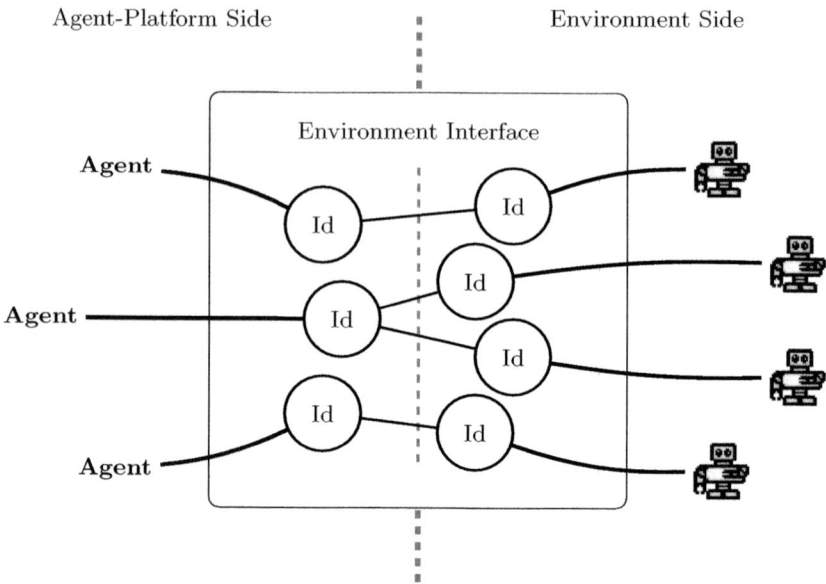

Fig. 4. The agents-entities relation. We distinguish between agents, which are platform-properties, and controllable entities, which are environmental properties. Agents have access to the entities effecting and sensory capabilities. In general the agents-entities-relation, depends on the specific environment-interface.

via observers. Listeners are useful when connecting to the *AgentContest* environment, since it is the simulator that actively provides agents with percepts.

Registering and Unregistering Agents: This step is the first to facilitate the interaction between agents and environments and establishing the agents' situatedness. It is necessary for the internal connection between agents and entities. The interface provides two methods: one for registering (`registerAgent`), and one for unregistering an agent (`unregisterAgent`). We note that the agents themselves are not registered to the interface; instead, identifiers as representatives are stored and managed. We note that only identifiers representing the agents are stored and managed by the interface.

Adding and Removing entities: Entities are added and removed in a similar fashion to agents. Again identifiers representing entities are stored instead of the entities themselves. There are two methods: the first (`addEntity`) adds, and the second one (`deleteEntity`) removes an entity. Again this is necessary to facilitate the connection between agents and entities. Once an entity is added or removed, any observing components (platform and/or agents depending on the design of the platform) are notified about the respective events. This is done in order to allow components to react to changes in the set of entities in an appropriate manner.

Managing the Agents-Entities Relation: Associating an agent with one or several entities is the second and final step of establishing the situatedness of agents by connecting them to entities that provide effectory and sensorial capabilities. The agents-entities relation is manipulated by means of three methods. The first method (called `associateEntity`) associates an agent with an entity, the second one (`freeEntity`) frees an entity from the relation, and the third one (`freeAgent`), frees an agent. This can be done by the interface internally and by other components that have access to it as well. Restrictions on the structure of the relation can be established by the interface. In the *AgentContest*, for example, one agent is supposed to control at most one virtual cowboy.

Performing Actions and Retrieving Percepts: The agents-entities relation is a connection between agents and the sensors and effectors of the associated entities. We establish two directions of information flow. Each direction corresponds to a typical step in common agent deliberation cycles. We have facilitated the management of the two directions of flow by following a unified approach whereby two methods are provided by the interface. The first one (`performAction`) allows an agent to act in the environment through the effectors of its associated entities. The second method (`getAllPercepts`) allows an agent to sense the state of the environment through the sensors of the associated entities. In the "cows and cowboys" scenario, nine actions are available. One for connecting to the server at a given IP address with valid username and password, and the other eight for moving the cowboy in each possible direction. The method `getAllPercepts` retrieves the last percept sent by the server.

Managing the Environment: Although different environments provide different support to manage the initialization, configuration, and execution of the environment itself, it is useful to include support for environment management in the environment interface. This allows agent platforms to provide this functionality by means of the interfaces that come with these platforms and relate environment functionality with similar functionality offered by the platform. For example, it is often useful to be able to "freeze" a running MAS simultaneously with the environment to which the MAS is connected by means of pause functionalities provided by the platform and the environment. As there is no common functionality supported by each and every environment, we have chosen to provide support for environment management by introducing a *convention* for labeling a set of *environment commands* and *environment events*. The commands that are part of the proposed environment management convention include *starting, pausing, initializing, resetting,* and *killing* the environment.

3.4   Implementation Details

The goal of developing an environment interface standard is to facilitate the easy exchange of environments. The interface would reduce the implementation effort of connecting agent platforms to environments. Of course, the effort of connecting to the environment through an environment interface should not substantially increase the effort needed for directly connecting agents to an environment. Below, we report on the experience we gained with adapting four agent platforms so that they support the environment interface as well as the experience gained with two environments that were adapted to support the environment interface.

In order to create an environment interface for a given environment, dedicated code that is specific to the environment is necessary. To that end, a particular Java interface has to be implemented. That interface enforces the functional contract introduced in subsection 3.3. Alternatively, the developer can inherit from a class that contains a default implementation for all of the contract's methods. Whatever path the developers follow, they need to establish a connection to the environment.

Supported Agent Platforms. To evaluate the ease of use and generality of the developed EIS concepts and components, we have connected four different APLs to example environments developed with the EIS. For 2APL, GOAL, JADEX, and JASON, a connection has been established with less than one day of coding effort each.

2APL proved to be compatible with EIS. In order to establish a connection a two-way converter for the interface intermediate language had to be developed. Furthermore, the environment loading mechanism of 2APL had to be replaced with the environment-interface loading mechanism provided by EIS. Percepts sent by EIS using the observer functionality are translated into 2APL events and handed over to the event-handling mechanism of the interpreter. Finally, special external actions have been added to facilitate the manipulation of the agents-entities relationship: (1) retrieving all entities, (2) retrieving all free entities, (3) associating with one or several entities, and (4) disassociating with one or several entities.

The original environment interface of GOAL did not fit with everything provided by the environment interface. It nevertheless proved quite easy to connect the interface to GOAL as most functionality provided by the interface is straightforwardly matched to that provided by the GOAL agent platform. Similar to 2APL, a two-way converter for the interface intermediate language had to be developed with little effort required. There were no percepts as notifications (like events in 2APL), prior to the adaptation to EIS. GOAL only allowed for retrieving all percepts in a distinct step of the deliberation cycle. Percepts as notifications are now collected and processed together in the step where all percepts are processed. Also, the MAS file specification of GOAL has been extended. Now one can use launch rules to connect specific agents with specific entities. This allows for instantiating agents even during runtime.

For connecting JADEX agents to EIS, it is sufficient to make all agents of one application aware of the concrete EIS object, implementing the current environment. In order to do this in a systematic way, the JADEX concept of *space* was used. A space may represent an arbitrary underlying structure of a MAS that is known by all agents. To support the EIS, a special EISSpace has been provided, which implements the required interfacing code for connecting to an EIS-based environment. Therefore, the participation in such an environment can now simply be specified in the JADEX application descriptor ("`.application.xml`"). When such a defined application is started, the initial agents as well as the EIS environment will be created. Agents can then access EIS by fetching the corresponding space from their application context and use the EIS Java API directly for, e.g., performing actions or retrieving percepts.

JASON's integration with EIS was straightforward since almost all concepts used in the EIS are also available in Jason. The integration consists essentially of: (1) the conversion of data types, and (2) the development of a class that adapts EIS environments to JASON environments. In regards to (1), all EIS data types have an equivalent in JASON. Although some data types in JASON (e.g., Strings) do not have a corresponding type in EIS, they can be translated to EIS identifiers. In regards to (2), the adaptor is a normal JASON Environment class extension that delegates perception and action to the EIS. The adaptor class is also responsible for registering the agents with the EIS as they join a JASON multi-agent system and wake them up when the environment changes (using the observer mechanism available in EIS). From all the concepts used in EIS, only that of "entities" is not supported by JASON as all actions and perceptions are relative to an agent and the overall environment rather than a particular entity therein. For sensing, the chosen solution was to add annotations to percepts that indicate the entity of origin. For actions, in case the agent is associated with exactly one entity, the action is simply dispatched to that entity. Otherwise, a special action that receives the relevant entity as a parameter must be used.

Implemented Environments. The environment interface comes with several very simple examples of environments for illustrative purposes. These examples are mainly provided for clarifying some of the basic concepts related to the interface. We briefly discuss here two EIS-enabled environments, that may be used by any agent platform that supports EIS.

The *elevator environment* is a good example of an environment that was not built specifically with agents in mind, and is available from [1]. The environment is a simulator of arbitrary multi-elevator environments where the elevators are the controllable entities and the people using the elevators are controlled by the simulator. It comes with a graphical user interface (GUI) and a set of tools for statistical analysis. The environment had been originally adapted for the GOAL platform. The additional effort required to re-interface that environment to EIS was very little. The main issue was the event handling related to the initial creation of elevators, a functionality provided and supported by the environment interface which required some additional effort for adapting the environment to provide such events. The environment provides actions that take time (durative actions) instead of discrete one-step actions, which illustrates that the interface does not impose any restrictions on the types of actions that are supported. Similarly, elevators only perceive certain events but not, for example, whether buttons are pressed in other elevators. The percept handling related to this was easily established, illustrating the ease with which to implement a partially observable environment. We have successfully used the elevator environment with GOAL and 2APL.

Connecting to the MASSim-server turned out to be easy. As already mentioned, the entities in the *AgentContest*-environment are cowboys that herd cows. From the implementation point-of-view each connection to an entity is a TCP/IP connection. Acting is facilitated by wrapping the respective action into an XML-message and sending it to the server. Perceiving is done by receiving XML-messages from the server and notifying possible agent-listeners. Furthermore, for the sake of convenience, percepts are stored internally for a possible active retrieval. Much effort had to be invested in mappings from the interface intermediate language to the XML-protocol of the *AgentContest* and vice versa. We have shown that the interface does indeed not pose any restrictions on the connection between itself and environments.

Finally, it is worth mentioning that an interface to Unreal Tournament 2004 [18] is under developmentGrown out of the need for a more extensive evaluation of the application of logic-based BDI agents to challenging, dynamic, and potentially real-time environments, this EIS interface might help putting agent programming platforms to the test.

Evaluation Summary. The relative ease with which the interface has been connected to four agent platforms and various environments already indicates that the interface has been designed at the right abstraction level for agent-environment interaction. The four agent platforms differ in various dimensions, regarding, for example, the functionality provided for handling percepts and actions (is the platform more logic-oriented or Java-based?) and how environments were connected to these platforms before using the interface. The environment interface nevertheless could be connected to each of the platforms easily, thus providing evidence of its generality and as well. Of course, we need more agent platforms to use the environment interface, and we have invited other platform developers to do so, but we do not expect this will pose any fundamental new issues. Initial experience with various environments has also shown that little to no restrictions are imposed on the types of environments that can be connected to an agent platform using the interface. The interface, for example, can support both real-time or turn-based environments, as well as environments that differ in other respects. Although we have mainly discussed software environments, there is no principled restriction imposed by EIS that would make it only applicable to such environments. It has been shown already in the past that it is possible to connect agent platforms to embedded platforms such as robots. EIS just provides another, more principled approach for doing so. In fact, it is planned to use EIS to connect to a robotic platform in the near future.

4   Related Work

The EIS was designed as a building block for an agent application, providing a standardized way of interfacing the agents with environmental components. In the context of agent applications, at least the following forms of environments can be distinguished: (1) environments in agent-based simulation models, (2) virtual environments such as testbeds or computer games, (3) real application components such as enterprise information systems, and (4) coordination infrastructures.

Agent-based simulation models can be used for performing experiments and analyzing the obtained result data. Agent simulation toolkits are specifically designed for this purpose and often employ custom agent models (e.g. simple task-based agents) and a proprietary form of defining the environment behavior. Usually, there is a tight coupling between agents and the environment that is designed to support these toolkit-specific models. Therefore, simulation toolkits are closed in the sense that they do not support (and are not meant to) connecting external agents to simulated environments or simulated agents to external environments.

The specialized architecture Koko [27] provides a reusable and extensible environment, aiming at an enhanced user experience by linking independent applications. With our work we neither focus on human interaction with agents or the environment, nor are we exclusively interested in multiplayer and/or social games. We see these only as a single class of test-cases out of many ones.

Agent programming testbeds and contests, such as TAC, [5], RoboCup, [4] and the Multi Agent Contest [3], are specifically designed to offer open interfaces for connecting different types of agents to the provided test environment. Moreover, some network-based computer games with remote playing capabilities (e.g. Unreal Tournament) offer interfaces for controlling entities in the game environment which have been adapted to connect to software agents instead of human players [11]. All of these interfaces are quite specific with regards to the testbed or game they were created for, and therefore agent platform developers have to repeat the implementation effort of connecting their agents to each of these interfaces.

To connect agents to an environment composed of real application components, different options are available. Application-centered approaches would directly use available component interfaces or domain specific standards (such as HL7 in the healthcare domain) for the connection. Depending on the severity of the "impedance mismatch" between the component interface and the agent platform, this can become quite laborious and additionally has to be repeated for each platform and each application. Agent-centered approaches try to "agentify" the environment components, leading to a more seamless and straightforward connection. For example WSIG (Jade) [2] is an infrastructure that allows agents to interact with web services as if they were agents and vice-versa.

One well known approach for coordinating agents is by using blackboard approaches, which offer agents a possibility to decouple their interactions in terms of time and potential receivers. Besides passive blackboards acting as information stores only, also more advanced tuple spaces such as ReSeCT [22] have been devised with which one can also capture domain logic in terms of rules. The Open Agent Architecture (OAA) [13] is another form of coordination environment, in which the cooperation among agents and also humans is facilitated by automatic task delegation and execution. In contrast to EIS, these approaches focus on information exchange and problem solving and do not tackle the question of how environments could be generically interfaced.

Organizational or institutional approaches such as Islander [16] and MOISE [19] regulate agent behavior at high-level allowing designers and/or agents to define, monitor, and enforce certain kinds of organizational constraints (e.g. norms and group membership). The latest platform for MOISE is founded on the notion of organizational environment where agents can perceive and act on their organization. This kind of environment can also contain artifacts specially developed to enforce some norms (e.g. a surgical room's door that forbids agents to enter if they do not play the role of doctor). Other approaches affect more directly agent behavior, for example biologically inspired approaches such as pheromone-based techniques to guide agent movement. While these approaches make use of the notion of environment, they are quite domain specific and do not allow for arbitrary environment development. In contrast, the A&A model [23] has been proposed as a generic paradigm for modeling environments. In the A&A paradigm, an application is composed of agents as well as so called artifacts. While the model makes no restricting assumptions with respect to the agents, the interface and operation of an artifact is intentionally quite rigidly defined. An implementation of the A&A model is available in form of the distributed middleware infrastructure CArtAgO [25].

We see EIS not as a competitor, but rather as a desirable complement to the above mentioned approaches. For example, one possible use of the EIS standard is reducing the required implementation effort for connecting agent to, say, virtual environments, as once an EIS-based interface has been developed for a contest or game, it can easily be reused by different agent platforms. Unlike FIPA-compliant approaches such as the WSIG, the focus of the EIS is providing a lean interface, i.e., when FIPA-compliant communication is not necessary, the EIS allows achieving similar openness and portability with much less effort. In particular, we see much potential in a combination of EIS and CArtAgO. Currently, there are specific bridges available for connecting agent platforms such as JADEX, JASON and 2APL to CArtAgO [24]. Implementing an EIS bridge for CArtAgO could lead to a universal implementation that could be used to connect CArtAgO to any agent platform (if it is already EIS-enabled). In general, the EIS standard will facilitate connecting any agent platform to all sorts of environments (A&A based as well as others).

5   Conclusion

The design and implementation of our proposal for an environment interface standard (see [8] for a more detailed exposition and more technical details) is motivated by the fact that it has been difficult to connect arbitrary agent platforms to many of the available environments. The design of the interface provides additional insight into the general problem of agent-environment interaction. At a conceptual level, the development of the environment interface has yielded insight, for example, into some of the distinguishing features of existing agent platforms. For example, where some platforms expect events initiated by the environment other platforms are based on a polling model for retrieving percepts.

The initial results of applying the interface to various agent platforms and environments have been very encouraging: they demonstrate the generality and usability of our interface. The environment interface standard allows the portability and reuse of application and testing environments across existing and newly developed agent platforms. Furthermore, it provides a basis for heterogeneous agent applications composed of agents implemented in different agent platforms. The experience so far has also shown that connecting to and using the interface requires minimal effort and can be implemented easily.

Although the environment interface proposed here provides a solid basis for agent-environment interaction, there are some topics that require additional work. One of these topics involves the environment management system which has only been partly supported by most agent platforms; it facilitates combinations of agent platform and environment functionalities such as combined resetting of MAS and environment, but this requires additional investigation. We also need to gain more experience with the dynamic addition and removal of entities and the handling of such events by platforms. Related to the previous point, there is the issue of managing various types of entities. For example, how can the interface be extended to support the identification of these different types? Finally, we need to get more agent platforms, including platforms from multiagent based simulation and other areas, involved and support the environment interface to establish our proposal as a genuine (de facto) standard.

References

1. Elevator simulator homepage, http://sourceforge.net/projects/elevatorsim/
2. Java Agent Development Framework homepage, http://jade.tilab.com/
3. Multi Agent Contest homepage, http://www.multiagentcontest.org/
4. RoboCup homepage, http://www.robocup.org/
5. Trading Agent Competition homepage, http://www.sics.se/tac/
6. Adobbati, R., Marshall, A., Scholer, A., Tejada, S., Kaminka, G., Schaffer, S., Sollitto, C.: Gamebots: A 3d virtual world test-bed for multi-agent research. In: Proceedings of the 2nd International Workshop on Infrastructure for Agents, MAS, and Scalable MAS (2001)
7. Banks, J., Carson, J.S., Nelson, B.L., Nicol, D.M.: Discrete-Event System Simulation. Prentice Hall (2009)
8. Behrens, T.M., Dix, J., Hindriks, K.V.: Towards an environment interface standard for agent-oriented programming. Technical Report IfI-09-09, Clausthal University of Technology (September 2009)
9. Bordini, R.H., Hübner, J.F., Wooldridge, M.: Programming Multi-Agent Systems in AgentSpeak using Jason. Wiley Series in Agent Technology. John Wiley & Sons (2007)
10. Braubach, L., Pokahr, A., Lamersdorf, W.: Jadex: A BDI-agent system combining middleware and reasoning. In: Unland, R., Klusch, M., Calisti, M. (eds.) Software Agent-Based Applications, Platforms and Development Kits (2005)
11. Burkert, O., Kadlec, R., Gemrot, J., Bda, M., Havlcek, J., Drfler, M., Brom, C.: Towards fast prototyping of IVAs behavior: Pogamut 2. In: Proceedings of 7th International Conference on Inteligent Virtual Humans (2007)

12. Buro, M.: Call for AI Research in RTS Games. In: AAAI 2004 AI in Games Workshop (2004)
13. Cheyer, A., Martin, D.: The open agent architecture. Journal of Autonomous Agents and Multi-Agent Systems 4(1), 143–148 (2001)
14. Dastani, M.: 2apl: a practical agent programming language. Autonomous Agents and Multi-Agent Systems 16(3), 214–248 (2008)
15. Dastani, M.M., Dix, J., Novák, P.: Agent Contest Competition: 3rd Edition. In: Dastani, M.M., El Fallah Seghrouchni, A., Ricci, A., Winikoff, M. (eds.) ProMAS 2007. LNCS (LNAI), vol. 4908, pp. 221–240. Springer, Heidelberg (2008)
16. Esteva, M., de la Cruz, D., Sierra, C.: Islander: an electronic institutions editor. In: AAMAS 2002: Proceedings of the First International Joint Conference on Autonomous Agents and Multiagent Systems, pp. 1045–1052. ACM, New York (2002)
17. Hindriks, K.V., Roberti, T.: GOAL as a Planning Formalism. In: Braubach, L., van der Hoek, W., Petta, P., Pokahr, A. (eds.) MATES 2009. LNCS, vol. 5774, pp. 29–40. Springer, Heidelberg (2009)
18. Hindriks, K.V., van Riemsdijk, B., Behrens, T., Korstanje, R., Kraaijenbrink, N., Pasman, W., de Rijk, L.: Unreal GOAL bots. In: Preproceedings of the AAMAS 2010 Workshop on Agents for Games and Simulations (2010) (to appear)
19. Hübner, J.F., Boissier, O., Kitio, R., Ricci, A.: Instrumenting multi-agent organisations with organisational artifacts and agents: giving the organisational power back to the agents. Journal of Autonomous Agents and Multi-Agent Systems (2009)
20. Mili, R.Z., Steiner, R.: Modeling Agent-Environment Interactions in Adaptive MAS. In: Weyns, D., Brueckner, S.A., Demazeau, Y. (eds.) EEMMAS 2007. LNCS (LNAI), vol. 5049, pp. 135–147. Springer, Heidelberg (2008)
21. Müller, J.: Towards a Formal Semantics of Event-Based Multi-Agent Simulations. In: David, N., Sichman, J.S. (eds.) MAPS 2008. LNCS (LNAI), vol. 5269, pp. 110–126. Springer, Heidelberg (2009)
22. Omicini, A.: Formal ReSpecT in the A&A Perspective. Electronic Notes of Theoretical Computer Science 175(2), 97–117 (2007)
23. Omicini, A., Ricci, A., Viroli, M.: Artifacts in the A&A meta-model for multi-agent systems. Autonomous Agents and Multi-Agent Systems 17(3), 432–456 (2008)
24. Ricci, A., Piunti, M., Acay, L.D., Bordini, R., Hübner, J., Dastani, M.: Integrating artifact-based environments with heterogeneous agent-programming platforms. In: 7th International Joint Conference on Autonomous Agents and Multiagent Systems (AAMAS 2008), pp. 225–232. IFAAMAS (2008)
25. Ricci, A., Viroli, M., Omicini, A.: CArtAgO: A Framework for Prototyping Artifact-Based Environments in MAS. In: Weyns, D., Van Dyke Parunak, H., Michel, F. (eds.) E4MAS 2006. LNCS (LNAI), vol. 4389, pp. 67–86. Springer, Heidelberg (2007)
26. Russell, S., Norvig, P.: Artificial Intelligence: A Modern Approach, 2nd edn. Prentice Hall (2003)
27. Sollenberger, D., Singh, M.: Architecture for Affective Social Games. In: Dignum, F., Bradshaw, J., Silverman, B., van Doesburg, W. (eds.) Agents for Games and Simulations. LNCS, vol. 5920, pp. 79–94. Springer, Heidelberg (2009)

Author Index